DIEPPE 1942
The Jubilee Disaster

Ronald Atkin

LUME BOOKS

LUME BOOKS

First published by MACMILLAN LONDON LIMITED in 1980

Copyright © Ronald Atkin 1980

This edition published in 2023 by Lume Books

The right of Ronald Atkin to be identified as the author of this work has been asserted by them in accordance with the Copyright, Design and Patents Act, 1988.

All rights reserved. No part of this publication may be reproduced, stored in a retrieval system, or transmitted in photocopying, recording or otherwise, without the prior permission of the copyright owner.

www.lumebooks.co.uk

Table of Contents

CHAPTER ONE: The Plan	1
CHAPTER TWO: Rutter	12
CHAPTER THREE: Jubilee	34
CHAPTER FOUR: Departure	51
CHAPTER FIVE: Yellow Beach	72
CHAPTER SIX: Orange Beach	91
CHAPTER SEVEN: Blue Beach	110
CHAPTER EIGHT: Green Beach	131
CHAPTER NINE: Red and White Beaches	147
CHAPTER TEN: Disaster	182
CHAPTER ELEVEN: Withdrawal	211
CHAPTER TWELVE: Surrender	236
CHAPTER THIRTEEN: Aftermath	250
Bibliography	273
Newspapers and Periodicals	277
Source Notes	279
Acknowledgements	299

Someday there will be two spots on the French coast sacred to the British and their Allies. One will be Dunkirk, where Britain was saved because a beaten army would not surrender. The other will be Dieppe, where brave men died without hope for the sake of proving that there is a wrong way to invade. They will have their share of glory when the right way is tried.

The New York Times, 19 August 1943

Just before sunset on Tuesday 18 August 1942 a small convoy slipped out of the German-occupied port of Boulogne. It consisted of five commandeered Dutch coastal motor vessels, escorted by an armed minesweeper and two submarine chasers of the German Navy. Their destination was Dieppe, and their scheduled arrival time 0500 hours next morning.*

Hugging the coastline of northern France to keep as far away as possible from the eyes of British radar and the threat of marauding torpedo boats, the convoy took up a loose formation permitting clear fields of fire in all directions in case of attack. Leading the group was submarine chaser UJ 1411, commanded by Lt Wurmbach, and bringing up the rear was UJ 1404, commanded by Lt Berner. The seaward flank was protected by the minesweeper 4014, under the command of Lt Bögel.

The early part of the voyage, on a bright moonlit night and over a calm sea, was devoid of incident, though the escort vessels were on constant stand-to in such clear visibility. That hazardous part of the Channel was known to the British as E-boat Alley. The Germans no doubt had their own name for it, too.

Around 0100 hours the moon went down, the convoy ran into a light sea mist and the German sailors breathed easier. Not too much danger of being attacked in conditions like these. The breather was short-lived. Soon after 0300 hours the sound of engines was picked up. The convoy, only ten miles from the haven of Dieppe, edged its way cautiously through the mist, the sailors crouched behind their guns and peering anxiously into the gloom.

At 0347 hours noises of nearby vessels registered on the escorts' direction-finding equipment and faintly discernible shadows appeared on the convoy's starboard side. That was enough for Lt Berner in UJ

---

* The time given in German accounts of the Dieppe Raid is Continental, which in the summer of 1942 was one hour ahead of the British clock. All times quoted in this narrative have been amended to British time for the sake of uniformity.

1404. He fired a star shell. Its quivering glare exposed the low profiles of ships, landing craft and motor boats. The convoy had blundered into the Dieppe Raid.

CHAPTER ONE
The Plan

'It will not advance the Russian or Allied cause if we embark on some operation which ends in disaster.'

– Winston Churchill

In the summer of 1942 the war was almost at the end of its third year and the position of the Allies was desperate. On the Russian front the Germans' offensive was driving towards the Volga and the oilfields of the Caucasus, threatening to link up with the Japanese in India and overwhelm the Middle East from the rear. In May and June U-boats sank more than a million and a half tons of shipping, and in a single week at the beginning of July Britain and the United States lost vessels totalling 400,000 tons. The rate of Atlantic sinkings exceeded the building capacity by two-and-a-half to one and the appalling toll in oil tankers alone threatened to bring the Allied war effort to a summary halt.

Singapore had fallen to the Japanese, the Royal Navy had suffered a series of embarrassing setbacks in the Far East and on 21 June Winston Churchill experienced his worst moment of the war so far. In Washington for talks with Franklin D. Roosevelt, the British Prime Minister sat in shocked silence as the American President read from a slip of pink paper brought into his White House office the news that Tobruk had fallen and the British Army in North Africa was in headlong retreat towards the Suez Canal. Churchill, who hurried back to London to defend himself vigorously and successfully in Parliament against a censure motion on his conduct of the war, subsequently wrote of that moment: 'Defeat is one thing; disgrace is another.'

The gloom was unrelieved and the Nazi propaganda minister, Josef Goebbels, announced gleefully 'England is on the toboggan'.

Yet the embattled Churchill was being urged by his new American allies to open a Second Front across the Channel to bring relief to the hard-pressed Soviet armies. The Americans were demanding an invasion of France in September 1942, an operation to which Churchill gave the stirring codename 'Sledgehammer' but about which he was understandably, and quite sensibly, cool.

Not that Churchill ever needed any urging to be positive in his conduct of the war. Only a few days after the Dunkirk evacuation in 1940 he was bombarding Maj-Gen. Sir Hastings Ismay, his right-hand man in the War Cabinet secretariat, with memos demanding 'a vigorous, enterprising and ceaseless' offensive against the coastline newly occupied by the Germans. 'We should immediately set to work to organise raiding forces along these coasts where the populations are friendly' Churchill wrote. 'What we have just seen at Dunkirk shows how quickly troops can be moved off (and I suppose on to) selected points if need be. How wonderful it would be if the Germans could be made to wonder where they were going to be struck next, instead of forcing us to try to wall in the Island.... Enterprises must be prepared with specially trained troops of the hunter class who can develop a reign of terror down these coasts.'

The immediate result was the formation of the Commandos, who sustained British morale in those grim days with a series of raids on the occupied coastline of Europe. Though most were no more than pin-pricks, and some proved embarrassing duds, they were testimony to Churchill's eagerness to attack, even at the most depressing of times, and helped to sustain the British people's determination.

Germany's invasion of Russia in June 1941 provoked instant demands for the establishment of a Second Front. Walls were plastered with the slogan SECOND FRONT NOW and even the Empire-minded *Sunday Express* urged Churchill to hurry to the aid of Britain's unlikely new ally: 'Where's that Second Front?' it asked on 6 July 1941.

Field-Marshal Alan Brooke, who had taken over as Chief of the Imperial General Staff in October 1941 ('when the horizon was black from end to end with only one shaft of light in the possible entry of America into the war') was the professional soldier whose bleak task it was to restrain Churchill's passion for premature offensives and 'an incurable wish to stick his fingers into every pie before it was cooked.'

Having deflected the Premier from launching a feint attack on the Cherbourg peninsula to relieve pressure on the Russians, Brooke then spent long nights debating with Churchill a plan to invade Norway and, in Churchill's words, 'unroll the Nazi map of Europe from the top'. Brooke complained in his diary 'It had no strategic prospects of any kind and yet he insisted on returning to it. Heaven knows what we should have done in Norway had we landed there.'

The CIGS, who acknowledged Churchill as 'quite the most wonderful man I have ever met', had no illusions about some of his master's strategy, however: 'Winston never had the slightest doubt that he had inherited all the military genius of his great ancestor, Marlborough. His plans and ideas varied from the most brilliant conceptions to the wildest and most dangerous ideas. To wean him away from the wilder plans required superhuman efforts.'

Brooke knew, however, that Churchill would never overrule the unanimous opinion of the Chiefs of Staff Committee – the supreme battle headquarters of the British and Commonwealth armed forces – on any purely military matter. The bitterness over Gallipoli, which had come so close to wrecking Churchill's political career in the First World War, had left a deep scar and he would permit no one, not even the Cabinet, to criticise his Chiefs of Staff.

The Committee had three members, the heads of each armed service, with Brooke as chairman. They met every morning in the Cabinet War Room in Great George Street, near St James's Park, and debated, until they were in unanimous agreement, the stream of problems that beset a nation at war.

The Committee acquired a fourth member, Lord Louis Mountbatten, in March 1942. Mountbatten, forty-one years old and the King's second cousin, had had a lively war with the Royal Navy until then. As captain of the destroyer HMS *Kelly* he had been sunk off Crete and machine-gunned in the water. Appointed commander of the aircraft carrier HMS *Illustrious* he went, in October 1941, to Norfolk, Virginia, where the vessel was being repaired after the Mediterranean campaign. Abruptly, he was ordered to hand over his ship and return to Britain at once.

Angry and disappointed, he reported to the Prime Minister's official residence, Chequers, where he was told by Churchill he had been chosen to replace the sixty-nine-year old Sir Roger Keyes as head of the recently-formed Combined Operations Organisation. 'I would rather go back to the *Illustrious*', was Mountbatten's reaction. 'Then you're a fool' replied Churchill. 'The best thing you can look for there is to repeat your last achievement and get yourself sunk.'

Despite Mountbatten's initial reluctance, the appointment was an inspired one. Combined Operations had been formed to provide muscle for Churchill's ambitions to assault the occupied coast of Europe, and Keyes, a hero of the Zeebrugge Raid in the First World War, was simply too old for the wearying complexities of commanding an organisation that had necessarily in 1940 to be developed virtually from scratch. Mountbatten's staff experience was limited but he possessed other qualifications in abundance. His courage and ability were unquestioned, he was handsome, popular, witty and imaginative, and he had the knack of being able to talk as plainly and persuasively to the ranks as to his fellow-officers. The fact that he bore a marked resemblance to his cousin, King George VI, was not exactly a disadvantage, either.

Mountbatten's enthusiasm for having a crack at Occupied Europe, a venture so dear to Churchill's heart, brought him a place on the Chiefs of Staff Committee in his new role as chief of Combined Operations, though the chairman, Brooke, while acknowledging the newcomer's energy and drive, sourly regarded his presence as 'rather a waste of time'.

Brooke, without question Britain's outstanding soldier at that time, was accustomed to waging war by more accepted, conventional and cautious methods, and it alarmed him to find a newcomer to his committee apparently eager to promote Churchill's plans. Was he not having enough trouble persuading Winston to operate within the confines of Britain's limited resources? At Mountbatten's first Chiefs of Staff meeting on 10 March, when Operation 'Sledgehammer' was discussed, either as a raid or a proposed lodgement in France to help out the Russians, Brooke recalled 'Dickie [Mountbatten] was hankering after a landing near Cherbourg, where proper air support is not possible'.

Instead, it was agreed to compile a list of seven ports, around the Calais and Boulogne area and therefore well within the Allied air umbrella, which could be the target of a raid and help provide valuable information for long-term invasion plans.

The costly, though spectacularly successful attack on St Nazaire at the end of March, when the obsolete former American destroyer HMS *Campbeltown* rammed and blew up the dry-dock gates, boosted Churchill's desire for further adventure to feed the suffering British public. Brooke arrived at one Chiefs of Staff meeting just in time to turn down a Churchill proposal to land the Brigade of Guards on the Channel Island of Alderney.

After spending three hours discussing invasion possibilities with Churchill and Mountbatten, Brooke wrote 'This meeting with Winston was typical of many others when all difficulties were brushed aside and many unpleasant realities, such as resources available, were scrupulously avoided. He was carried away with optimism, and established lodgements all round the coast from Calais to Bordeaux with little regard to strength and landing facilities.'

So where could the armed forces strike next to appease the Prime Minister? The list of suggested Channel ports had been forwarded to Combined Operations, where the Naval Adviser, Capt. John Hughes-Hallett, who had masterminded the planning of the St Nazaire operation, argued with much reason that none of the ports should be selected since there was no knowing how many unauthorised people had glimpsed the list. So Hughes-Hallett and the other members of the target committee at Combined Operations Headquarters set about finding an alternative. When COHQ's Air Adviser requested somewhere within fighter range and the Military Adviser suggested a target not so far away that the soldiers would get seasick, Hughes-Hallett stabbed a finger at Dieppe on the map and said 'Right, let's take the old peace-time route – Newhaven to Dieppe and back. It's less than seventy miles away.'

Dieppe's proximity would permit the attacking force's Channel passage to be undertaken almost entirely under cover of darkness, and the fact that it was an excellent port with good rail and road communications and an airfield nearby made it ideal as a prospective target for full-scale invasion.

On 4 April Mountbatten gave his approval for plans to be drawn up for a Combined Operations attack on Dieppe. 'It's on,' was the wording of his terse note to Hughes-Hallett.

Dieppe, described in the *Blue Guide* to Normandy as 'a seaport, fishing harbour and fashionable watering-place' is situated, like Dover on the other side of the Channel, in a break between high chalk cliffs. The town lies at the mouth of the river Arques in a valley which is less than a mile wide and is dominated by headlands rising to more than 300 feet on the western side and a slightly less imposing height on the east.

The gap in which Dieppe is situated is easily the biggest in the formidable chain of chalk stretching along that part of the coast. There are other, smaller gaps. At Puys, about 2,000 yards east of the Dieppe harbour entrance, a gully leads down to a tiny beach, and at the village of Pourville, some two and a half miles to the west, there is a larger break where the river Scie flows into the sea.

Dieppe faces almost due north towards the English coast. The entrance to the harbour, between a pair of jetties, is on the extreme eastern end of the seafront (or the left-hand side if approached from the sea) and immediately beneath the cliffs of the Eastern headland. The town's impressive promenade, the Boulevard Maréchal Foch, stretches westwards from the harbour entrance for some 1,200 yards and most of Dieppe's leading hotels stood in 1942, and still stand, on the Boulevard de Verdun which forms the southern side of the 150-yard wide, well-grassed front. Interrupting the row of hotels along the Boulevard de Verdun was the town's tobacco factory, easily identifiable with its pair of tall chimneys. At the western end of the promenade, close under the cliff and beneath the Old Castle, was the Casino, a large white building which lay between the beach and the front of the town, breaking the clear sweep of the promenade between the headlands.

The beach in the Dieppe area is of large pebbles, hard on the feet and tossed into steeply shelving mounds by the action of tides and storms. The pebbles, found only along a hundred kilometres of Normandy coastline, were exported for use in the manufacture of porcelain. Though the people of the area feared that the constant removal of the pebbles would spell the end of their beaches, the seas continued to throw up new ones and in 1942 the Dieppe seafront remained an unattractive mass of stones, slippery, shifting and difficult to negotiate.

The town itself, its bars, cafés, shops and houses, huddles around the two harbours, outer and inner, and when the British painter Benjamin Robert Haydon went there in 1814 he noted 'Dieppe turns its back upon the sea as if in disgust at the sight of an element on which its country has always been beaten'. Its architecture was a hotchpotch, testimony to sufferings at the hands of the English. At the time of Joan of Arc, Lord John Talbot bombarded it for nine months. In 1694 Lord Berkeley, returning with his fleet from an unsatisfactory encounter with the French off Brest, vented his anger on Dieppe, setting it on fire after a three-day bombardment from the sea.

England's friendlier, and enduring, connection with Dieppe began after Napoleon's abdication in 1814 and grew with the development of a regular Channel ferry service to the port. There was an English quarter and two Anglican churches, British business houses flourished and British goods were prominently displayed in the shops. It was a favourite resort and painting scene of Turner, Oscar Wilde stayed there after his release from prison, Lord Salisbury built a house at Puys and Winston Churchill married Clementine Hozier, one of four children of Lady Blanche Hozier, who went to live in Dieppe with her daughters in 1899.

Churchill's comments on the selection of Dieppe as a target have not been recorded but he knew the place well enough at the turn of the century, occasionally visiting the town with his wife to see his mother-in-law. Churchill was not popular with the English residents of Dieppe, being described as 'bumptious and opinionated' and 'a tiresome young journalist'. He displeased the women even more as he sat outside the Hozier cabin on the promenade reading the daily papers, 'his bathing costume rolled down to expose an unusual amount of bare flesh, roasted to an unlovely scarlet'.

Two alternatives were swiftly drawn up for the Dieppe Raid by Combined Operations' planning staff. The first, designed on Mountbatten's instructions to avoid a frontal assault on the port, proposed to land a battalion of the new 40-ton Churchill tanks, as yet untried in combat, and a battalion of infantry on the beach at Quiberville, eight miles to the west, another two battalions in Pourville, two miles west, and two more at Puys, immediately east of the port. A further two battalions of infantry would remain at sea as a floating reserve. The intention was to take Dieppe by overrunning the headlands on either side. The second plan involved a smashing frontal blow at Dieppe over the town's main beaches, supported by flank landings at Pourville and Puys and attacks by parachutists and gliderborne troops against two heavy coastal batteries, situated at Berneval, six miles east of Dieppe, and Varengeville-sur-Mer, three and a half miles west, which commanded the sea approaches to Dieppe and, unless subdued, were in a position to destroy the invasion fleet.

Mountbatten set the project before his fellow members of the Chiefs of Staff Committee, who approved it and secured Churchill's enthusiastic backing. But Brooke, still displeased at the arrival on his tiny, select committee of war planners of the breezy young Mountbatten, insisted that the army's role in the operation should come under the direction of Home Forces rather than Combined Operations because the number of soldiers to be involved would be considerably greater than Combined Operations' commandos. Since the Chiefs of Staff Committee refused to grant the necessary unanimous approval to an outline plan until this point was conceded, Mountbatten went along with Brooke's wishes.

On 14 April a meeting at Combined Operations Headquarters at 1a Richmond Terrace, Whitehall, supported the project as 'attractive and worthwhile'. As Brooke had insisted, a representative of Home Forces sat in on the session.

Four days later it was agreed to pursue the plan for a frontal assault which was being vigorously pushed by Home Forces. The man delegated to see it through was Lt-Gen. Bernard Montgomery, who had been appointed chief of South-Eastern Command four months previously. The argument in favour of a frontal attack was that the risk of landing tanks eight miles away at Quiberville was too great. Bridges across the rivers Scie and Saane would have to be seized to prevent their being blown and halting the armoured column. Such a landing would also render a surprise attack on Dieppe itself out of the question.

Gen. Montgomery thought the idea of envelopment of Dieppe from the flanks would prove too protracted; there were also too many chances of unforeseen hold-ups. Having asked Combined Operations whether a raid of forty-eight hours' duration would be feasible and having been told that it would not, Montgomery then pressed for the frontal assault. He was sustained in this thinking by intelligence information that Dieppe was held by no more than 1,400 low-category German troops who could not be reinforced significantly until eight hours after the attack had gone in.

Still Mountbatten objected. 'On 25 April I called a meeting, at which I took the chair, to thrash out the pros and cons of the two plans. I came out strongly against the frontal attack but the Home Forces planners stuck to their guns, maintaining that a heavy bombing attack of maximum intensity on the defences immediately before the landing craft touched down and followed by low-flying attacks would counter-balance the risks of frontal attack.'

As the Chiefs of Staff had given Home Forces the authority to make the plan, Mountbatten was forced to yield. The frontal assault was put into the outline plan and approved by the Chiefs of Staff, so Mountbatten ended up by officially approving a scheme of which he strongly disapproved in order to achieve his cherished reconnaissance in force against the German-held coast of France.

Now it was time to give the operation a name. The one chosen was 'Rutter'. Although it was an old German word for a mercenary horse soldier it possessed no special significance, happening merely to be the next in line on a list of approved code names at Combined Operations Headquarters.

It had been Mountbatten's intention to use Commandos and Royal Marines 'who were well trained for the job' on Operation 'Rutter', but the decision about which troops to employ was now the responsibility of Gen. Sir Bernard Paget, Officer Commanding Home Forces, who had been pestered by commanders of the Canadian troops based in Montgomery's South-Eastern Command to be given a crack at the enemy. Mountbatten termed it 'a high-level political decision, and not one in which I was involved'. Montgomery also strongly denied after the war that the choice of Canadians had been his: 'Some people say it was me, which is totally untrue. I don't know who decided, it certainly wasn't me,' the inference being that it must therefore have been Paget.

Capt. John Hughes-Hallet considered it 'a bold decision, to say the least, to employ troops who hadn't been in action before on an operation which called for a great deal of experience' and in later years he recalled the vital decision this way: 'Monty claims he told Paget he didn't think it right to use the Canadians, not because they were not fine chaps but because they were totally inexperienced. Paget's view was that the Canadians had been a long time in England, were very well trained and were becoming impatient.'

However, the recollection of Lt-Gen. Harry Crerar, commanding the Canadian 1st Army Corps, is different. He claimed that on 27 April he was summoned to Montgomery's headquarters, told of the plan to raid an enemy-held port and asked briskly, 'Do you want it?' 'You bet' Crerar replied.

Three days later Montgomery called on Lt-Gen. Andrew McNaughton, in command of Canadian troops in Britain, to put the offer formally. Montgomery told McNaughton he had been 'pressed to agree' to a composite British and Canadian force but since he preferred to maintain unity of command he felt that Canadian soldiers were those best suited, Montgomery revealed that he had already contacted Crerar, who had suggested the Canadian 2nd Division for the operation. Suitably flattered, McNaughton cabled his superiors at Canadian Military Headquarters in Ottawa. Although he was authorised to commit Canadian forces in Britain to action on his own judgement, it had been agreed that, where possible, McNaughton would notify his government. Within two days Ottawa had given its approval without even knowing the nature of the operation, with the proviso that McNaughton should bear in mind 'whether prospects of success are sufficient to warrant risks involved'. On 15 May McNaughton again cabled Ottawa with the news that the outline plan for 'Rutter' had been approved. He told his government that he considered the objective worthwhile, land forces sufficient, sea and air forces adequate and arrangements for co-operation between all branches of the forces 'satisfactory'.

The Canadian government was delighted. At last the country's demand for action for its soldiers was to be gratified. A speech by Churchill to the Canadian House of Commons only four months previously in which he told the nation 'The Canadian Army in England is chafing at the bit and is burning to come to grips with the enemy' had been widely publicised.

So had his further promise: 'In a few months' time, when the season of invasions returns, the Canadian Army may find itself engaged in one of the bloodiest affrays the world has ever known.'

At the time of its utterance Churchill could hardly have realised how devastatingly that comment would be borne out.

CHAPTER TWO
Rutter

'No plan could be more unpromising than the plan of frontal attack.'

– Winston Churchill

The war was still less than four months old when the first Canadians arrived in Britain, and by the summer of 1942 more than 200,000 of them had been ferried across the Atlantic to mount guard in Fortress Britain. It was impressive growth from distinctly modest beginnings. At the outbreak of war the Canadian Army consisted of only 4,500 permanent troops and the rush to volunteer swamped Canada's meagre and outdated military resources. Recruits to the Royal Regiment of Canada were issued with jackets and trousers in different shades of khaki, while many men did their drill instruction in their civilian clothes and shoes until these fell apart. One regiment had to purchase its own cap badges, and another dipped into its funds to buy gloves so that rifles could be gripped comfortably in sub-zero temperatures.

The shortages were not confined to recruits. Lucien Dumais, a sergeant instructor with the French Canadian regiment, Les Fusiliers Mont-Royal, conducted his drills wearing an army cap and civilian suit with stripes pinned to the sleeves. The situation was laughably grim. Dumas recalled: 'We had no equipment, apart from a rifle for every fourth or fifth man, and about ten old, worn-out machine-guns left over from the 1914 war. Six months later, when I was commanding the anti-tank platoon, we not only had no trucks to tow the guns – we had no guns! We learned the mechanics from a handbook and carried out sham drill in front of a picture of a gun. Nobody in the platoon had ever seen a real one. It was difficult to keep up the men's interest with this sort of thing; they tried hard, though, and took up position around the picture imagining things as best they could. The loading of ammunition was an easy job, since we had none.'

Strategical thinking was sometimes equally ludicrous. The Director of Engineering Services at the Defence Department in Ottawa exhibited some trench-bound thinking with the comment that 'the ultimate weapon which wins a war is the bayonet on a rifle ... no one knows how useful tanks will be'. Soon afterwards most people realised how useful tanks were, as German armour smashed through and around supposedly impregnable static defences to reach the Channel coast in the brilliantly conceived 1940 *Blitzkrieg*.

By then the Canadian 2nd Division was well in the process of formation, though its advance elements were dismayed to learn that, rather than join the 1st Division in Britain, they had been assigned to garrison duty in Iceland. The gaffe was a brief one, remedied when Churchill complained, 'It would surely be a very great mistake to allow these fine troops to be employed in so distant a theatre.'

By the end of 1940, sometimes direct from Canada and occasionally via a brief stay in Iceland, the 2nd Division was gathered at Aldershot, traditional military depot for British forces since the Crimean War. Despite their lack of training and some trying experiences en route, the Canadians impressed their superiors. The Commander of the 2nd Division, Gen. Victor Odlum, who had served in both the Boer War and the First World War, and would shortly be swept away to the less demanding position of Canadian High Commissioner in Australia, exclaimed proudly as he watched the Royal Regiment march into Aldershot after an overnight train journey from Scotland, 'My men of steel!'

The newly-arrived troops found conditions at Aldershot not at all to their liking. The weather was cold and damp, the people in this garrison town cold and indifferent. Their barrack buildings, warmed by a larger ration of coal than that allocated to British troops, did not impress men only recently separated from the central heating and civilian comforts of life in Canada. There was a lot of grumbling in the early stages, and much illness caused by the damp weather. The problems persisted, even when the various regiments were dispersed into Sussex to assist with the coastal defence of that area of southern England. Postal censors noted an antipathy towards their lot, caused by a combination of bad food, poor health, depressing weather, homesickness and boredom.

There were other problems. The Royal Regiment brought with them to England, via Iceland, their regimental mascot, a St Bernard dog named Royal, who had been presented to the regiment on mobilisation in September 1939. The animal settled happily into a large, specially-built kennel on the lawn in front of the regiment's officers' quarters at Aldershot. Soon the commanding officer, Lt-Col. Hedley Basher, received a letter from the Ministry of Health in London ordering that the dog be surrendered to undergo its compulsory six months quarantine, in accordance with the strict British regulations in this matter.

This, and two subsequent communications, were ignored. Eventually an official arrived from London and demanded the immediate transfer of the animal to a government quarantine station. When all pleas failed, Col. Basher left the official holding and admiring the huge dog and went away to collect his loaded pistol. If Royal was taken away from the Regiment for six months, explained Basher, he would only pine away, so the simplest thing would be to have the dog destroyed at once. He handed the health official the gun and invited him to shoot. The startled man announced that he needed to return to London to report to his superiors. Nothing futher was heard, and Royal proudly accompanied Col. Basher into Sussex at the head of the regiment.

So, in Sussex, began the 2nd Division's earnest training for war, a combination of defensive instruction to counter the fading German threat against England and offensive exercises to prepare them for the day when they would storm ashore in Europe.

The prairie men of the South Saskatchewan Regiment (known as the Sirloin Steak Rustlers to the Sussex locals who could not pronounce the name of the province from which the soldiers came) immersed themselves cheerfully, and with some success, in their route marches and exercises. According to the regimental history the scout platoon became so efficient at camouflage that, when demonstrating for a group of senior staff officers, one major general 'obeyed a call of nature' on a tree which turned out to be a member of the platoon.

Discipline was not all it might have been during those days in 1941. In its offence report for July the Essex Scottish Regiment, from Windsor, Ontario, noted punishments meted out for striking an officer, failing to get out of bed at reveille after being warned, smoking a cigarette on route march, insolence to an NCO, and being dirty on parade.

On one exercise, a group of Canadians was forced to leave shelter and parade in the rain when Gen. Montgomery and Gen. Crerar arrived. As the British general prepared to address the parade he was greeted by rude noises and someone shouted, 'Hey Monty, for Christ's sake go home, willya?' The embarrassed Crerar attempted to identify and punish the culprits, but his letter of apology to Montgomery brought a dismissal of the matter as 'high spirits'. Monty said he considered it nothing more than soldiers letting off steam – 'and the best target is always an officer, the more senior the better'.

Montgomery must have found the Canadians a puzzling bunch. On one visit to the South Saskatchewans, he held a long conversation with the officer in charge of a special operations company, who chewed a large wad of gum during their talk. Eventually the ever-proper Monty turned to the Saskatchewans' commanding officer, Lt-Col. Sherwood Lett, and asked what the officer was chewing. Fingers crossed, Lett replied that it was gum, and that all Canadian and American athletes chewed gum because it was good for their health. Very impressed, Montgomery commented that in that case all soldiers should be chewing it.

There were praiseworthy attempts to find reasonable outlets for the Canadians' spare-time energy and entertainment, despite an acute shortage of helpers. One unit chaplain noted that he also served as education officer, mess secretary, welfare officer and sports officer: 'I have organised canteens, been in charge of broadcasts, distributed libraries, promoted shows, entertainments and dances – anything and everything to help our men and promote their welfare.'

Four voluntary organisations in Canada, the Salvation Army, Knights of Columbus, YMCA and the Canadian Legion, sent their representatives over to England to organise entertainment and recreational facilities, their fine work occasionally spoiled by duplication of effort and even, on occasion, unseemly rivalry for the soldiers' custom.

Pubs, clubs and other licensed establishments were highly popular with Canadian servicemen as, of course, they were with all Allied troops in wartime Britain, though the Canadians were saddled with a reputation for worse behaviour than any other overseas group.

From the time they first arrived in England in December 1940 until the Dieppe Raid in August 1942, 71 officers were tried by court martial. Of these six were cashiered and 21 dismissed the service. A large number of offences concerned careless handling of their bank accounts and non-payment of cheques and debts. During the same period 3,238 Canadian servicemen were tried by field general courts martial. Easily the most prevalent offence was absence without leave, accounting for more than half the cases. Next came misconduct, and drunkenness was third – 'accounting for a remarkably small percentage of the total' according to an official report.

In those 20 months the Canadian 1st Division in Britain committed 23,039 offences, and the 2nd Division 21,492, figures which were described as 'substantially better than those for troops in Canada for the same period'. Early in 1943 an officer at Canadian Military Headquarters in Britain said that under all circumstances the disciplinary situation was good. 'When the fact is taken into consideration that many of the cases reported are of chronic or repeating offenders, only a relatively small number of Canadian troops in the United Kingdom is giving trouble.' His estimate of Canadians who had become involved with the civil authorities was one-third of one per cent of those stationed in Britain.

The citizens of Sussex could perhaps be forgiven for thinking that the Canadians' share of crime in their county was rather greater than official statistics showed. Week after week reports were published in their local papers of Canadian misbehaviour. The tragedy was that these stories appeared alongside articles about Sussex servicemen who had been killed, captured or wounded in action.

Drink was the root cause of most civil offences, which varied from the trivial and even mildly amusing to the extremely serious. Alcohol was advanced as the excuse when Albert Blunt was fined £5 for assaulting a widow 'through a broken glass panel of a telephone kiosk' (while making a call to her sister, the woman felt a hand 'touch her bare flesh at the top of her stocking' and she saw Blunt crouched outside the phone box).

The alcohol intake frequently rendered the apprehension of the offenders a simple matter. George William White, sentenced to fifteen months hard labour at Sussex Assizes for rape, was found by police fast asleep on the pavement a few yards from his victim's home, his head cradled on his gas mask, and the woman's hat, gloves and handkerchief close by.

Lt-Col. John Durnford-Slater, commanding officer of No. 3 Commando, billeted in Seaford awaiting the Dieppe Raid, recalled in his autobiography: 'one night I had just gone to bed when I heard curious noises in the hall. I put on my slippers and went down in pyjamas to find an enormous Canadian walking around the hall. He had broken in through a small window. Fortunately he was extremely drunk, so I spoke to him nicely and gave him a little push into an armchair, where he slept most amiably. I started to telephone the police and most unwisely ended my message with the words "I will detain him until you come". This brought the Canadian to life in a big way, and he jumped to his feet shouting "Detain me nothing. Say, I could knock hell out of you."

'Mentally I quite agreed with him, as I did not feel my best in pyjamas in the middle of the night and faced with an angry man six inches taller than myself. I measured him for a blow strictly forbidden in the Queensberry Rules, but suddenly he again became amiable and another gentle push put him back in the comfortable armchair, where he slept heavily, and in the end went off with a small and rather elderly special constable.'

The winter of 1941–42, the third of the war and the third uncommonly cold winter in succession, probably marked the low point of morale in Britain among civilians and soldiers alike. On Christmas Day Alexander Wallace, a 44-year-old Calgarian, shot himself in a fit of depression and the Sussex coroner commented, 'All these soldiers very unselfishly came to this country for the purpose of giving us aid. We are apt to forget because they speak our language that they are, to all intents and purposes, in a foreign country, just as much as we should be in Libya.'

The sentiment was lost on some of the Sussex constabulary, whose Deputy Chief Constable complained about serious disturbances in Brighton during which police had been assaulted by gangs of drunken Canadians. 'These disturbances at night are getting very serious,' he said. 'On several occasions recently officers have had to draw their truncheons.' In his Notebook column in *The Brighton and Hove Gazette*, 'Gazetteer' deplored the Canadians' misconduct, calling for drastic action 'to infuse a little discipline into men who seem to believe that enlistment in the army releases them from all obligations of order and decency' and closed with the scathing, and typical, comment of those times directed at Canadians and Americans alike, 'The root of the trouble seems to be that they have too much money and spend it wrongly.'

Complaints became so vociferous that the Canadian Army's public relations officer, Maj. W. G. Abel, was sent to address Hove Rotary Club on the subject 'Why Canadians Seem Boisterous'. In the course of his speech Major Abel claimed that Canadian soldiers received only a shilling a week more than their British counterparts, adding, 'So if Canadians seem rather more boisterous it is not because they have plenty of money but because they used to lead a tougher life and still have the instincts of the cowboy or the frontiersman.'

The frontier spirit certainly seemed to be rampant in Mervyn Shopland Gibbs, who was refused a drink at the Richmond Hotel. When the licensee told him, 'No Canada, you've had enough, now go away like a good little boy,' Gibbs became abusive and told her 'I'll wreck the joint and when I've done that I'll shoot you.' He then locked the door, smashed chairs, tables, glasses and windows and when the police arrived put up a fight that lasted twenty minutes.

The Germans made gleeful propaganda of this sort of thing, and Lord Haw Haw advised his British listeners, 'If you really want to take Berlin, give each Canadian soldier a motor cycle and a bottle of whisky; then declare Berlin out of bounds and the Canadians will be there within 48 hours.'

During that bleak winter of 1941–42 the 2nd Division's new Commanding Officer, Maj-Gen. John Hamilton Roberts, inherited these reports of misbehaviour together with a host of other problems. 'Ham' Roberts, aged fifty, was one of the first to benefit directly from a visit to Britain a few months earlier by Canada's Prime Minister, Mackenzie King, who had been told in typically blunt fashion by Gen. Montgomery that most of Canada's commanders in the field were 'rather too old for this war'. On his return to Ottawa, King set about correcting that. Gen. Odlum was removed from command of the 2nd Division and replaced by Roberts, who was described by one of his Canadian contemporaries as 'a big hefty guy like one of your Rugger forwards'. Roberts, a Manitoban by birth and a resident of Vancouver, had served with the Royal Canadian Horse Artillery in the First World War, was wounded and won the Military Cross.

So rapidly did Roberts and his superiors, Crerar and McNaughton, weed out the older officers under their command that one RAF officers' mess, which numbered among its honorary members seven Canadian colonels with an average age of thirty-five, hung a sign over the bar: 'We earnestly regret that Canadian colonels under twenty-one cannot be served spirits unless accompanied by their parents.'

Roberts organised a vigorous round of exercises and manoeuvres designed to permit his wilder elements to work off surplus energy. Those elements were very much in the minority. For instance, by the summer of 1942 5,000 Canadian servicemen had married in Britain. In the Sussex Downs village of Firle, Kate Lusted recalled, 'They were very nice boys and they liked to come to our home and play cards, though all we could give them were things that weren't on ration, like buns and cocoa. But the French Canadians were more of a problem. They used to go round emptying the orchards, get one of their trucks and take the fruit somewhere where they knew they could sell it.'

Another Firle resident, John Hecks, a twenty-year-old in the Home Guard at the time, said, 'They were a happy-go-lucky lot of chaps and we got on very well with them,' though he too remembered instances of law-breaking: 'Some of them would catch the train back from Lewes, pull the communication cord, get out and take the short cut through the fields to their camp at Firle Place.'

The Canadians in 1942 have been described as 'the most exercised, untried army in the war'. They could easily have been sent to the Middle East, but Churchill was sensitive to world opinion about appearing to wage the North African campaign with Dominion soldiers only. So they remained stuck in Sussex, discouraged and, as far as they were concerned, forgotten. Ross Munro, a Canadian Press war correspondent in Britain, wrote, 'You could sense the lethargy. The most exciting thing that could happen was a weekend trip to London and a round of pubs and clubs.'

Or as one private in the Fusiliers Mont-Royal, Ray Geoffrion, put it, 'We enjoyed going out with girls and visiting pubs but that wasn't what we had come to England for. We wanted to fight.'

Planning of Operation 'Rutter' was now moving ahead quickly. The Canadians became involved officially for the first time on 8 May, too late to do anything to affect the Outline Plan. The man delegated to represent Gen. Roberts at the planning sessions as Chief Operations Officer was Lt-Col. Churchill Mann, a talented thirty-six-year-old staff officer who specialised in planning, but as yet knew nothing about raiding operations. His first reaction on being shown details of 'Rutter' was 'a fantastic conception'. The disadvantage, he was quick to note, was the proposal to attack the enemy frontally, where penetration would be most effectively obstructed, but he felt that in an English coastal town a similar attack would have good prospect of success 'providing the engineer tasks were suitably dealt with'.

So 'Rutter' wafted forward on its wave of optimism. Next day, 9 May, the joint Force Commanders were appointed: Roberts as

Military Commander; Air Vice-Marshal Trafford Leigh-Mallory, head of No. 11 Group of Fighter Command, as Air Force Commander; and Rear-Admiral H. T. Baillie-Grohman, who had to be summoned from the Middle East to take up his duties, as Naval Commander. They were responsible for all further planning, except for the vital and ultimate decision whether or not 'Rutter' should sail. This, at the insistence of the Chiefs of Staff Committee, was the responsibility of the Naval Commander-in-Chief at the nearest home port, in this case Admiral Sir William James at Portsmouth.

The official Outline Plan for 'Rutter', submitted to the Chiefs of Staff Committee the same day, 9 May, contained a bland misconception in its very first line: 'Intelligence reports indicate that Dieppe is not heavily defended and that the beaches in the vicinity are suitable for landing infantry, and armoured fighting vehicles at some.'

Having assumed that one of the most important ports on the Channel coast would not be adquately defended, the Outline Plan next detailed the objectives of the raid: to destroy enemy defences and radar installations, power stations, dock and rail facilities and petrol dumps in the vicinity of Dieppe, collect secret documents and prisoners, and, most ambitious of all, remove 'for our own use' forty invasion barges reported to be lying in Dieppe harbour.

The allocation of the assault force was slightly changed from that originally submitted by Mountbatten. Two infantry brigades, of three battalions each, would be involved in the landing: two battalions going ashore at Pourville, west of Dieppe, and one at Berneval, to the east of the port, in flank attacks intended to subdue anti-aircraft, coastal defence and mobile batteries on the cliffs before linking up with the frontal assault force in Dieppe. In this task they would be assisted by parachutists.

Two battalions were to land on the main beach in front of Dieppe half-an-hour after the flank attacks went in, to be followed by thirty Churchill tanks and whatever engineering support was deemed necessary. Another battalion of infantry and thirty more tanks would be held offshore as a floating reserve.

When Dieppe had capitulated it was proposed to re-embark troops and tanks either over the beaches or from inside the harbour. The earliest date for this ambitious venture, because of the combination of tides and moon, was the night of 20–21 June or any of the six nights following.

To persuade the Germans to keep their heads down while the assault went in, the Royal Navy allocated the pop-gun firepower of six Hunt Class destroyers, which carried only 4-inch armament insufficient to dent heavily-protected defensive emplacements. In an attempt to persuade the Navy to release a battleship to support the landings with adequate fire-power, Mountbatten went to see the First Sea Lord, Sir Dudley Pound. As a sailor himself, Mountbatten fully recognised the Navy's objections to exposing a capital ship in the confines of the Channel, but the Germans had just proved that it could be done with the successful 'Channel dash', when the warships *Scharnhorst, Gneisenau* and *Prinz Eugen* achieved something which no enemy of England had pulled off for three centuries by passing safely through the Dover Strait.

Sir Dudley, terrified of losing his mightiest weapons to air attack and mindful of the recent fate of the *Prince of Wales* and *Repulse* against Japanese aircraft in the Far East, was appalled at the suggestion: 'Battleships by daylight off the French coast? You must be mad, Dickie.'

So the crucial mistakes began to multiply. First, a frontal assault against a defended target; now the refusal to provide enough weight of shell to back up that landing. But there still remained the promise of support from the air. Or did there? Because of Churchill's unwillingness to incur French wrath by inflicting heavy civilian casualties through indiscriminate air raids there was a Cabinet ruling that targets in Occupied France could only be bombed when weather conditions were such that accuracy could be expected. Anxiously, permission was sought of the Prime Minister, who was reminded that the raid on St Nazaire in March had been affected by this restriction; the bombers which arrived over the town were able to do nothing more than wake up the garrison since low cloud prevented their identifying their targets in the dock area.

Grudgingly, Churchill gave his approval for the night bombing of Dieppe, whatever the weather, though he reiterated his general opposition. At least that part of the heavy support was saved. On 13 May the Chiefs of Staff approved the Outline Plan for 'Rutter'. The same day the Canadian 2nd Division was ordered to move to the Isle of Wight for secret training.

Canada's top soldier in Britain, Gen. McNaughton, fully approved of 'Rutter', as he told his government in a 'very secret' cable, though because of what McNaughton termed 'the most stringent measures to preserve secrecy' the Canadian government still did not know where their soldiers were about to be sent.

The force chosen by Roberts from the 2nd Division to undertake the raid on Dieppe consisted of the 4th Brigade (battalions from the Royal Regiment of Canada, the Royal Hamilton Light Infantry and the Essex Scottish – all Ontario regiments) and the 6th Brigade (Fusiliers Mont-Royal from the French-Canadian province of Québec, Camerons of Canada from Winnipeg and South Saskatchewan Regiment), plus the Canadian 14th Tank Battalion, known as the Calgary Tanks.

The brigade commanders were Sherwood Lett (4th) and William Wallace Southam (6th). Brig. Lett was forty-six. He joined the Army in 1913 as a private and rose to the rank of captain in the First World War, winning the Military Cross. A Rhodes Scholar at Oxford and student at the University of British Columbia, Lett gave up his law career to rejoin the Army in 1939. He had commanded the South Saskatchewans in Britain for a short time before taking over the 4th Brigade.

Brig. Southam, from Toronto, was forty-one and a member of the newspaper publishing company which bore his name. A graduate of the Royal Military College in Kingston, Ontario, Southam went overseas as a major with the 48th Highlanders of Toronto.

Col. Hedley Basher, another First World War veteran and conqueror of Britain's quarantine laws in the 'battle' over the regimental mascot, led his battalion of the Royal Regiment so quickly from their Billingshurst barracks to new quarters near Freshwater on the Isle of Wight that they arrived on the afternoon of 19 May several hours before Gen. Roberts turned up on the island to establish training headquarters at Osborne Court, Cowes. The South Saskatchewans were next, moving thankfully from Wykehurst Castle which according to the regimental history 'was inhabited by a middle-aged woman who kept an incredible number of cats' and settling in at another stately home, Norris Castle, once one of Queen Victoria's favourite summer homes. The Saskatchewans had a new commanding officer, the thirty-two-year-old Lt-Col. Cecil Merritt, another former lawyer and an outstanding athlete from the West Coast province of British Columbia who, at the outbreak of war, was a militia major with his father's old regiment, the Seaforth Highlanders of Vancouver. When he set out for the war, Merritt's wife saw him off at the regimental armoury with sandwiches, a flask of coffee and the plea, 'Don't try to win medals. Just come home'. They were not to see each other again for six years and Cecil Merritt would become the first Canadian Victoria Cross of the war.

By 20 May all the Canadian infantry units had arrived on the Isle of Wight; the Royal Hamilton Light Infantry, commanded by the thirty-nine-year-old Lt-Col. Robert Ridley Labatt, who had been in charge of the first Canadian detachment to stand guard at Buckingham Palace during the Coronation celebrations in 1937; the Essex Scottish, under the quiet, bespectacled Ontario lawyer, Lt-Col. Fred Jasperson; the Camerons of Canada, commanded by Lt-Col. Alfred Gostling, once a Winnipeg radio repair man; and the French Canadians of the Fusiliers Mont-Royal under Lt-Col. Dollard Menard, who had come to the Second World War via the Khyber Pass.

Menard, a professional soldier who became restless with the peace-time Canadian army, had volunteered for service with a Sikh regiment. When the war broke out Menard's request that his government should bring him back to Canada was ignored, so he made his own way home by managing, at one brief stage, to become a member of the Royal Navy. When he took over the Fusiliers, where command had always been a matter of succession, he was regarded with suspicion as an outsider, but his readiness to exceed his men's output of energy in training quickly endeared him to the battalion.

Completing the gathering of youthful commanders was the thirty-three-year-old John Gilbey Andrews, colonel of the Calgary Tanks. Andrews, a professional soldier, had been in the army for eleven years after abandoning his previous job of bank clerk.

The Isle of Wight had been chosen as the Canadians' training ground for three reasons: its isolation enabled a tight clamp to be kept on security, its beaches provided natural facilities for amphibious training and landing exercises, and its sheer chalk cliffs were similar to those at Dieppe. The 5,000 strong contingent of the Canadian army, known as 'Simmerforce' (a name which might have been borrowed from an Evelyn Waugh novel) was augmented by hundreds of sailors and other auxiliaries required for the training. Only civilians who lived or worked on the Isle of Wight were allowed to remain; then it was sealed off. As a means of emphasising the need for security, all the troops were obliged to see a propaganda film called *Next of Kin* in which those taking part in a combined operation were annihilated because the enemy had been alerted by careless talk.

The Canadians were pitched into violent programmes designed to increase their stamina and ability. They tackled obstacle courses, bayonet fighting, unarmed combat, cliff climbing, firing on the run and from the hip, embarking and disembarking from landing craft, demolition practice and river crossings.

After a week of this furious activity Roberts noted in his diary, 'Although the condition of the men is reasonably good, the assault courses and speed marches have shown that there is a great improvement to be made in this direction. In the speed marches units are able to do five miles in forty-five minutes, but took from one and a half to two hours to do the remaining six miles. In the assault courses, troops were able to complete the course but were, in many cases, unable to fight or fire effectively when finished.'

By the end of the second week Roberts had noted a dramatic improvement, while Ross Munro, the Canadian Press correspondent, termed the training, 'a revelation'. He wrote, 'Nothing as advanced as this had ever been done in combined operations. The massive

Churchill tanks lumbered off the tank landing craft ... the base areas rocked with test demolitions. The infantry were out every day, practising street fighting; Sten guns chattered and grenades banged from morning till night.'

There were mistakes and muddles, especially on the beaching exercises. Landing craft put in at the wrong places, collided with each other or even came ashore stern first, so that the troops who had been crouched down inside the boats dashed straight out into water over their heads.

Gradually, however, the training had its effect. One man in the Royal Regiment wrote home, 'You wouldn't know the regiment now ... all dead wood weeded out and now we're the trimmest and fightingest little unit you ever did see.' Capt. John Foote, the immensely popular chaplain of the Royal Hamilton Light Infantry, who insisted on participating in the most rigorous exercises, remembered, years later, 'We were welded, like a good Rugby team.'

Welded they may have been, unobserved they certainly were not. The Germans maintained a sharp aerial reconnaissance over the Isle of Wight and on the evening of 24 May, Empire Day, the Royal Regiment's encampment was bombed by two planes but no one was hurt.

On 5 June a crucial planning meeting was convened at Combined Operations Headquarters in London. General Montgomery was in the chair, and the three force commanders, Roberts, Leigh-Mallory and Baillie-Grohman, also attended. The subject under discussion was the proposed night bombing of Dieppe. Leigh-Mallory, worried that the bombing might be inaccurate, which would only serve to alert the Germans, suggested to the meeting that such a raid 'was not the most profitable way of using the bombers'. Instead of objecting, as he should have done, to the proposed withdrawal of his air strike force, Roberts, as Military Commander, then actually supported the abandonment of the air raid on the grounds that indiscriminate destruction of Dieppe would hamper the movement of his tanks through the streets.

Roberts recalled later, 'After discussing it with Leigh-Mallory, I said "No, I wouldn't take a chance if they could only hit Dieppe and not the headlands and places where I wanted their bombs".' And so was taken the fateful decision to abandon the bombing, even though it had previously been recognised as the one factor capable of helping a frontal assault to succeed after the refusal of the Navy to provide heavy fire support.

In his memoirs Montgomery wrote, 'I should not myself have agreed with these changes. The demoralisation of the enemy forces by preliminary bombing was essential (as was done in Normandy in 1944 just before the troops touched down on the beaches).' But as a Combined Operations historian has noted, 'This is one passage in Montgomery's book where his memory has played him false. Far from not agreeing to the change he was in the chair at the meeting and is not on record in the minutes as having demurred.' Monty's biographer, Ronald Lewin, also commented, 'This appears to be one of those not infrequent occasions when Montgomery has had a convenient lapse of memory – as some shut off a hearing aid to exclude a disagreeable noise.'

In place of the bombers there would now be dawn strikes against the beach and headland defences by cannon firing fighters, while bombing raids would be mounted against Boulogne as a diversion and against the nearby airfield of Abbéville, to hamper its use during 'Rutter'.

So now the plan had come down to a proposal to attack a defended port, dominated by cliffs, without any meaningful preliminary bombardment. But so keen were the Canadian commanders and their soldiers to get into action that Goronwy Rees, one of Montgomery's aides involved in the Dieppe planning, was convinced 'the operation would have proceeded even if the troops had been asked to land with no better weapons than their bare hands and fists; in the event, they had little more'.

Mountbatten had missed the fateful 5 June meeting. He was in the United States attempting to deflect Roosevelt and the US Joint Chiefs of Staff from their intentions to open a Second Front that autumn. Having been frustrated in his bid to obtain the promise of an early invasion from Churchill, the Russian Foreign Minister Molotov had taken himself to Washington, where the American President, seeking to take an initiative before the Congressional elections in November, had categorically authorised Molotov to tell his leader, Stalin, that he expected a Second Front later that year and had cabled Churchill suggesting August as the latest landing date.

On 3 June Mountbatten arrived in Washington to explain why a cross-Channel sacrifice landing to assist the Russians was impossible in 1942. One point which he stressed was the severe shortage of landing craft, and he extracted a promise from the United States government to provide more of these vessels as a matter of urgency.

On his return to London Mountbatten was 'really taken aback' to learn of the decision to abandon the Dieppe air bombardment, but when he raised the matter with Field-Marshal Brooke, the Chief of the Imperial General Staff insisted that the force commanders of 'Rutter' should be allowed to plan the operation their way.

After almost a month on the Isle of Wight the 'Rutter' forces were considered ready to test their new skills and fitness in a full-scale exercise. It took place near Bridport, in Dorset, an area as closely resembling the Dieppe coastline as possible, on 12 June. Given the code name 'Yukon', it was witnessed by Generals Paget, McNaughton and Crerar. What they saw in the dawn light was a shambles. The flanking battalions were landed at the wrong beaches, the Royal Regiment was put ashore two miles to the west of the intended spot, the South Saskatchewans were almost a mile away from where they should have been, the tank landing craft got lost and arrived an hour and a half late, liaison was poor and the rate of progress inland extremely slow.

Mountbatten, who had missed 'Yukon' because of his Washington visit, decided on his return that 'Rutter' should be postponed in order to mount a second exercise, 'Yukon II', on 23 June despite the considerable risk of a breach of security in the interim. With the Chief of Combined Operations and Gen. Montgomery joining Paget, McNaughton and Crerar as observers, 'Yukon II' was considerably smoother, though the landing craft carrying the Essex Scottish lost their way and the troops landed late.

Mountbatten was satisfied enough to give 'Rutter' the go-ahead on the first available combination of moon, tides and weather, but McNaughton was not so happy. 'These are anxious days', he told Ross Munro of the Canadian Press afterwards. 'There is great peril when the Navy does not land our men on the right beaches at the right time.' Munro shared his apprehension: 'I had probably been on as many landing exercises as anyone in the Canadian Army during the previous year or more, and they never seemed to go according to schedule. Difficulties always cropped up during the run-in to the beaches and put the troops at a disadvantage from the start.'

But the Canadians' very inexperience infected them with the dangerous conviction that if the Navy could only put them ashore at the right place the battle was won. Montgomery's staff assistant, Goronwy Rees, recalled after 'Yukon II': 'We sailed back to Cowes by destroyer, lying on deck stripped to the waist under a blue and cloudless sky; all of us suffered from the same fatal lack of imagination which prevented us from translating the depressing lessons of the rehearsal into the murderous consequences they would have in battle … like an amateur dramatic company we assured ourselves that everything would be all right on the night.'

On 27 June Roberts called all the officers of his division to his headquarters in Cowes, where in a room with the windows blacked out and in stifling heat he outlined the complete plan, without actually naming Dieppe. Pointing to a scale model of the area he said, 'Gentlemen, we have waited more than two years to go into battle against the Germans. The time has now come.' He emphasised the need for the strictest security and revealed that the other ranks would not be told of the operation until after they had boarded ships for what was ostensibly another exercise, 'Klondike'. As Ross Munro recalled, 'Everyone left the room with a feeling of high elation. Here was the big job at last; all this training was now to be put to use as the real thing on a daring operation.'

On 30 June Montgomery spent the day on the Isle of Wight going over the details of 'Rutter' with the force commanders. Despite his private reservations, expressed after the war, about 'launching against a defended port in the Atlantic Wall a Canadian division which had done no fighting and which was commanded by a major-general who had never commanded a division in battle, and never even commanded a battalion in battle', Montgomery forwarded a guardedly optimistic report to his superior, Paget: 'I am satisfied that the operation as planned is a possible one and has good prospects of success given (a) favourable weather (b) average luck and (c) the Navy put us ashore in roughly the right places and at the right times.' Beneath his signature he penned the postscript, 'The Canadians are first-class chaps; if anyone can bring it off, they will', a comment which hardly matched his post-Dieppe statements.

That same evening Churchill, just back in London from doing his best to dissuade the Americans from their cross-Channel ambitions, called a meeting at 10 Downing Street to discuss the Dieppe Raid. Mountbatten, his Combined Operations naval planner Capt. John Hughes-Hallett and the CIGS, Field-Marshal Brooke, were among those who joined the Prime Minister around a table while Mrs Churchill hovered in the background arranging flowers. Churchill, depressed by the fall of Tobruk, asked Mountbatten whether he could guarantee success at Dieppe, saying he was afraid of 'another Tobruk'. Mountbatten revealed that Hughes-Hallett had taken part in training exercises with the Canadians in the guise of 'Private Charles Hallett' of the Camerons, and Hughes-Hallett assured his war leader that the Canadians 'would fight like hell'.

Brooke now made one of his forceful interventions. If anyone could guarantee success there would be no object in doing the operation, he pointed out. When Churchill grumbled that this was not a moment at which he wanted to be taught by adversity, Brooke replied, 'In that case you must abandon the idea of invading France, because no responsible general will be associated with any planning for invasion until we have an operation at least the size of Dieppe Raid behind us to study and base our plans upon.' The argument was won. Churchill gave the raid his blessing.

Operation 'Rutter' was set for 4 July. On 2 July the Canadians began boarding their troopships, mainly converted Channel ferries, and by the next day more than 200 assorted vessels involved lay off the Isle of Wight. There were late security flurries when an Isle of Wight resident, Mrs E. M. Hans-Hamilton, reported that she had heard from her servants and her daughter about Canadian troops being involved in an operation against France, and the island's Chief Constable passed on another story that Parkhurst Prison was going to be evacuated to receive German prisoners. Asked to check the sources of these rumours, the Chief Constable wondered where he was expected to start 'when two brigades leave an open quay in broad daylight and practically every one of these soldiers has told his girlfriend that he is off to a certain place'.

There was a flutter, too, among Canadian military and security personnel when, in a Dominion Day speech in Ottawa on 1 July, Premier Mackenzie King warned the Axis powers, 'The Canadian Army is not an instrument built only to resist attack.... The day is coming – and it may be close at hand – when it will have an honoured place in the van of attack.'

Aboard the troopships the battalion commanders officially revealed to their cheering soldiers that 'Klondike' was, in fact, to be Dieppe. Roberts and Mountbatten later toured the ships, which were then sealed off ready for departure.

Now, however, the weather intervened. The sort of problems faced in mounting an operation such as 'Rutter' were pointed out by Professor Solly Zuckerman, whose first assignment on joining Combined Operations as a civilian scientific liaison officer was a request from Mountbatten to estimate the number of nights in a month in which conditions would be suitable for cross-Channel raids. 'It took a month or so, working on tides, wind forces and directions and moonless nights. In the end I proudly presented the results to Mountbatten with the words "Well, it turns out that there will never be a night suitable".' On the evening of 3 July, wind strength was the trouble. In the opinion of the commander of 1st Airborne Division, which was to supply the paratroops to be put down on the headlands on each side of Dieppe, an accurate air drop would have been impossible, though Major Brian McCool of the Royal Regiment did not agree: 'You never had better weather in your bathtub.'

Two more days passed, with the Canadians sealed aboard their ships. On a tank landing craft (described by its commander, the actor Peter Bull, as 'a cross between a coal shovel and an empty water-trough') about fifty Canadians were crammed in the well-deck among tanks and other vehicles in conditions of great secrecy, covered over by canvas and sweltering in the heat.

Ross Munro was aboard the Channel ferry *Prince Charles* with the Essex Scottish as the days of waiting dragged by: 'In the wardroom the barometer is our idol. We worship before it every hour of the day and wear a patch on the carpet praying to it that the weather will break.'

Continued inclement weather and an air attack combined to deliver the death blow to Operation 'Rutter' on 7 July. At 0615 hours that morning four Focke Wulf 190 fighter bombers swept low over Yarmouth Roads where the converted ferries *Princess Astrid* and *Princess Josephine Charlotte* lay at anchor with the Royal Regiment on board.

The attack was devastatingly accurate. *Princess Astrid* suffered one hit and a near miss, the bomb piercing the sea deck and going out through the side before exploding in the water. *Charlotte* was struck by a bomb which went through the mess decks, into the engine room and out through the bottom of the ship, exploding beneath it and severely damaging the engine-room.

Four soldiers of the Royal Regiment were slightly injured – the only casualties of Operation 'Rutter'. Sgt Charles Surphlis was aboard *Princess Astrid* when she was hit: 'I was still in kip at the time; we didn't know what the hell it was. I jumped out of my bunk and straight into some water which had been spilled out of a dish when the bomb struck. I thought we were sinking already.'

The Royal Regiment was hurriedly disembarked and moved to Cowes for re-embarkation in new vessels, but the weather was still not considered good enough for the raid to proceed. Since the morning of 8 July presented the last possible favourable tide, the decision to cancel was taken in Portsmouth by Admiral Sir William

James: 'It was a hateful decision to make when all those gallant fellows were keyed up and trained to the last button, but I could not stop the westerly wind blowing, and that was the deciding factor.'

There was disbelief and dismay among the Essex Scottish aboard *Prince Charles*. 'God, what a blow to these troops!', Ross Munro wrote in his diary. 'Men break down and cry on the decks, they take the disappointment so hard. In the wardroom the officers drink innumerable double scotches (at eight cents a glass – Navy prices). "Let us hate" is the toast.'

The raiding force was dispersed from the Isle of Wight and back to the mainland of Southern England. Advising Gen. Crerar of this in a 'most secret and personal' letter, Brig. Maurice Chilton of Montgomery's South-Eastern Command noted that, as it would be impossible to maintain security among the large force which had already been briefed about its target, 'the Army Command had therefore recommended to the powers-that-be that the operation be off for all time'.

Montgomery was 'delighted, absolutely delighted' at the news of 'Rutter's' cancellation. 'I had never been happy about this difficult operation being done by such inexperienced commanders and troops. You see, bravery alone is no substitute for battle experience ... none.'

Within a week, however, the operation which was to have been 'off for all time' would be remounted.

CHAPTER THREE
Jubilee

'Dieppe gave the Allies the precious secret of victory. If I had the same decision to make again I would do as I did before.'
— Earl Mountbatten of Burma

With the cancellation of 'Rutter', newspapers in Canada were given permission on 14 July to publish reports of the forces' training programme for the operation. The story was picked up and appeared two days later in the British national press. The *Daily Telegraph* gave it great prominence, calling the training exercise 'a prelude to what may be major military operations on the European coast', and some of the units participating were named.

Yet the same day steps were being taken, in strictest secrecy, to remount the Dieppe Raid. 'Rutter' was the third consecutive operation against the German-held coastline to have been cancelled, and Churchill considered it 'most important that a large-scale operation should take place this summer', both for military planning and pressing political reasons.

Churchill's view was discussed at a 'Rutter' post-mortem held at Combined Operations Headquarters, as a result of which, according to Mountbatten, 'I made the unusual and, I suggest, rather bold proposal that we should remount the operation against Dieppe.' Mountbatten's reasoning was that, unless a test attack could be launched against Europe before the end of the summer 'raiding season' the Allies' return to the Continent in strength would be further delayed.

'I put the idea to the Chiefs of Staff and then we discussed it with the Prime Minister', said Mountbatten. 'Candidly, all were startled and at first argued against it on security grounds.'

After persuading his fellow Chiefs of Staff and Churchill that there was no alternative target that could be scouted by Combined Operations in time to mount a raid that year, Mountbatten argued that, even if the Germans had known in advance that an operation had been planned against Dieppe, the last thing they would imagine would be that the British would be stupid enough to attempt the same operation again. Mountbatten also secured Churchill's agreement to abnormal security measures. Nothing about the remounting of the operation was to be put in writing anywhere. 'It was all done verbally be me', Lord Louis said. 'Not even the First Lord of the Admiralty knew about it. He read about the raid for the first time in the newspapers when it happened.'

To help maintain secrecy it was suggested that no further exercises should be held by the Canadians and Gen. Roberts was asked if he would agree to this. Not only did Roberts concur, but he reiterated his anxiety 'to get cracking as soon as possible'. Once more, Canadian enthusiasm was outrunning judgement.

There was a good deal less enthusiasm in other quarters. Roberts's 4th Brigade commander, Sherwood Lett, admitted, 'When the fact that the actual Dieppe operation was on again sank in, I knew at once that we were in for it.' So did many of the officers and men of the Canadian regiments involved, and they remain convinced to this day that the Germans knew all about Dieppe well in advance. Jack Poolton, a private in the Royal Regiment, claims that when he got back to the mainland from the Isle of Wight after the 'Rutter' dispersal, people said to him 'Oh, you didn't go to Dieppe, eh?'

While it is undoubtedly true that, within the highest circles of British defence commands, security over Dieppe had never been so good, it is equally undeniable that, on the outside, rarely can an operation have been so freely discussed by so many. Lord Lovat, the Commando leader, remembered, 'The Canadians made no secret of where they had been going and though I wasn't involved in Dieppe at that stage I even got lavatory rumours up in Scotland that a raid had been postponed.'

Lt-Col. Robert Labatt of the Royal Hamilton Light Infantry visited 'Rutter' headquarters at Osborne Court just after the operation had been cancelled. Where armed guards had once barred entry, anyone could now walk in. 'Doors were open … and 'Rutter' papers stamped 'cancelled' were scattered everywhere.'

Churchill's urgent need for something, anything, of a positive nature to appease Britain's impatient allies, Russia and the United States, was probably decisive in pushing forward the Dieppe Raid. He was locked in a bitter argument with the Americans over their ill-judged 'Sledgehammer' project to invade the Continent in the autumn of 1942 and Operation 'Roundup', the plan to cross the Channel in force in May 1943. The Prime Minister agreed with his CIGS, Field-Marshal Brooke, who considered 'we are hanging on by our eyelids … and could stage no large-scale operations without additional shipping', and he finally managed to torpedo 'Sledgehammer' with this note to Roosevelt:

'We hold strongly to the view that there should be no substantial landing in France this year unless we are going to stay. No responsible British military authority has so far been able to make a plan for September 1942 which had any chance of success unless the Germans became utterly demoralised, of which there is no likelihood. Have the American Staffs a plan? At what points would they strike? What landing craft and shipping are available? Who is the officer prepared to command the enterprise?'

'Sledgehammer' was formally abandoned on 22 July. The following evening Churchill received a telegram from Stalin again demanding a Second Front to relieve his hard-pressed armies. The Prime Minister replied to the Russian leader that action was in hand. Two days later he approved the remounting of the Dieppe Raid. Indisputably, Dieppe was being offered as a sop to frustrated Americans and angry Russians.

Churchill's eloquence and doggedness eventually persuaded the American military leaders and their President to attack the Germans instead in North Africa in late 1942, at the cost of going personally to Moscow to explain the details of the African venture to Stalin, a journey which he described as 'rather like carrying a large lump of ice to the North Pole.' When Churchill broke the news that there would be no invasion of France that year, Stalin complained that the Soviet

Command had based all their plans of summer and autumn operations on the assumption that a Second Front would be launched in 1942. When the British leader stressed the dangers of a Channel crossing Stalin replied contemptuously, 'If the British would only fight the Germans as the Russians had done … they wouldn't be so frightened of them.' Stalin's attitude, if not his rudeness, could be appreciated. The sacrifice of a few thousand men thrown against the French coast only amounted to the sort of casualty rate being suffered daily by the Russians in their struggle to stem the German summer offensive.

The Dieppe operation was given a new title. 'Rutter' became 'Jubilee'. The choice of code name, a Hebrew word for the time of celebration announced by a blast on a ram's horn, was a little unfortunate, implying as it did that, at a flourish of the Jubilee trumpets, Germany's Atlantic Wall would fall down. There were changes, too, among the commanders. Rear Admiral Baillie-Grohman went to another job and his place as Naval Force Commander was taken by the man who had had more to do with the Dieppe planning than anyone else, Capt. John Hughes-Hallett. Baillie-Grohman was thankful to be relieved of the task: 'Had I been asked to take on the responsibility of Naval Commander once more I am very doubtful if I could have agreed.… Any commander, German or British, who once got the news that there had been a plan to raid his port, whether it had been cancelled or not, would most certainly look again, not once but twice or thrice, at his defences and they would be strengthened. The great probability that this news would leak out, combined with the absence of heavy supporting fire and poor training would, in my opinion, make this operation not feasible as an act of war.'

Command of the Royal Regiment's battalion was taken over by Lt-Col. Douglas Catto, a former Toronto architect, who replaced Col. Hedley Basher just in time to see the Royals win the annual brigade sports meeting at Horsham, but the biggest personnel change was at the very top, where Montgomery was replaced by the Canadian,

Crerar. As soon as the 'Rutter' force had dispersed Montgomery considered the project cancelled for good 'and I turned my attention to other questions'. When he heard about the operation being remounted Montgomery wrote to his superior, Paget, pleading 'At least if they want to do something on the Continent let them choose another target than Dieppe.'

Montgomery's unhappiness was noted by his aide, Goronwy Rees: 'I suspected that behind Monty's calm lay a wish that the formal responsibility for the operation had not fallen on him.' That wish was granted. Mountbatten, McNaughton and Roberts had discussed the question of more direct Canadian command over the 'Jubilee' troops, and McNaughton secured Paget's permission to install Crerar in Montgomery's place.

As it happened, Montgomery was not even in the country when the Dieppe Raid took place. On 10 August he left for the Middle East to keep his appointment with destiny at El Alamein.

There were changes, too, in the plan. The most important was the decision to delegate the flank-attack tasks of knocking out the coastal batteries to seaborne Commando groups rather than parachute troops. 'Rutter' had taught a hard lesson here, with the raid cancelled because the wind conditions, rather than the sea, had proved unsuitable.

The Commandos chosen were No. 3, under Lt-Col. John Durnford-Slater, and No. 4, led by Lt-Col. the Lord Lovat. Durnford-Slater, known as 'Torchy' because of his red hair, claimed to be the first Commando. His career was transformed in mid-June 1940 when he left the Royal Artillery, and what he called 'a valuable but painfully dull' job as adjutant of an anti-aircraft unit with instructions to form a Commando group. Sturdily built and balding, he still played Rugby with gusto. According to one of the officers of his unit 'his ideas were old-fashioned; in any raid he must always be the first man ashore and the last away'.

On occasion, his ideas were also rather irregular. After leading 3 Commando on the successful raid against Vaagso in northern Norway in December 1941 he found himself with about 80 vacancies in men he had lost either killed, wounded or, as he put it, 'who did not measure up in battle to the stiff requirements of the unit'. To replace them, he gave his officers extra leave on condition that they returned with suitable recruits poached from other units. 'It did not take over-long to fill our ranks,' he reported.

Simon Fraser, twenty-fourth Chief of the Clan Fraser of Lovat, was heir to an historic estate and worldwide clan. Tall, handsome, aristocratic and a stickler for the sort of taught discipline that saves lives in battle, Lord Lovat had, within a year's training in Ayrshire, transformed 4 Commando from what he termed 'a rabble in arms' into a formidable unit.

Hours after being told they were to take part in a raid, Lovat and Durnford-Slater were bound for London on the night train from Scotland. The atmosphere at Combined Operations Headquarters was not to the liking of Lovat after the outdoor life further north. He found it 'honeycombed with rooms filled with every branch of the Services, including the powder-puff variety, who looked elegant in silk stockings.... There was said to be a fair proportion of drones among the inmates'.

The Commando leaders were welcomed by Mountbatten's vice-chief, Maj.-Gen. Charles Haydon, who locked the door of his office, disconnected the telephone and then outlined the operation plan, which he admitted he did not like, without naming the target. They were shown photographs, picture postcards and models of their attack areas. 'I saw at a glance it was Dieppe', Lovat recalled. 'Haydon asked how the devil I knew that. It was simple. Those bloody postcards had it written on the back.' So much for the cloak of secrecy.

On 24 July Lovat and Durnford-Slater were introduced to the other 'Jubilee' commanders at a conference, when these forthright individuals secured two major concessions. They were given permission to plan and execute their operations independently, and to land under cover of darkness. At this meeting there was no support for the opinion of the Air Force Commander, Leigh-Mallory, that 'the Canadians are going to have a bad time.' Neither Lovat nor Durnford-Slater was impressed by his first view of Roberts, the Military Commander. Lovat considered him 'a nice fellow but very thick; he sat there looking very bovine and solid'. And Durnford-Slater noted of the meeting, 'Roberts took practically no part when asked to say whether the plans suited him. Like the rest of us, he was convinced of the possibility of carrying it out but, as opposed to Leigh-Mallory, he did not raise the least objection.'

When Leigh-Mallory persisted in his argument that the Canadians would be pinned down on the main beach in front of Dieppe Gen. Crerar, now responsible overall for the operation, interrupted testily, 'What the hell do you know about it? You're an airman.' To which Leigh-Mallory replied, 'I'm an airman now but I happen to have fought in the First World War as a subaltern.' As Lovat commented, 'That made Crerar look pretty old-fashioned.'

In addition to the Commandos, a token detachment of fifty US Rangers was also drafted into the raiding force. Brig.-Gen. Lucian Truscott, the senior of a group of American officers attached to the Combined Operations staff to gain invasion experience, was asked by Mountbatten to provide a group of Rangers for 'Jubilee' to give them an insight into battle conditions. It was fitting that the request should have gone to Truscott, who had only recently formed the Rangers with men 'borrowed' from units which had already crossed the Atlantic and were in Northern Ireland. Though the troops were to be Commando-type soldiers, the use of that name was deliberately avoided. 'I selected the name Rangers because few words have a more glamorous connotation in American military history', said Truscott.

He nominated six officers and forty-four other ranks of the 1st Ranger Battalion, who had undergone punishing training at the Commando centre at Achnacarry House in Invernesshire, spiritual headquarters of the Clan Cameron and home of the clan chief, Cameron of Lochiel. Their first view of Achnacarry was a sobering one – a long row of graves alongside the trees that lined the driveway. Nailed to each cross was a small board bearing name, rank and number and cause of death, such as 'He showed himself on the skyline'.

Lovat and Durnford-Slater left the 24 July meeting to rejoin their respective Commando, who had made a high-speed transfer to

Southern England, carrying with them a proposed date for 'Jubilee', between 17–19 August, and the news that, in the interests of security, the raiding force would not be concentrated in one spot, as had happened on 'Rutter' when it had been bombed as it lay at anchor off the Isle of Wight. Instead, it would sail from several different ports in an assortment of vessels. Whereas on Rutter all units had been embarked in converted Channel ferries, with the intention of transferring them to smaller craft just off the French coast, it was now planned that some of the attacking units would make the whole crossing in their assault boats. Durnford-Slater's 3 Commando drew the short straw here, as did two Canadian battalions, the Cameron Highlanders and the Fusiliers Mont-Royal.

Because briefing of the raid was to be deferred to the last possible moment, the Canadian units relaxed in ignorance of their approaching fate at their camps in Sussex and Surrey, with little to disturb the training routine, though the Royal Regiment, luckless all along the line in its association with Dieppe, suffered two low-level bombing and machine-gun attacks by FW 190s at its camp at Littlehampton.

While the Canadians were still debating their wretched luck over the cancellation of 'Rutter', the two Commando detachments were hard at work on meticulous preparations for 'Jubilee'. Durnford-Slater's 3 Commando had moved from Largs to Seaford, which their commanding officer found 'most invigorating, as frequent visits from low-flying German aircraft gave us the necessary warlike atmosphere which had been lacking in the West of Scotland'. They rehearsed the land part of the operation on the Sussex Downs, and to simulate as far as possible the conditions on the Channel crossing they were loaded into cramped boats which circled the Isle of Wight all night.

No. 4 Commando, already specialists at rock climbing and street fighting, moved from Troon to Weymouth and carried out eight full-scale rehearsals of their role in the Dieppe Raid, using Lulworth Cove, once the property of Lovat's great-uncle, for the landings. As Lovat pointed out, 'Usually a battle is fought at short notice, with little or no plan of action. Here the data had been sorted out and sifted like a jigsaw puzzle.... When intelligence is available, only fools fail to take advantage. We were playing for high stakes. All knew it.'

Lovat's men learned by heart every aspect of their task; the precise distances to be covered, the contours of the countryside through which they would launch their attack, and rapid crossing of barbed wire with the aid of netting and in some cases human volunteers in leather jerkins. They became so accurate in their weapon training that the mortar squad could drop eighteen out of twenty shots into a 25-foot square at a range of 200 yards, a skill which was to pay spectacular dividends. In the middle of all the activity stood their commander, wearing a sweater with the word LOVAT printed across it in phosphorescent characters for ease of identification during exercises.

Sgt Bill Portman, a demolitions expert, did his training carrying an 85 lb pack of explosives on his back. 'We used to do five mile sprint marches every day before we started training. That was with full equipment, everything, and you tried to do it in 45 minutes. The object was to do seven miles in the hour. You cursed a lot when you were doing it but it was good fun, actually.

'There is a lot of nonsense talked about Commandos, as though they were six foot between the eyes or something, but in actual fact all they were was a bunch of highly-trained blokes dedicated to the idea of getting fit and doing their job.' Donald Gilchrist, a section leader in 4 Commando agreed: 'They were not supermen. They were ordinary men who had been super-*trained*.'

Though they had not been told their destination, some Commandos were as perceptive as Lovat. George Cook, a private in 4 Commando, recalled, 'One or two blokes looked at the map and worked out that we were going to Dieppe because of the sort of places we were practising our landings at.'

Donald Gilchrist was not convinced that the exercises would ever amount to anything serious. 'Then, quite suddenly, as I was hurrying towards the hotel where the officers were staying, I saw something that stopped me in my tracks. Three Commandos moved across my line of vision carrying something that glittered in the sunshine. Armfuls of British bayonets. Sheffield steel, guaranteed. This was it.'

Early in August the new plan for 'Jubilee' was completed. It was an ambitious and immensely complicated operation, rendered even more difficult by the fact that the reported presence near Dieppe of a Panzer division persuaded the planners to reduce the time to be spent ashore. Nevertheless, the operation order still ran to almost 200 foolscap pages.

Eight landings were planned along a ten-mile front.* On the eastern extremity (or the left-hand side if approached from the sea) 3 Commando were to go ashore at Berneval and Belleville-sur-Mer to attack and destroy the group of giant guns dubbed by the planners the Goebbels Battery. The target beaches were known as Yellow 1 and 2.

Between Berneval and Dieppe itself stood the small community of Puys above a cleft in the line of cliffs. This was Blue Beach, the destination of the Royal Regiment of Canada, whose task was to force their way to the clifftop, overrun a small battery known as Rommel and take the eastern headland overlooking Dieppe from the rear.

For the purpose of 'Jubilee', the long beach of Dieppe itself was divided in two, Red and White. Red Beach, the eastern half, was where the Essex Scottish would go ashore. White Beach, dominated by the large Casino building, was the target of the Royal Hamilton Light Infantry. These two battalions, to be followed in by tanks and accompanying engineering and demolition units, were to capture the town and hold the harbour to assist a Marine cutting-out party to remove German invasion barges and other craft to be towed back to England. The Fusiliers Mont-Royal would be held off Dieppe's main beach as a floating reserve.

To the west of Dieppe, at the mouth of the river Scie, lay Pourville. This was designated Green Beach, the western inner flank landing, which would be the responsibility of the South Saskatchewan Regiment. Their task was to swing left and overrun Dieppe's western headland. The Cameron Highlanders would follow the Saskatchewans ashore, move through the territory they had cleared

---

* See maps between pages x and xii.

and pass up the Scie valley to capture the aerodrome at St Aubin and what was believed to be the German divisional headquarters at Arques-la-Bataille.

On the extreme western flank, or the right-hand side viewed from the sea, lay Orange 1 and 2, the beaches at Varengeville and Quiberville, where 4 Commando would land to execute a pincer attack on the group of heavy coastal guns known as the Hess Battery.

With so many ships of different speeds involved, finely-judged synchronisation needed to be the keynote of the planning. The four flank attacks at Yellow, Blue, Green and Orange beaches would be carried out in the pre-dawn period known by the French as '*entre chien et loup*' and by sailors as nautical twilight, when experienced mariners are able to detect first light though the sun is still well below the horizon. Dawn, or civil twilight, is seen much later by the layman, roughly forty-five minutes after the onset of nautical twilight.

These early landings could expect no supporting bombardment from the air or sea, so they depended totally on sufficient darkness and achieving surprise. The assault on the main beaches was due to go in at 0520 hours, half an hour after the flank landings, when there would be just enough light for bombs, rockets and a smokescreen to be delivered from the air.

In addition four destroyers and a gunboat would bombard the front of the town from the time the landing craft were a mile offshore until the moment of touchdown, and would then shift their aim to the East and West headlands for a further fifteen minutes.

Once a perimeter had been established inland of Dieppe parties of engineers would carry out a detailed programme of demolition: docks, bridges, railways, gas works and telephone exchange were to be destroyed, as well as military and naval objectives. Plans to blow up a railway tunnel to interrupt communications with Rouen and Le Havre were abandoned when it was discovered that the explosion would take place immediately beneath the proposed shore headquarters of the Royal Hamilton Light Infantry.

The engineers were commanded by Maj. Bert Sucharov, a flamboyant, moustachioed character who always wore a gunbelt with a pair of pistols, cowboy fashion. Sucharov's spearhead group of 94 men were detailed to be first off the tank landing ships carrying the Churchills and armoured cars of the Calgary Tank Regiment, clear a way through any beach minefields and also lay chespaling to assist the tanks to obtain traction on Dieppe's pebble beach. The chespaling had been devised by Sucharov after the Churchills had run into problems on the exercise beaches, and consisted of strips of wood about four feet wide, held together by wire and rolled up into bundles 250 feet long, and needing four men to carry them. On exercises the engineers had been able to lay a hundred feet of this temporary pathway in three minutes.

A highly complex system of communications had to be devised for this extremely complicated operation: from raid headquarters in the control room of Fighter Command's No. 11 Group at RAF Uxbridge to the destroyer HMS *Calpe*, the ship on which Gen. Roberts would establish his headquarters off the beaches, and from there to the brigade and battalion command posts ashore. There were other wavelengths to keep *Calpe* in touch with the tanks, Commandos, aircraft and other ships, and the whole system had to be duplicated in HMS *Fernie*, the reserve headquarters destroyer, so that it could take over running 'Jubilee' if Roberts's command ship was put out of action.

Nothing, apparently, had been overlooked. Both *Calpe* and *Fernie* were to carry a pair of homing pigeons to fly messages back to England if all else failed.

The plan was minutely detailed. It was also, unfortunately, totally lacking in flexibility in the event of something going seriously wrong with one particular phase of the operation.

Gen. Crerar found nothing wrong with it, however. After going over the 'Jubilee' arrangements he felt that the revisions to the old 'Rutter' project 'added to, rather than detracted from, the soundness of the plan as a whole; given an even break in luck and good navigation the demonstration should prove successful'.

As Ross Munro of the Canadian Press pointed out, 'Everyone was so confident in those July days that it would be a nice easy raid. One found oneself making complete plans to run around Dieppe as if it were a manoeuvre in Brighton.... I even made a date to meet one of the sergeants from the Essex Scottish at the corner just outside German naval headquarters and get the latest dope from him there.'

Among all the tasks of remounting the Dieppe Raid none was more difficult than reassembling the supplies and ammunition needed. All the equipment brought together for Operation 'Rutter' had been returned to depots. Now, without explanation, it had to be recovered. The tragedy of this arrangement was that the Canadians had spent weeks with the same weapons during training and had worked hard at making them serviceable for individual requirements and preferences. This was particularly true of the Sten guns, which had a nasty tendency to jam.

The Stens, and most of the other weapons issued for 'Jubilee', were brand-new. The consequences were frustrating and, in some cases, fatal. For the purposes of security Combined Operations requisitioned the Warnford Park estate in Hampshire as a stores depot. Because of the need for secrecy, Canadian depots were not touched and all the supplies came from British sources. The equipment rolled into Warnford Park steadily from the beginning of August and the final consignment beat the 15 August deadline by less than three hours.

Some quite extraordinary steps were taken to preserve the security of 'Jubilee'. Lt Tony Smith, Intelligence Officer of 4 Commando, was unhappy about the situation at Weymouth, where Lovat's men were billeted out in private homes. So, at his request, two Norwegian soldiers were sent from London to parade around ostentatiously with the Commandos and create the impression that a raid was planned against Norway.

Smith's scheme was totally undermined when, on 17 August, two days before the raid, three Free French Commandos wearing shoulder flashes arrived to join Lovat's group. Though Smith considered them 'most excellent fellows in every way' there was no doubt they compromised his carefully constructed security screen, so the bewildered Frenchmen were bundled into a police car, whisked away to Dorchester and collected by the Commandos the next morning as they moved towards embarkation.

Though counter-espionage agents mingled with the Canadians, Commandos and naval personnel in pubs and at dances, and a postal censorship was imposed from Weymouth to the Thames Estuary, a few indiscretions were reported. One Canadian soldier, arrested by Seaford police on the night of Sunday 16 August, told them 'You can't keep me here, I'm going on a raid on Dieppe Wednesday'; the same night an NCO of the Fusiliers Mont-Royal visited a Brighton boarding-house and told the landlady he was off on a raid and would not be back; and the Intelligence Section of the Royal Regiment handed over a security area to their counterparts in the 48th Highlanders with the comment, 'You can have the job, we're going to Dieppe.'

An officer of 3 Commando suffered court martial, a severe reprimand from Col. Durnford-Slater and the ignominy of being returned to his former Army unit after telling two naval lieutenants in Newhaven that a large-scale operation was about to take place.

There was a more serious breach when a Royal Navy officer went ashore in Newhaven with a copy of the naval operation orders in his pocket and left them lying on the bar of a hotel. They had been spotted and picked up by some Royal Regiment officers before the officer rushed back to retrieve them. When he returned to his ship several hours overdue he could not remember where he had been. He was detained until after the raid and subsequently invalided out of the service when medical evidence revealed he was on the edge of a nervous breakdown.

In the final days before 'Jubilee' the edginess over security reached a peak. In its edition of 15 August the *Daily Telegraph* published a two-column advertisement for the washing powers of Sylvan Flakes. It was headed 'Beach Coat from Dieppe' and the illustration showed a woman wearing what was described as a Dieppe Coat and pruning a tree. When the matter was investigated one British intelligence officer argued that the branches of the tree in the picture fitted accurately on a scale map of Dieppe. A further check convinced MI 5 that it was a coincidence, but Sylvan Flakes dropped the suspect advertisement.

Gradually the circle of those in the know about Dieppe widened from the original handful as senior officers were briefed about their role in the raid. Col. John Andrews broke the news to his Calgary Tanks officers in dramatic fashion. Standing beside a relief model of the area, Andrews told them 'Take a last, long, lingering look, gentlemen. The next time you see this, it will be on a larger scale.'

Aboard his tank landing craft at Newhaven, the actor Peter Bull was 'staggered' by the news that Dieppe had again been chosen: 'I knew that our previous episode was pretty widely known by careless talk and I thought the German espionage system must have been poor not to have garnered the information. In any case, reconnaissance planes had frequently flown over Newhaven harbour and it only needed a member of the Baedeker family to say '*Ach, Newhaven. Also das macht Newhaven-Dieppe*' for the fat to be in the fire.'

Major Guy Vandelac of the Fusiliers Mont-Royal shared Bull's astonishment: 'My God, I never thought they would put it on again. After the first operation was cancelled the matter of Dieppe was casual talk.'

The troops were not to be told until they were either aboard the transport vessels or immediately before embarkation. For example, only five senior officers in the South Saskatchewan Regiment knew they were going to Dieppe when they were ordered out of camp near Pulborough. To cover the troop movements the Canadians were told they were off on a three-part exercise lasting a month.

The preliminary order to prepare the expedition for sailing went out on the morning of 17 August. Though the weather forecast had been given as 'not very favourable' Mountbatten, the Force Commanders and Admiral Sir William James, the Portsmouth C.-in-C. who had cancelled 'Rutter' on the advice of the meteorological experts, decided to press ahead when they were told that rising winds would probably mean even less satisfactory conditions on succeeding days.

After a final conference, at which Gen. Roberts again rejected the offer of preliminary heavy bombing on the grounds that it would block the passage of his tanks through Dieppe, the senior officers met on the morning of 18 August to review the latest weather situation.

'We had a number of rather contradictory reports from the meteorological experts', said Admiral James, 'but eventually we decided to give the executive order. I suggested to Mountbatten that these experts should never be told why they are being asked for special reports; a met. chap would only be human if he saw only the gloomy side if he knew that a major operation in which thousands of lives are involved depended on his reading of the weather charts.'

And so, on that morning of 18 August, the message went out to the various commanders. 'The show is on.' The Canadian Army was finally getting into action. Operation 'Jubilee' would provide what Field-Marshal Brooke termed, 'The landing in France for which the uninformed had been clamouring.'

50

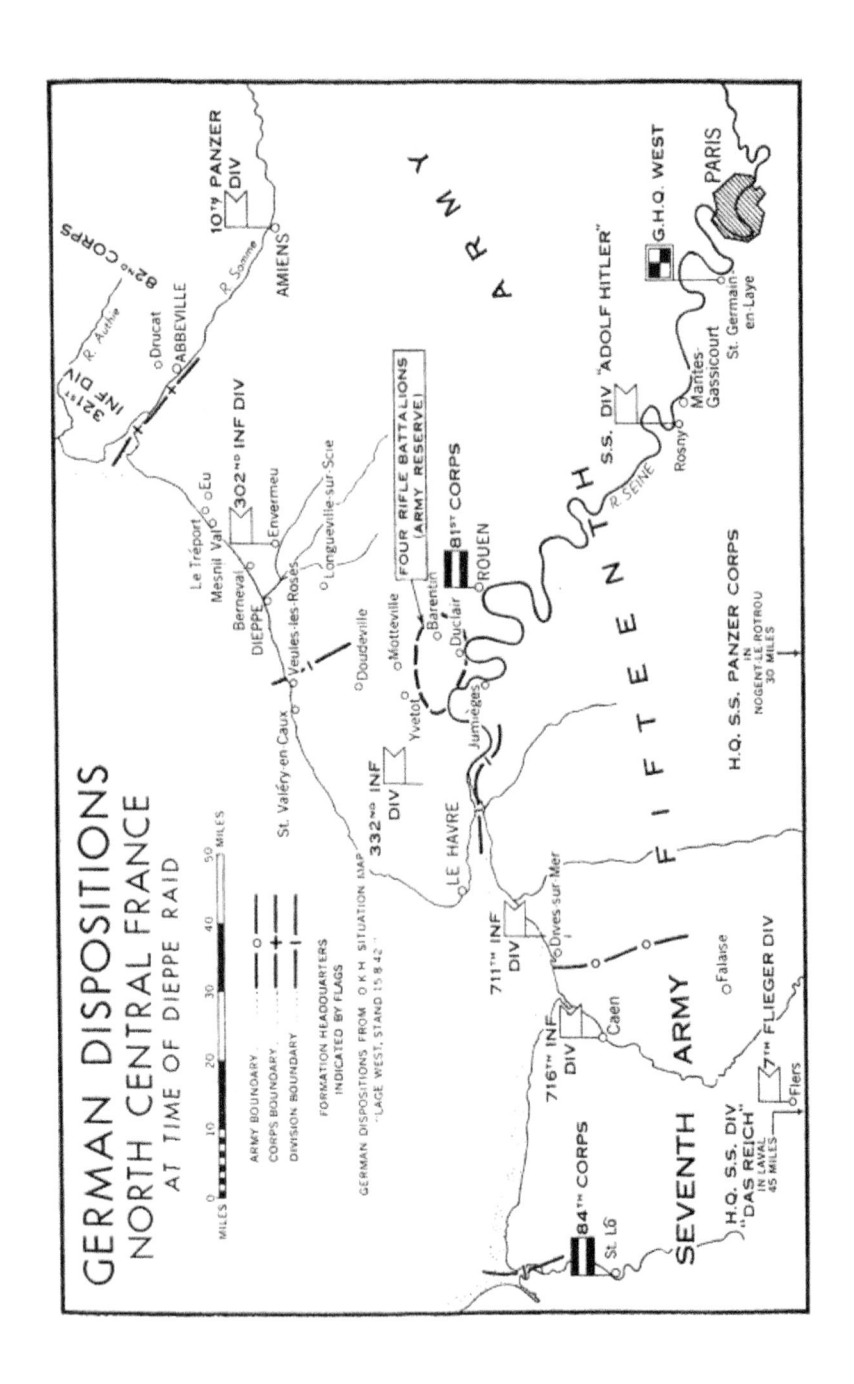

CHAPTER FOUR
Departure

'Invasion mustn't be done half-heartedly. Either you should land and smash the defending forces to hell or you should leave them alone.'

– German propaganda broadcast,
19 August 1942

Neither the repeated Russian pleas for a Second Front nor the build-up of shipping and landing craft along England's South Coast had escaped the notice of the German High Command. Despite his summer of spectacular triumphs in Russia and North Africa, even Hitler was becoming increasingly nervous about an Allied intervention in the West.

On 9 July, two days after the cancellation of Rutter, Hitler ordered a strengthening of defences in France and the Low Countries. The Führer, personally supervising the Russian campaign from a secret headquarters deep inside occupied territory, issued a perceptive summary of the probable dangers in France: 'As a result of our victories, England may be faced with the choice either of immediately mounting a major landing in order to create a Second Front or of losing Soviet Russia as a political and military factor. It is highly probable, therefore, that enemy landings will shortly take place.'

Because of the need to provide air cover and the range limitations of invasion barges, Hitler forecast that the most threatened areas were the Pas de Calais, the sector between Dieppe and Le Havre and Normandy.

Hitler's officially-expressed alarm merely hastened the strengthening of Fortress Europe, a process which had been under way for some months, until by midsummer Field-Marshal Gerd von Rundstedt, the C.-in-C. West and highest German military authority from Holland to the Spanish border, had under his command thirty-six divisions, including elite armoured, airborne and S.S. troops.

Under the control of von Rundstedt, the Dieppe sector was part of the responsibility of the Fifteenth Army, commanded by Col.-Gen. Curt Haase, whose three corps covered the coast from the Scheldt in Holland to Caen in Normandy. One of these three Corps, the 81st, commanded by Gen. Adolf Kuntzen from its headquarters in Rouen, was directly charged with the defence of the Dieppe area, and the 302nd Infantry Division was the section of 81 Corps actually based around Dieppe. The 302nd was commanded by Maj.-Gen. Conrad Haase, who was not related to the Fifteenth Army's Curt Haase. To differentiate between the two, the Germans nicknamed the Fifteenth commander 'Der Grosse Haase' and the 302nd's 'Der Kleine Haase' (Big and Little Haase).

A daunting length of coast, some fifty miles, had been allocated to the 302nd Division, which had been formed in southern Germany in November 1940 and moved into France in April 1941. Although the 302nd had been stationed at Dieppe for a year when Combined Operations began to plan their raid, British intelligence continued to advise that the area was defended by the 110th Infantry Division, which was on the Russian front. Nor was the divisional headquarters at Arques-la-Bataille, as intelligence indicated. It had been moved in April 1942 to Envermeu, nine miles from Dieppe. So the Cameron Highlanders had been briefed to attack a non-existent headquarters. Mountbatten was to admit in later years that the intelligence reports on Dieppe were 'woefully inadequate'.

In one respect, however, intelligence was correct in referring to the German defenders of Dieppe as 'low category troops'. The demands of Russia were already being felt in the German army and, though von Rundstedt had at his disposal some elite soldiers, the 302nd Division was far from elite. Gen. Joachim Lindner, who in 1942 was a captain and the adjutant of the 571st Regiment which formed part of the division, admitted, 'The coastal defence divisions were second class. This is a hard word but it is essentially true.' When Hermann Goering visited Dieppe in March he was much put out to discover that regiments of the 302nd Division were minus whole companies and even a battalion, all posted to the Russian front. In July and early August the division was brought up to strength with the arrival of some 2,500 reinforcements, most of them such raw recruits that part of their daily programme had to be devoted to elementary lessons like 'Recognition of Badges of Rank'.

The replacement group which arrived in Dieppe just before the raid was largely made up of *Volksdeutsch* (ethnic Germans), or out-and-out foreigners. An indication of the percentage may be gathered from the fact that of the four prisoners brought back to England from the main beaches at Dieppe only one was a 'true' German. The others were all Poles, Otto Samulewitsch, Bronislav Wesierski and Max Kussowski.

Samulewitsch had fought in the Polish army against the German invaders in 1939 and was made a prisoner of war. In exchange for accepting German 'citizenship' as a *Volksdeutscher* in an area of Poland which had become part of the Greater German Reich, Samulewitsch was released. Three months later he received his call-up papers.

Kussowski and Wesierski were given the alternative of a concentration camp or service in the Wehrmacht. When they agreed to army service they joined 1,200 other Poles being assembled in Rostock. Two hundred of these arrived in Dieppe on 10 August after a six-day journey from Germany. They had been soldiers for only three weeks.

All were poor physical specimens and none, according to the officer who interrogated them in England, would have passed a medical test for service in the British army. Kussowski had been rejected by the Polish army because of chronic bronchitis. He mentioned this when he was being examined by a German doctor, only to be told 'For cannon-fodder all are good.' Wesierski, who had flat feet and heart pains and who had collapsed on arrival in Rostock, was also given short shrift by the examining physician, being told that if Germans were fighting and being killed, Poles could do the same.

One ten-man section in Dieppe consisted of a German NCO, two other Germans (one a former priest), five Poles, a Belgian and a Czech. Though the Germans did not seem to mind putting weapons into the hands of people they had previously oppressed, they were generally careful to regulate the distribution of foreigners among their units.

Understandably, morale was low and discipline poor among this exceedingly mixed bag. Maurice Mallet, who lived in Pourville during the war, got to know the Germans who had taken over a hotel in the village as their headquarters:

> 'One young soldier was a shoemaker and a Communist. He used to sit all evening with his fist raised, all alone. Another lad of the same age had worked on a pig farm. He was not at all a Nazi, not at all a Hitler supporter. There was another one, a very nice lad, a stage manager from the Essen theatre. I asked him once if all Germans supported Hitler and he said there was no choice. One night the pig farmer was sitting in a chair in the hotel kitchen and getting into a mood. He said he was not going to stand up ever again for an officer and if the war wasn't over in six months he would kill himself. In our area the Germans weren't too bad, just blokes who were afraid because they had been called up. There were very few Fascists, just the odd one. We weren't occupied by the really nasty elements.'

If the German defenders were a motley assortment, their armament was equally mixed. 'We had a lot of captured weapons, from Czechoslovakia, from France, from the British, everything', said Joachim Lindner. 'There was a great shortage of ammunition for these weapons, some of which were pre-war models.'

The 302nd Division possessed only half its requirement of carbines and anti-tank rifles and such was the shortage of transport that their 7.5 cm. guns were towed round by commandeered French trucks. The transport was mainly horse-drawn. According to Lindner, 'We were not mobile. Horses and bicycles were the only means of transport.' What few vehicles they did possess were admitted to be in 'extraordinarily poor shape' and since they had no spare tyres for their lorries they were reduced to attempting to purchase them in the civilian market.

But the Germans had had plenty of time to organise a comprehensive system of defence. 'With the weak forces under our command we knowingly didn't defend every ravine', said an 81st

Corps report. Instead, they concentrated their weaponry around Dieppe itself, with reserves based inland.

The sector was particularly strong in artillery, with three heavy and four smaller batteries grouped in a semi-circle around Dieppe. The town's seafront was guarded by a complicated array of pillboxes and machine-gun nests and gun sites, but these defences were positioned mainly to draw the attention of landing parties. The main fire-power was concentrated on the heights. An old French tank had been cemented into the sea wall near the west jetty of the harbour as a static defence position. 'This was the only tank we had in Dieppe,' Lindner recalled.

The rambling white Casino, considered an obvious target in case of attack, had not been converted into a strongpoint. Most of the building was empty, though there were defence positions in and around it. The caves which riddled the East and West headlands held the artillery, machine-guns and mortars which were Dieppe's strength. Though air reconnaissance pictures had revealed these caves, the Combined Operations planners did not pay enough attention to what they might contain. A Canadian intelligence officer, Maj. Reginald Unwin, who was the adviser to the military planners on Dieppe's defences, warned of the potential danger of the caves, but his comments were dismissed as those of an over-cautious pessimist. So strongly did Unwin feel about this threat that he refused to sign the final appreciation of German defences when it was submitted for inclusion in the Combined Operations plan.

In the autumn of 1941 the Todt Organisation, the German forced labour movement, arrived in the area to begin construction of what was to be known as Fortress Dieppe. Concrete fortifications, emplacements and pillboxes studded the coastline and by March 1942 the two headlands had been converted into strongpoints, as had the Quatre Vents Farm between Dieppe and Pourville.

Neither Dieppe's main beach nor the ones at Pourville and Puys were mined, but some mines were planted at the unguarded landing points chosen for the Commandos' flank attacks at Berneval and Varengeville. The exits up the gullies from those tiny beaches were also choked with heavy wire and booby-trapped. In front of Dieppe a double row of wire barred access to the promenade, one on the beach itself and another, a formidable obstacle seven feet thick, along the sea wall.

Although the garrison of Dieppe, commanded by Lt-Col. Hermann Bartelt of the 571st Regiment, consisted of only 1,500 men, there were strong reserves along the 302nd Division's 50-mile-sector. They totalled some 6,000 men and the 10th Panzer Division, which was resting and refitting at Amiens, 60 miles from Dieppe, after being badly mauled in Russia.

The mile-long stretch of Dieppe's main beach was defended by No. 7 Company of the 571st Regiment, only 150 strong, of whom 15 were Polish. Though not the finest of physical specimens, these troops were perfectly capable of firing automatic weapons from behind concrete, and the beach defence company was bolstered by a naval unit which possessed eight 37 mm. anti-tank guns.

Elsewhere the defenders were spread even more thinly. At Pourville, the summer resort at the mouth of the river Scie which lay outside Fortress Dieppe, only a small detachment of the 571st formed the garrison, though the heights between Pourville and Dieppe, which included Dieppe's West headland, were a fortified redoubt containing Col. Bartelt's headquarters. A platoon-strength garrison of some 50 troops was assigned to cover the beach at Puys, but Berneval nearby did not even possess a permanent infantry garrison.

Inter-service jealousies and squabbles were by no means the prerogative of the Allies, and the presence in Dieppe of army, air force and naval units with their overlapping responsibilities caused trouble. 'The air force did not like to be defended by army men, and it was difficult for the army to go into the port at Dieppe, that was naval territory', said Joachim Lindner.

The heavy coastal batteries at Berneval and Varengeville, targets of the Commandos, lay outside the Dieppe defence zone and were therefore vulnerable, since infantry could not be spared to protect them. They were the responsibility of the navy and for three months before the Dieppe Raid the German naval commander of the Channel coast had repeatedly demanded the transfer of 813 Battery from Varengeville closer to Dieppe since, in his opinion, 'It was tactically and absolutely wrongly sited.' Three proposals were submitted by the navy for a new site within the defensive perimeter, and an indication of the bad feeling existing between the services was the naval commander's comment that 'for three long months the 302nd Division had declined each of three suggestions without even making one positive proposal'. Finally, the army agreed to a fourth proposal and though a new site was agreed nothing further had been done by 19 August. As a result 813 Battery was the scene of the Germans' only severe setback of the Dieppe Raid.

The defenders around Dieppe were kept in a constant state of alarm by rumours and reports of Allied activity during the spring and summer of 1942. Warning of the dangers of an impending landing, von Rundstedt issued an order on 2 July stressing the importance of destroying attacks 'before, or *at the lastest*, immediately after, they have reached the beach'. He forbade any withdrawal, warned of the severe penalties for what he termed desertion of posts and concluded, 'We must keep the watch in the West while our comrades in the East and Africa have to fight bitterly. We must at all times be prepared to destroy the English when they land. We must under all circumstances prevent the formation of the Second Front. That is our historical task. To that task belongs our whole energy, our whole personality and our life.'

Von Rundstedt's instructions were interpreted literally and dramatically by Gen. Conrad Haase, commander of the 302nd Division. All his officers were summoned to headquarters and made to swear to defend their positions to the death. Haase concluded the occasion by taking an oath to die rather than retreat or surrender.

On 20 July Gen. Curt Haase issued a Fifteenth Army order demanding 'the highest degree of watchfulness and readiness for action' during three periods of favourable tide and moon: 27 July to 3 August, 10 to 19 August and 25 August to 1 September.

Curt Haase was 60 and had served in the First World War. According to British intelligence he had 'all the characteristics of an old and worried German general' and was given to issuing rather hysterical documents intended to rally the morale of his soldiers, such as 'Be on guard! Eyes and ears alert! Kick the Anglo-American and his helpers in the snout!'

On 10 August, to bring his troops to the alert for the latest period of danger, Haase again warned of an impending landing:

> The troops **must** realise that it will be a **very sticky** business! Bombs and naval guns, sea weapons and Commandos, assault boats and parachutists, airborne troops and hostile citizens, sabotage and murder will have to be coped with. Steady nerves will be required if we do not want to **go under.**
>
> Fear does not exist! When the hail of fire pours down upon the troops, they must wipe their eyes and ears, clutch their weapons harder and **defend themselves as never before!**
>
> **WE** or **THEY!** That must be the slogan of all!
>
> The German Army has in the past received all kinds of tasks from the Führer and has always carried them out. The Army will carry out this task too. **My soldiers won't be the worst!** I I have looked into your eyes! You are German men! You will willingly and bravely **do your duty! And thus remain victorious!**
>
> Long live our people, our Fatherland and our Führer!

Despite the repeated alerts life was good for the occupiers of Dieppe. 'It was a paradise compared with Russia,' said Joachim Lindner. A sergeant, Friedrich Waltenheimer, recalled 'We were provided with enough food, but were able to buy more on the open market if we needed to. We used to barter with fishing boats. The fishermen were not officially permitted to sell their catch to us but they used to exchange the fish for cigarettes. If you could speak French, as I did, the connections were very good.'

Fresh fruit and vegetables could be bought in Dieppe's markets and there was a thriving black market in silk stockings and cognac. Also in great demand in the army canteen for dispatch to Germany, where they were in short supply, were such things as notepaper, toothpaste, perfume, sweets and chocolate and ladies' underwear.

The garrison had their own cinema, which provided two shows a week, and their own brothel. 'Our relationship with the French population was so good that I could never understand why British intelligence over Dieppe was so poor,' said Capt. Richard Schnösenberg.

The greatest problem was keeping the defenders at the proper pitch of readiness. 'It was very quiet, day after day nothing,' according to Joachim Lindner. 'We had a problem with the men guarding the coast, the poor man walking with his rifle along the cliffs. Nothing happened but the waves coming and going, coming and going. Sometimes he slept. Yes, we had a problem to keep them awake.'

Though Operation 'Jubilee' did not get the go-ahead until the morning of 18 August, the movement preparations of the Calgary Tanks were, of necessity, undertaken much earlier. On the evening of 16 August, as 18 of the Churchills were hauled from unit lines at Seaford by tank transporters to Gosport, west of Portsmouth, for embarkation the latest intelligence reports were still being assessed.

The tank officers accompanied the column in staff cars, and Major Allan Glenn remembered: 'All of a sudden the bloody column comes to a halt and we were called to a conference in a little air raid shelter by the side of the road, no lights or anything. We were shown some aerial photographs, taken that afternoon over Dieppe, and there was something new on them that had everyone in confusion. Right on the promenade there was a round structure. Watch that, we were told. So when we got to Dieppe we looked out and sure as hell there was that round structure. We put thousands of rounds of everything through it. Then, after we were captured, we were marched past it. It was a bloody latrine. You could have grated cabbage on what was left of it.'

The remaining tanks of the battalion rumbled the short distance from Seaford to Newhaven under their own power and were embarked, together with the unit's beach party, scout cars and ammunition, the following evening.

The Calgary Tanks adjutant, Capt. Austin Stanton, was so pessimistic that, shortly before leaving Seaford, he went back to his quarters and changed all his clothes. 'I knew that if you were taken prisoner two things were hard to get, one was food and the other was clothing. So I put on a complete new set of battledress, everything from the skin out, which I was very glad of afterwards.'

Clearly, Stanton did not like the revised Dieppe operation, and said so. 'In my opinion there was no hope of security, and because of this I was really ticked off by my colonel, Johnny Andrews, the night before we left.'

All across south-eastern England on Tuesday 18 August men and stores were moving towards the five places from which the raid was to be launched – Southampton, Portsmouth, Gosport, Newhaven and Shoreham. There was considerable congestion at Newhaven, where the Cameron Highlanders and 3 Commando were both embarking in their small landing craft.

The Camerons had a particularly bad day. Because the promised transportation had not arrived at their camp near Fittleworth in Sussex by the afternoon, the battalion hastily set out for Newhaven in an assortment of commandeered vehicles. They arrived about 1700 hours when, according to their second-in-command, Major Tony Law, they were given 'a very poor meal, consisting of stew, the meat in which was very tough, and tea which was almost undrinkable'.

There was similar chaos over the collection of the Camerons' weapons at Newhaven. The equipment was dumped in a pile, and the explosives not labelled. The Sten guns and other weapons had not been cleaned since being taken out of storage and were covered in grease. Their commanding officer, Lt-Col. Alfred Gostling, was the only man in the regiment who had actually fired a Sten during the 'Rutter' exercises, and the Camerons spent most of the Channel crossing attempting to clean and to familiarise themselves with their new guns in the dark, surrounded by hand grenades, high explosive, scaling ladders and even bicycles which had been loaded with them.

Such was the congestion at Newhaven that 3 Commando had to queue in the streets outside the docks for half an hour. As the Commandos' leader, John Durnford-Slater, recalled, 'The people emptied their houses and, sensing the importance of the occasion, watched us in dead silence from the kerbside.'

The lack of security alarmed two of the Toronto Scottish Regiment's machine-gunners who were to provide extra fire power aboard the tank landing craft. According to Cpl J. R. Corbett, 'On arriving at Newhaven I was quite surprised to see what I thought was a public demonstration of how we were going to pull off a big raid. People all around the dock could plainly see what was going on. After all the trouble taken around camp to maintain secrecy it seemed very foolish.' Corbett's opinion was shared by Pte R. W. Church: 'Some girls were standing on the corner of the street where we got off the trucks and they were crying. It seems their boy friends told them they were going on a raid. Altogether, I think it was a little too open at Newhaven. There were no guards to prevent the public mingling with the troops as they embarked.'

As the soldiers moved towards Newhaven they had passed cinema hoardings promoting that week's attractions in Brighton. Currently showing was *Beyond the Blue Horizon*. The next presentation was *Reap the Wild Wind*.

The Camerons and 3 Commando were loaded aboard personnel landing craft (LCPs) known as Eurekas. These wooden boats could carry twenty-five soldiers, were fast, manoeuvrable and quiet and could operate right inshore, as they drew little water. All this had been achieved at the expense of protection for their occupants, however.

On the other side of Brighton at Shoreham the French Canadians, the Fusiliers Mont-Royal, were loaded aboard similar cramped and unprotected vessels. Before boarding, they were assembled at a school and briefed about their destination by their commanding officer, Lt-Col. Menard, when, according to the regiment's War Diary 'everybody acclaimed with joy'. The padre, Father Major Armand Sabourin, held Holy Communion after which the Fusiliers were given a meal at the school, served on white tablecloths with Wrens as waitresses. Pte Ray Geoffrion remembered it well 37 years later: 'It was a most delicious meal and the last decent one I was to get for a long time.' As they boarded their frail craft late in the afternoon the French Canadians were singing.

The bulk of the raiding force was carried in considerably greater comfort aboard nine former Channel ferries converted into infantry landing ships; six of these sailed from Southampton and three from

Portsmouth. The troops in these would transfer to landing craft just off the French coast.

As his Commando travelled to Southampton to board *Prince Albert* Lord Lovat reported that his convoy noticed empty Canadian trucks outside pubs all the way to the docks. 'One can only guess what was being said inside' said Lovat, who subsequently criticised the Canadians for their 'light-hearted approach' to Dieppe. For their own refreshment the Commandos had to make do with apples thrown into the trucks by women as they passed through one small town.

Also loaded at Southampton were the South Saskatchewans (in *Princess Beatrix* and *Invicta*) and the Royal Hamilton Light Infantry (*Glengyle*). The RHLI were accompanied by their chaplain, Capt. John Foote, a remarkable man who played the trumpet in the regimental band and clarinet in the orchestra and who quietly ignored orders that he was not to go on the raid. 'I didn't take notice of red tape like that,' Foote said. 'I just packed up and went along with the rest of them. I always intended to go. From the time I went into the army, whatever the men were doing I did. I don't think I would have been a very popular padre if I had stayed on shore and greeted them when they came back.' John Foote would win the Victoria Cross on Dieppe's White Beach and learn to play yet another instrument, the French horn, as a prisoner of war.

The Essex Scottish Regiment embarked in two sections (*Prince Leopold* at Southampton and *Prince Charles* at Portsmouth) while the group which was to land on Blue Beach at Puys was divided into three ships. The Royal Regiment went aboard *Queen Emma* and *Princess Astrid* in Portsmouth, while a party of the Black Watch of Canada attached to the Royals were loaded on to the *Duke of Wellington* at Southampton.

Portsmouth was also the assembly point for the 18 officers and 352 other ranks of the Royal Marine Commando. The Marines were led by Lt-Col. Joseph Picton Phillips, nicknamed 'Tiger' and the son of a Marine colonel. Phillips had had his men under canvas in all weathers to toughen them up (and had objected when attempts had been made to house them in heated buildings the previous winter) so the thought of being assigned to the most daring part of an extremely ambitious operation – stealing German barges from the port – could hardly have worried them. Phillips crossed with part of his force in HMS *Locust*, a river gunboat whose shallow draught had enabled her to get close inshore at Dunkirk and evacuate more than 2,000 soldiers in five trips. The remainder of the Marine Commando were carried in seven Chasseurs of the Free French Navy. The 150-ton Chasseurs were armed with a 75 mm gun and machine-guns and had sailed to British ports after the fall of France in 1940.

The detachment of US Rangers, who were divided among the raiding groups, completed the army force, which numbered 6,106, of whom the Canadian army provided 305 officers and 4,658 other ranks, the rest being made up of Commandos and assorted extras such as the Americans and groups of official observers.

Not included in the total was the party of war correspondents and photographers who had been briefed at the last moment. They included five Americans, invited at the special request of the Canadian army's public relations section. Among them were Quentin Reynolds, one of the best-known American correspondents, who was covering the story for *Collier's* weekly magazine, and Drew Middleton of Associated Press. Fleet Street was allowed to send only one man, A. B. Austin of the *Daily Herald* as 'pool' contributor. Covering the story for Canada were, inevitably, Ross Munro of Canadian Press, Fred Griffin of the *Toronto Daily Star* and Wallace Reyburn of the weekly *Montreal Standard*. Political considerations led to an invitation being issued to M. Bondarenko, London correspondent of the Soviet news agency Tass, but he refused to go unless he was provided with advance information about the operation. When this request was turned down Bondarenko said that, in any case, Russian people were not interested in raids but only in an actual invasion of Europe.

Wallace Reyburn, a New Zealander who made his way to Britain in 1941 from Canada as a freelance war reporter, recalled how he got involved in Dieppe:

'When I got the job with the *Montreal Standard* Canadian troops weren't in the war, so I wrote mainly about "Britain can take it", that sort of thing, plus what I called Little Joe stories. I used to visit the Canadians and do stories about Little Joe from Kokomo, keep his family happy. The poor buggers, they weren't doing anything except rioting every now and then, getting drunk, getting arrested.

'Then one day I was sitting in this flat that I shared with three other journalists when a fellow phoned me and said "Do you want to do something dangerous?" A couple of days later I was at Dieppe. I didn't even have a uniform, so I borrowed one from Ross Munro, sewed a couple of captain's pips on the shoulders and eventually returned it to him with a couple of shrapnel holes, one in the shoulder and one in the bottom.'

To transport and protect Operation 'Jubilee', the Royal Navy had assembled 252 ships and landing craft. Eight Hunt class destroyers, *Calpe, Fernie, Albrighton, Berkeley, Bleasdale, Brocklesby, Garth* and the Polish ship *Slazak*, supported by a gunboat *Locust*, a sloop *Alresford* and four steam gunboats, comprised the main naval assault and protection force. It has quite rightly been called 'a peashooter armada'. The destroyers were an unusually small type of only 900 tons, mounting four 4 in. guns. The 500-ton *Locust* carried two 4 in. guns and a 3.7 in. howitzer, while the 700-ton *Alresford* possessed only one 4 in. gun.

Aerial cover and assistance was to be provided by 63 squadrons of the Royal Air Force, comprising five squadrons of Boston and Blenheim light bombers, two squadrons of bomb-carrying Hurricanes and 56 squadrons of fighters, a concentration of fighters larger than the entire command which had won the Battle of Britain in 1940. Flying alongside the British pilots were Canadians, Americans, Australians, New Zealanders, South Africans, French, Poles and Norwegians.

In the docks there was last-minute confusion over the allocation of stores and personnel because of the short notice at which the operation had been mounted. Lt J. R. Ferguson, commanding the 53rd Light Anti-Aircraft Battery of the Royal Canadian Artillery, was placed aboard his tank landing craft, LCT 20, with the 52 men of his battery sharing 25 Bren guns. The trouble was that they had done all their training with Bofors guns, quite different weapons. Ferguson had been given no orders 'at any stage' about the role of his group. The Brens, which had come straight out of storage, were covered with grease. No cleaning material of any kind had been provided and the men worked far into the night by torchlight on the Channel crossing trying to clean the weapons by using petrol borrowed from the tank crews and their own torn-up shirts as rags.

One Canadian battalion (which remained unnamed in the Combined Operations Report on the raid), under the impression that it was merely taking part in yet another boring exercise and anxious to save weight on the journey, had even turned up for embarkation with empty ammunition boxes.

The preparation of explosives caused tragedy on two of the troop transports. At 1710 hours, before the force had sailed, men of the Black Watch of Canada were priming their issue of hand grenades aboard *Duke of Wellington* when a soldier primed a grenade, put it down and, after being momentarily distracted, picked up the same one and began priming it again, effectively setting in motion its detonation. When he realised what had happened, he attempted to throw the grenade through an open porthole but it hit the bulkhead, bounced back and exploded, killing one man and injuring 18. Shortly before midnight, aboard *Invicta*, similar carelessness among Lt Leonard Kempton's platoon of the South Saskatchewans while cleaning grenades caused an explosion which wounded 17 men.

Though the Essex Scottish greeted the news that they were going to Dieppe 'with high spirits and considerable eagerness' and Col. Cecil Merritt was cheered when he announced the destination to his South Saskatchewans, there was little jubilation among the Royal Regiment personnel. Ross Munro was aboard *Queen Emma* and wrote, 'Few of the Royals seemed to be in as confident a mood as I had know them in "Practice Dieppe". The rush to the port and the mass of details, which had to be crammed into a few hours, left everyone rather ragged. Even before we put to sea some had an ominous feeling about what was ahead of them.'

The attitude of Pte Ron Beal was typical: 'In June when we were told we were going on a raid against Dieppe everybody was cheering, light-hearted and eager. But when they got us to Portsmouth in August and told us where we were going there was no cheering, no riding on a high. It was just "Ok, I guess we have to go".'

There was a similar reaction aboard LCT 3 when Lt Jerry Wood of the Royal Canadian Engineers briefed his men: ' "It's Dieppe again, men!" I looked into stolid dead-pans.'

During the summer the Germans had sown an extensive system of minefields in mid-Channel, mainly to afford their own coastal convoys some protection from British torpedo boats. Early in the evening of 18 August minesweepers sailed from Portsmouth to clear two channels, each almost half a mile wide, through the danger area. Only one mine was seen during the sweep.

Worries about the armada being spotted by the Germans' routine evening reconnaissance caused the imposition of deceptions such as fitting the troopships with false extra funnels so that they resembled merchantmen, though *Prince Albert*'s fell off soon after departure.

Because of the ships' different speeds and the complicated timetable of landing the force sailed in 13 groups. The first four comprised the troopships and armed escorts; groups 5, 6 and 7 were the personnel landing craft (LCPs) carrying Cameron Highlanders, Fusiliers Mont-Royal and 3 Commando; groups 8 to 12 were the tank landing craft, and group 13 was the Royal Marine Commandos in HMS *Locust* and the Chasseurs.

As one of the finest evenings of the summer drew to a close, the expedition got under way. *Princess Astrid* carrying the Royal Regiment was first to clear Portsmouth at 2110 hours. According to Ross Munro, 'The sea was smooth, the sky was clear and there was the slightest of breezes ... in the wardroom the officers sat around the tables and dined in navy style as the last sunshine poured through the open portholes.' As the ships moved out of Portsmouth an air raid siren wailed the All Clear. The enemy's evening reconnaissance had been just too early to discover the gathering of the fleet.

Aboard HMS *Fernie* the American general Lucian Truscott, who was travelling on the deputy command ship as an observer, was impressed by the medley of hunting songs played over the loudspeaker system as the Hunt class destroyer moved towards battle.

Aboard HMS *Calpe*, the headquarters ship, the Naval Force Commander, Hughes-Hallett, confessed to a feeling of relief mixed with exhilaration – 'relief that all the preparations were at last successfully completed; of course I was aware that there were shortcomings in the plan, particularly the lack of heavy supporting fire, but the moment of sailing was no time for jogging backwards and I put my fears behind me'.

By Hughes-Hallett's side Roberts, the Military Force Commander, read a message from his superior, Crerar: 'Good luck and give him the works.'

Roberts dictated the reply: 'Thanks, we will.'

The Germans manning the Atlantic Wall operated their defensive system in three stages of alert. The Continuous State of Alert, which was normal routine; Threatened Danger (troops to be ready for action); and Highest Degree of Alert, or action stations.

On the evening of 18 August, because the weather conditions (light wind, little cloud, moon setting at 0100 hours, high tide at Dieppe at 0403 hours and early morning haze on 19 August giving way to good visibility) made a landing a 'possibility', coastal commanders were ordered to maintain a Threatened Danger alert.

Capt. Richard Schnösenberg, commanding the area from Dieppe harbour's East mole to the village of Puys, was assiduous in following his instructions. The German Army Command had ordered that defence alarm drills should be carried out weekly, and Schnösenberg chose the night of 18–19 August to sound the alarm in his sector round Puys. So the defenders in that vital area were in a state of readiness which considerably exceeded the ordered alert. 'All units stationed near Puys – a rifle platoon, a heavy machine-gun squad, an air force signals company – all were in position,' said Schnösenberg.

In a pillbox on the Dieppe beach east of the Casino Pte Leo Marziniak did sentry duty from 2100 until 2300 hours, and again from 0100 to 0300 hours. While off duty he slept fully clothed, as instructed for the state of Threatened Danger, on the floor of the pillbox.

Not all were so well prepared, however. Since the forecast for 19 August called for an overcast afternoon following a fine morning, not the best of conditions for aerial operations, many Luftwaffe personnel were given the night off to attend a dance at a village near Dieppe where a group of *Helferinnen*, the Women's Auxiliary Air Signals and the German equivalent of WAAFs, were stationed. The occasion was turned into a propaganda session by the presence of a group of formally white-jacketed war correspondents, photographers and cameramen, in the area to publicise the *Helferinnen* and boost recruitment and morale back home.

In 813 Battery up on the cliffs at Varengeville, guards returning from night patrols ignored the Threatened Danger alert, undressed and went to bed. They would need all the rest they could get.

The passage of the British fleet through the minefields was accomplished without loss, if not without incident. *Queen Emma*, carrying the Royal Regiment and commanded by a Royal Navy officer brought out of retirement, set off at such speed that she led the entire fleet towards the danger area, lost touch with accompanying destroyers and went through the eastern, rather than the scheduled western swept channel, overtaking HMS *Fernie* and several tank landing craft, fortunately without collision.

The shallow-draught gunboat *Locust*, unable to keep up with the troopships or find either channel, sailed safely straight through the minefield. This section of the force, carrying the Royal Marine Commandos, had been late getting under way and had to go flat out to keep up, causing what the official report called 'alarming sparks from the funnels and an alarming glow from the exhaust pipes'. The engines of one of the Chasseurs were not up to this extra labour. It broke down and had to return to England.

Safely through the minefield, the force fanned out towards the allotted beaches. On ships and landing craft, the Jubilee raiders composed themselves for the morning. Aboard *Glengyle* padre John Foote brought the Royal Hamilton Light Infantry together for the prayer 'The Lord is my light and my salvation'. Others wrote letters home. Pte Harold Price of the Royal Regiment remembered, 'We were assured that if anything happened to us the letters would get home to our next of kin. I aways recall that the guys in my company, the guys that were close to me, were writing letters. Do you know, every guy I can remember who wrote a letter got killed, every guy.'

Makeshift meals were available for those who felt like eating. There was a washtub of sandwiches on the deck of *Queen Emma* for those who wanted to help themselves. 'I don't think anybody took or ate any', said Pte Jack Poolton. Aboard LCT 3 Lt Jerry Wood of the Royal Canadian Engineers praised the naval personnel for providing, without prior knowledge of the operation, 'a first class dinner of soup, bully, biscuits, butter, jam, lashing of hot tea, sugar, milk.... I had my first taste of white bread in England.' After dinner Wood settled himself into a hammock he had scrounged and started to read the book he had brought with him, *Last Train From Berlin*.

Aboard *Glengyle* Col. Robert Labatt, commanding the Royal Hamiltons, had been offered the captain's cabin in which to have a meal and prepare himself. Labatt shaved, bathed and changed his clothes ('I remembered hearing that the navy did this in case of wounds') before sitting down to eat at a table prepared with stiff white linen and silver cutlery. Joined by his adjutant, Capt. Herb Poag, Labatt had bacon, eggs and kidneys served from an electric chafing dish, porridge and mugs of coffee. 'Hot toast, butter and marmalade completed the last meal Herb would ever eat and my last civilised meal for many months to come,' said Labatt.

Aboard HMS *Calpe* the American journalist Quentin Reynolds drank brandy and listened as Gen. Roberts assured him, 'The plan is good, the men are keen, and they know what to do.'

Roberts' opinion was not shared by Labatt. 'There was no doubt about the officers knowing the job thoroughly but I had no time to satisfy myself about the men. It seemed fantastic. Units were being launched into an involved operation, the success of which depended on two factors, surprise and the thorough knowledge of each man of his particular job. Yet no time had been made available for him to study his task.'

Bill Stevens, a Royal Regiment private who was only 17, agreed: 'I had been posted to the regiment only three weeks before the raid. I missed all the training on the Isle of Wight, but being with C Company I just went with them. I had no idea what I was supposed to do. On board ship I was shown some intelligence pictures, not that they helped much either.'

Units worked late into the night completing their preparations as best they could in the darkness. There was a moment of black humour on *Queen Emma* when some of the Royal Regiment were priming their hand grenades on deck. 'There were chaps squatting down, all in different positions,' said Jack Poolton. 'I was away up in the bow. We didn't want to get too close to anybody. To put those little detonators in was a very touchy thing, especially in the dark.' Just how touchy was discovered by Bill Stevens: 'When I was priming mine I suddenly thought, what the hell am I sitting on? I reached down and felt a depth charge, so I just moved myself away.' As Pte Reg Hall noted, 'If we had dropped one grenade the whole damn ship would have gone up.'

Many of the troops had been issued with French money and escape kits, consisting of silk handkerchiefs with maps of France and Germany printed on them, compasses and tiny files. Others slid steel mirrors into each breast pocket of their battledress as extra protection.

In the luxury of his cabin on *Glengyle* Col. Labatt prepared himself for action: 'I struggled into my battle kit, skeleton web, Colt 45, two extra mags, water bottle, prismatic compass, maps in oiled silk and field message book in left leg pocket; pencils, pen, torch, cigarettes, chocolate, wallet and escape kit in breast pockets. In the haversack, sandwiches, more chocolate and cigarettes; message pads, Sten mags, two grenades and one smoke canister, binoculars round the neck, Mae West around the chest, Sten gun in hand and there I was, the 1942 amphibious soldier.'

Aboard *Prince Albert* the mess decks, according to Lt Donald Gilchrist, resembled the setting for a Hallowe'en party rather than a Commando raid: 'Everywhere men were applying greasepaint to their faces. It varied in depth of colour. Some had achieved the desired nigger minstrel effect. Others looked more like Red Indians.'

At 0300 hours, while the Luftwaffe and their *Helferinnen* continued to dance the night away in France, hundreds of Allied pilots were roused for breakfast at stations throughout southern England in preparation for the biggest encounter since the Battle of Britain two years previously.

At the same moment, the 'Jubilee' Force passed the point of no return. If, by 0300 hours, nothing had gone seriously wrong and no troopship losses had been suffered because of mines or torpedo boats, the plans of the operation stipulated that the attack on Dieppe would go ahead, no matter what.

Nothing had gone amiss. The various groups were proceeding on course and in reasonable condition towards the French coast. 'Jubilee' was beyond recall.

CHAPTER FIVE
Yellow Beach

'From a political point of view the Dieppe Raid was unwise to say the least because it was bound to end in heavy losses without producing any visible success.'

– War Diary of the German
Naval Operations Staff

The Mission of No. 3 Commando was to land on Yellow Beach 1 and Yellow 2 at Berneval and destroy Battery 2/770 (the so-called Goebbels Battery) which dominated the eastern approaches to Dieppe. Most of the Commandos and the handful of US Rangers who accompanied them were loaded for the Channel crossing in the plywood Eureka boats, which were so vulnerable that one Commando, Sgt Wally Dungate, felt 'a rifle bullet would go right through about ten of them'. Aboard Steam Gunboat No. 5, which was to lead the force, were Col. Durnford-Slater, the senior naval officer for the Yellow Beach group, Cdr D. B. Wyburd, and the Rangers' leader, Capt. Roy Murray. Though more comfortable than most of his men, Durnford-Slater was scarcely happier about the protection afforded by what he termed 'a fast but vulnerable boat, laced with steam tubes'.

They sailed from Newhaven at 2030 hours. The steam gunboat led the way, followed by 23 landing craft in four columns with a flak landing ship (LCF No. 1) and an armed motor launch (ML No. 346) to provide protection at the rear. Because the group was delayed outside Newhaven harbour and then had to sail into a slight headwind, Cdr Wyburd pushed his force towards the minefields at just under ten knots which, as he admitted later, 'was just more than the landing craft could make comfortably'. A number of the Eurekas dropped back with engine trouble and at one time Wyburd could see only 15 of the 23 boats through binoculars.

Aboard one of the boats plagued by engine trouble was Capt. John Smale: 'Although we were left behind and on our own we didn't worry because we were bound to hit France sometime. Then we came across a destroyer which told us we were heading into a minefield, but since the boat was flat-bottomed we decided to go ahead.'

Four of the boats were forced back to Newhaven, but by the early hours the other nineteen were still more or less formed up behind SGB 5 as it steamed towards the heavily-used sealanes down which the Germans moved almost six million tons of shipping a year.

British radar on the Kent coast had detected the German convoy of five motor vessels and its escorts shortly after it left Boulogne that evening and had plotted its movement south-westwards. After the dots faded beyond the range of the radar screens in Dover about midnight, Portsmouth radar took over and when these unidentified ships were seen to be moving towards the 'Jubilee' fleet two signals were sent to *Calpe* at 0127 and 0244 hours to alert the force commanders. Neither signal was received because of defective communications, and though *Fernie* plotted the second signal, no action was taken because it was assumed that *Calpe* had received it safely. Nor had the destroyers *Slazak* and *Brocklesby*, which had been detached from the main force at 0330 hours to protect the extreme left flank of the fleet, been warned.

At 0347 hours, the British and German ships collided. As soon as Lt Berner in submarine chaser UJ 1404 saw shapes on the starboard side of his vessel he fired a starshell, illuminating the area in what a Canadian naval officer Sub-Lt David Lewis called 'a horrible quivering semi-daylight'. The leading British vessel, SGB 5, took the brunt of the Germans' short-range fire. Durnford-Slater, having been awakened shortly before, was standing on deck, his face blackened ready for the landing, when the German flare went up, at which the captain, Lt G. H. Hummel, shouted, 'My God, now look out.' At first it was thought that the raiding force's covering destroyers had opened fire on their own ships by mistake but, as Cdr Wyburd recalled, 'It soon became very apparent that this was not the case.'

Within minutes SGB 5's armament had been knocked out, she was badly holed, and, according to Durnford-Slater, 'steam hissed like a thousand snakes out of the pipes'. The Commando chief, who had been busy trying to dodge the tracer flying in his direction, said 'I was lucky. Only a few small fragments from bursting shells hit me. I seemed to be alone on the deck. A naval officer on the bridge saw my plight. "Come on up here," he yelled. "The bridge is armoured." I did not hesitate to accept his kind invitation. When I reached the bridge I saw that the armour-plating was not preventing considerable carnage. One of the naval officers was quite windy. He kept shouting "This is the end, this is the end."

'I was inclined to agree with him. I blew up my Mae West and undid my boots. All around me the bridge was piled up with wounded like a collapsed rugger scrum. There must have been ten casualites there, all hit when looking over the top of the armour-plating. One officer, whom I knew to be of considerable naval experience, stood with his head and shoulders exposed and directed the ship. Then he fell to the deck. "I'm hit," he groaned. He was bleeding where a shell splinter had penetrated his skull. Brutally, I pushed him upright again. I felt he was our last remaining hope.'

Larry Maier, a correspondent for the International News Service, who had been planning to cover the raid from SGB 5, wrote: 'Suddenly there was a blast in my face. I was knocked semi-conscious and thought I was a goner but I recovered, thinking I was lucky to escape. I happened to put my hand to my face. I discovered something wet and hot, then my chest felt wet and I realised I'd been shrapnelled ... the explosion had blown off my glasses, which were lost.'

In the unprotected little boats behind SGB 5 there was tumult as startled Commandos threw off blankets and grabbed for helmets and weapons. Pte Dennis O'Connor had the dubious distinction of being the first soldier to be hit on the Dieppe Raid: 'I was in the leading landing craft, standing right up forward, raring to go. Right beside me was a chap without his tin helmet and I bent down to pick it up for him and rouse him. Then boom, boom, boom, I was hit in the left leg, arm and throat.' O'Connor was later transferred to the flak ship

LCF 1. 'There they gave me some tea laced with brandy, which came straight out of the wound in my neck.'

When a shell killed or wounded all the naval personnel in his boat, Sgt Clive Collins took over the wheel and was given a course to steer for France by the commander. The compass was smashed, however, and when he saw that the group had been scattered, Collins turned round and headed for England, using a prismatic pocket compass. He made a remarkable landfall at Beachy Head and the craft limped into Newhaven at 1000 hours, six hours after the fight.

Capt. John Smale's landing craft, delayed earlier by engine trouble, caught up with the others just in time to run into the German submarine chaser 1411. 'One of the first bursts hit the two naval personnel in our boat,' said Smale. 'I was jolly lucky because I was standing next to them. After that we got as low as possible and Cpl Tom Gerrard steered as best he could while lying on the deck. We hoped that, having given us a few bursts, the German boat would go away but it changed course and came straight at us to ram. Gerrard saved everybody's lives by jamming the lever into reverse, so it just missed us. That was when I decided to jump overboard. There didn't seem much point waiting about because as they went by they gave us another burst or two.'

Smale was followed into the water by most of the Commandos aboard the Eureka. On a previous expedition against Guernsey he had almost drowned of waterlogged boots and leggings and had benefited from the experience. 'I got my trousers and boots off straight away, which saved my life. Remembering the Guernsey incident, I just had on a shirt and a Mae West.'

Having survived the gunfire Smale and Gerrard decided to stick together and strike out for the French coast. 'There were a lot of boats of one sort or another in the area and I wasn't too worried,' he said. A strong swimmer, Smale was in no difficulties but Gerrard had not had time to remove his boots. When he tried to do so the laces had swelled and he was unable to untie them. 'I tried to keep him up,' Smale recalled, 'but after a while I just couldn't hold him any longer. I think he was unconscious at the time and finally he just drowned.'

Within ten minutes of the first shot being fired SGB 5 was a shambles, the wireless equipment and all her guns put out of action and crippled by a direct hit on her boilers, though the gallantry of ERA Roy Eastlake in the engine room ensured that the gunboat could at least still navigate. Although wounded and badly scalded by escaping steam, Eastlake managed to keep the damaged machinery going. Forty per cent of those on board had been wounded, but miraculously only one was killed.

Before being silenced, the guns of the British gunboat had inflicted considerable damage. On submarine chaser 1411 First Lt Wurmbach was unable to put out an emergency signal because his antenna had been shot away in the first seconds. Lt Bögel, commanding the armed minesweeper 4014 presumed the encounter would be one of the 'usual torpedo boat skirmishes' so common in that part of the Channel but was swiftly disabused. As he moved to the lower deck to get better recognition of the enemy silhouettes a shell demolished his bridge, wounding his chief mate and helmsman and knocking him to the deck. Two of Bögel's crew were killed and ten wounded.

By this time the flak landing ship LCF 1 and the armed motor launch ML 346 had moved through from the rear of the British force and added their fire-power to the battle. LCF 1's two twin 4 in. guns set on fire Lt Berner's UJ 1404, which blew up and was lost with all hands. Outnumbered, outgunned and with the safety of their convoy paramount, Wurmbach and Bögel broke off the fight. An indication of the fierceness of the short battle can be gained from the fact that UJ 1411 expended 307 3.7 cm. tracer shells, 470 2 cm. shells, about 3,000 rounds of machine-gun bullets, four depth charges and six hand grenades.

The destroyers *Slazak* and *Brocklesby*, whose task it was to guard against the sort of collision with enemy naval forces which had just occurred, took no part whatever in the battle. The senior of the two commanders, Capt. Romuald Tyminski on the Polish destroyer *Slazak*, thought the firing was coming from shore and when Capt. Nigel Pumphrey ('a daredevil, always eager to attack,' said Tyminski) turned *Brocklesby* about and fired starshells towards the distant action he was ordered to cease firing and resume his station. Tyminski's explanation was that his ships were too far away to affect the outcome of the clash and that he did not want to reveal to the enemy the presence of major vessels in the vicinity of the flare-up. So the two destroyers continued to mount a preventive patrol against a disaster which had already happened.

Though the Commandos had been scattered and suffered casualties, astonishingly not one of the wooden landing craft had been sunk. Aboard *Fernie* two miles away Brig. Churchill Mann had what he termed 'a ringside seat' for the flare-up: 'Although it was a thrilling and spectacular display it filled us with foreboding, as we all realised that the chance of our effecting surprise was greatly diminished.'

The Yellow Beach landings had indeed been compromised, but so slow were the Germans to react to what they considered no more than 'a customary attack on a convoy' that an hour had passed before it was realised that the incident was not a 'customary attack' at all. The C.-in-C. West, von Rundstedt, maintained that as a result of the noise of battle at sea the alarm was given in the coastal area. It was a piecemeal alarm, however. In the immediate target area of Berneval German defenders were alerted by the proximity of the shooting but elsewhere the imminence of a landing was still not recognised.

To Wyburd and Durnford-Slater on the crippled SGB 5 the situation could not have looked gloomier. Only five of the original 23 landing craft still clustered around their mother ship and the two commanders quickly agreed that a landing at Berneval was now out of the question. Having been unable to pass on a signal to the Force Commanders aboard *Calpe*, Wyburd and Durnford-Slater transferred into a landing craft at 0445 hours, five minutes before their attack had been due to go in, and set off in search of the headquarters ship lying somewhere off Dieppe to deliver their grim message in person to Roberts.

The attack on the Berneval battery was still very much alive, however. When the sea battle died down Lt Alexander Fear, commanding officer of ML 346, set about rounding up stray landing craft. As a

Commando private, Albert Moore, recalled 'This naval launch came alongside and said through a loud hailer "Those who are mobile, follow me".' Altogether Fear collected five Eurekas containing a total of 96 Commandos and six US Rangers and headed through the early dawn for his target, Yellow Beach One to the east of Berneval.

Also on course for Berneval and Yellow Beach Two, west of the village, was a single landing craft commanded by Lt Henry Thomas Buckee and containing 20 Commandos under Maj. Peter Young. Buckee's boat LCP 15, was embarked on what was later praised as 'perhaps the most outstanding single feature' of the Dieppe Raid.

LCP 15 had been leading the starboard column of landing craft when the sea fight erupted and was immediately enveloped in 'the hottest tracer fire I have ever seen' according to Sub-Lt David Lewis. 'The air was filled with the whine of ricochets and the bang of exploding shells, but the flak was flying ahead and astern of us. Putting on full speed we went under the stern of the disabled steam gunboat and tore away from the lashing beams of flak.'

The startled Commandos, scrambling for their weapons, had been ordered to hold their fire by Young, who gave his men no outward sign that it was 'the most unpleasant moment of my life'. Above the noise of battle he yelled 'All right you lot, the first bastard who fires back and gives away our position will have me to deal with. We are going in.' Unmarked except for fragments of shrapnel and with nobody aboard hurt, LCP 15 sailed through the fight, carried clear of trouble by Buckee's swift reactions and Young's common sense.

Guided by the Dieppe harbour lights, flashing in ignorance of events to welcome into port the German convoy, Buckee headed for a black patch on the coast which he insisted, over Young's doubts, was Yellow Two. 'There you are, that's your beach,' said Buckee. 'My orders are to land even if there's only one boat.' Not to be outdone, Young replied 'And *my* orders are to go ashore, even if we have to swim.'

There was certainly no need to swim, or even get their feet wet, as, five minutes ahead of schedule at 0445 and in rapidly growing daylight, Buckee ran his craft right onto the pebbles of Berneval beach. The landing was totally unopposed. Briskly declining Buckee's offer of himself and his four sailors to swell the numbers of the pathetically small party, Young stepped ashore. With him were two other officers, Capt. John Selwyn and Lt 'Buck' Ruxton, an adventure-minded Ulsterman who had been lately frustrated in an ambitious plan to blow up the German embassy in Dublin and who had been with Young's unit less than a week.

Among the seventeen assorted other ranks were Young's batman, Pte Sidney Clark, and his runner, Pte Alfred Craft. The armament with which they proposed to attack the three 170 mm. and four 105 mm. guns of the heavily-defended battery consisted of one Bren and six Thompson sub-machine-guns, ten rifles, three pistols, a 3 in. mortar and a 2 in. mortar.

Though the gully leading from the beach was undefended, the obstacles blocking it were formidable. Barbed wire ten feet high protected the entrance and the cleft itself was choked with coils of wire. Since their landing craft contained neither wire-cutters nor any of the wire-blowing devices known as Bangalore torpedoes, Young set the example by climbing up the right hand side of the gully, using the pegs with which the Germans secured the wire to the cliffs as makeshift steps and pulling himself up bare-handed on the wire itself. 'The bars were very close together but fairly blunt and this, though it cut my hands, was not as unpleasant as it sounds,' said Young, who admitted that the climb was 'rather an ordeal' as he had no head for heights.

On reaching the top after some twenty minutes, Young was informed by a notice board in French and German that he had just traversed a mined area. Half an hour had elapsed before the whole party, their hands bloodied and their battledress torn, stood atop the cliff. They had been forced to leave their 3 in. mortar behind on the beach and L/Cpl 'Chalky' White, whose responsibility this weapon was, went into action against the battery totally unarmed. Another Commando, Pte Victor Adderton, carried only a pistol.

At least Young's party knew by then that they were not alone on a hostile shore. As they paused on the cliff they saw five more Eurekas running in towards Yellow One beach just along the coast.

Young led the way into a nearby wood and organised his men into three groups under Selwyn, Ruxton and himself. 'Some of the soldiers did not look particularly pleased at the turn of events,' he said, 'so I gave them a pep talk, telling them ... it would be something to tell their children about.' As one of the party, Gunner Stephen Saggers, pointed out 'Young was flamboyant but he was a bloke you could have confidence in.' Their morale restored, the group moved towards the village of Berneval. As they did so, the mighty guns of the battery opened fire with a deafening roar.

Though they had the benefit of the presence of ML 346 with its 3-pounder gun and machine-guns, the five landing craft chugging towards Yellow One were well behind schedule. As they neared the shore they were half an hour late and it was daylight.

Sgt Wally Dungate remembered, 'When we were going in you could actually see the defenders standing on the cliffs. The amazing part about it was that they never blew us out of the water but waited until we got right into the beach. You could see the Germans through binoculars, watching us come in.'

The beach towards which they were heading was not mined, the only wire was a heavy mass blocking the exit up a narrow gully, and there was no German garrison as such in Berneval. But the defenders in that area had been thoroughly alerted by the sea battle. Four men and a machine-gun were dispatched from the battery to cover the exit from the beach and they were joined by eight Luftwaffe personnel from a nearby radar station, ordered to delay the Commando landing until reinforcements could be brought up. Already in position on the cliff top, and spotted by Dungate, was a ten-man picquet which opened up on the landing craft with a machine-gun and rifles as they covered the final few yards to shore.

One of their first victims was Lt-Cdr C. L. Corke, who was mortally wounded on the run-in. The coxswain in the same vessel was killed and a Commando took the helm. 'When we landed the first bloke to get killed was a man called Harrison,' said Dungate. 'He was the first one off and a rifle bullet hit him right between the eyes, just like you see at the pictures.'

Once the Commandos had crossed a short expanse of beach they were able to get under the cover of the cliffs, out of the line of fire and regroup to tackle the wire. Crucial delays were encountered in getting off Yellow One beach because the landing craft which had reached the shore were not the ones carrying ladders to scale the cliffs or Bangalore torpedoes to blow the wire. Sgt Major Ron Grove, tired of waiting for the wire to be cut by hand, climbed to the top of the cliff to see if another route could be found to the battery. 'It was absolutely stinking with landmines,' he said. 'I came back down and told them "We *cannot* go that way." So we had to queue behind others cutting the wire, which took some time because it was really tough.'

The fire-power of ML 346 was highly effective in keeping quiet the German picquet who were spraying the beach from the shelter of a clifftop house, but the lone machine-gun covering the beach exit proved more difficult to subdue. Eventually it was silenced single-handed by a corporal, 'Banger' Hall, using grenades and bayonet.

Half an hour after the first five craft had landed, a sixth Eureka appeared and, despite heavy fire, succeeded in putting a further group of Commandos ashore. Almost simultaneously another vessel loomed through the smoke of battle off Yellow One. At first Lt Fear on ML 346 thought she was a British flak ship and closed her for news of the raid's progress until a German flag was seen flying. It was the 200-ton coastal tanker *Franz*, one of the German convoy, which had been damaged in the battle and was being beached.

As ML 346 opened fire at less than thirty yards range, the crew leapt overboard and swam for the shore, suffering the double indignity of being shot at by the German defenders as they went. *Franz* eventually ran aground on fire and a British boarding party removed the German ensign as a war trophy. Apart from the submarine chaser which had been blown up during the engagement, the tanker was the only other loss among the convoy, which reached the safety of Le Treport despite the tremendous Allied air and sea activity in the area.

One of Maj. Peter Young's favourite sayings, 'Young soldiers will follow their commanders out of the innocence of their hearts' was about to be put to the test as his tiny force moved out of the shelter of the woods above Yellow Two beach and towards the Dieppe-Berneval road. When they reached it, a French youth was passing on a bicycle. The terrified boy was grabbed by two Commandos and explained that his mother had been wounded by a stray bomb and he was on his way to get a doctor. He pointed out the whereabouts of the battery, said there were about 200 Germans in it (the actual strength was 127) and when Young told him he could go on his way, the youth kissed Young on the cheek, jumped on his bicycle and pedalled off furiously.

Having pushed forward cautiously into the village of Berneval-le-Grand, cutting telephone wires on the way and passing a woman calmly milking a cow, and still encountered no resistance, Young decided that to save time he would advance up the main street at the double. Village fireman in bright brass helmets were extinguishing the blaze in the house struck by the wayward bomb and the young cyclist's wounded mother was being carted away in a wheelbarrow as the Commandos jogged into the midst of the startled Frenchmen.

Another local inhabitant confirmed the exact position of the battery. 'As a reward we gave him a telescope which we had brought with us but which was no good and this greatly pleased him,' said Capt. John Selwyn. Turning the corner by the village church, the Commandos were fired on for the first time by a machine-gun further up the road. The bullets knocked a shower of tiles on to the head of the party's Bren gunner, Pte John Abbott as Young's men dived into the cover of the churchyard. A few rounds from the 2 in. mortar quickly subdued the machine-gun.

'The doubling had done the men good,' Young reported. 'They had now got their blood up and quite recovered their spirits. They were beginning to enjoy themsleves.' Young's plan to fire down into the battery pits from the tower of the eleventh-century church was frustrated because the staircase began ten feet up the tower and no ladder could be found to bridge the gap, so he attempted to advance on the battery through the orchards on the edge of the village. When the group came under fire again, Young decided to change his tactics.

'There seemed to me to be no future in advancing blind through these orchards against a hidden enemy, and it occurred to me that we might be better off in the cornfields.... In the army you are told that two bricks will stop a bullet. I then announced that nine feet of corn would stop a bullet. Fortunately my soldiers believed this, or appeared to. We ran into the cornfield and opened a fairly heavy fire on the battery, but not rapid because I hadn't got much ammunition.'

The remaining rounds of the 2 in. mortar were pumped in the direction of the Germans and the Commandos were then reduced to harassing fire delivered from a kneeling position because of the height of the corn. The Germans were plainly startled by the attack from the cornfield and eventually one of the huge artillery pieces was swung round and pointed inland. 'There was a bloody great bang and orange and black smoke came out of this thing,' said Young. 'The shell wandered over our heads and burst in a valley somewhere in France behind us. I thought, what a good thing because if they are firing at us *and* missing they are certainly not firing at the British fleet.' A dozen shots were loosed off at the Commando group before the Germans realised they could not obtain sufficient depression to achieve any success and gave up.

After an hour and a half of this action, during which the battery was reduced virtually to impotence, Young's men began to run out of ammunition and were in danger of being outflanked by enemy reinforcements.

So Capt. Selwyn was sent back to form a small bridgehead around the beach and ordered to fire three white Very lights if their boat was still waiting for them. In his landing craft, Lt Buckee had stayed offshore, taking cover behind a smokescreen from the sporadic shelling directed his way, and at 0745 hours when the Very lights went up Buckee moved in towards the beach under covering fire from ML 346. The increasingly embattled Young reported 'I never saw a more heartening sight' as the Very lights hung bright in the morning sun.

Gathering together his force, Young headed briskly for the cliffs a few hundred yards away 'followed at a respectful distance by some of the enemy', and from the cliffs he covered the withdrawal and embarkation of Selwyn's party. By now the Germans were closing in quickly on what they belatedly realised was a small group. Gunner Stephen Saggers recalled, 'When we began to withdraw down the cliff we found the enemy were coming after us quite fast. Most of us came down the same way as we went up, but one or two of them were a bit scared and 'Chalky' White ran across a minefield.' Though he stepped on an anti-personnel mine White was only slightly wounded and, once on the beach, loaded the 3 in. mortar which had been left behind during the landing and fired off his bombs at the approaching Germans.

Re-embarkation was complicated by the fact that the tide had gone out, leaving the beach ribbed with rocks, and as the naval personnel pulled the Commandos aboard, the landing craft stuck fast so they were told to throw away their weapons to lighten the load. Young, Ruxton and the Bren gunner John Abbott were the last off the beach and as they began to wade out the boat was moving away to avoid the bullets. 'It was like those dreams you have of trying desperately to walk and making no progress,' Young remembered. Lifelines were thrown to the three men and they clung on as the vessel accelerated away from the shore, dragging them in its wake. About 300 yards out, the boat hove to, just in time to save the exhausted Abbott from drowning, and they were hauled aboard. The clifftop snipers had now got the range. The boat's petrol tank was holed eight times and the coxswain, a yard from Young, was badly wounded in the thigh. As the landing craft surged out into the Channel, carrying away every man it had put ashore, the battery which the Commandos had for so long immobilised gave them a parting salvo of four shots, but the nearest fell a hundred yards away.

Buckee's homeward-bound boat passed not far away from the lone, bobbing figure of Capt. John Smale, who had leapt overboard from his landing craft during the night battle more than four hours earlier. Smale was close enough to feel the repercussion of the shells through the water but his comrades failed to spot him: 'Automatically I waved and shouted but I didn't expect to be seen.'

The group transferred to ML 346 for the run back to England and docked in Newhaven at 1045 hours. Young, who recalled that he felt 'distinctly warm, if somewhat tight, having been entertained nobly on whisky, cocoa and rum' was taken at once to London to report in person to Mountbatten. He was asked to return the next day to attend a conference and when he asked permission to wear his battledress 'which was rather the worse for wear' the Chief of Combined Operations told him 'What the hell, there's a war on.'

As Young headed for his home at Oxshott and a night in his own bed, the journey of the marathon swimmer John Smale was coming to an end. After the landing craft carrying Young's party had passed him, there was a spell when Smale could see nothing and nobody.

'Then eventually I had a rather strange meeting. A chap loomed up in the water, an American, and we had a long chat as we swam on together. He was an airman and talked about having been in the Eagle Squadron. As far as I remember we tried to keep together but drifted apart. By that time the current was carrying me down the coast and parallel with it.

'Almost at the entrance to Dieppe harbour I came across a German rubber dinghy with three or four aircrew in it. I waved and they definitely saw me. I hoped I could hitch a lift because I was getting a bit tired by then. But they just looked at me, picked up their paddles and pushed off in the other direction.'

The battle for Dieppe had long been decided as Smale floated past the town front, exhausted, suffering hallucinations and ill from having swallowed too much sea water. 'I was only a couple of hundred yards from shore when a German patrol boat came in sight,' he said. 'I waved at it, thinking it was one of ours. They waved back, came alongside and pulled me on board. They gave me a drink of rum and I remembered the captain waving to me to come up to the bridge. From my point of view that was a major operation, to climb up a small ladder. I just passed out and fell back on the deck. The next thing I knew I was being carried ashore on a stretcher.'

John Smale had been in the water for thirteen hours when he was picked up.

Because the Berneval area was not heavily defended, the 120 Commandos and US Rangers who landed at Yellow One were able to make good initial progress once they had cleared their way through the beach obstacles. Two of the three-man picquet at the hamlet of Petit Berneval were killed attempting to delay the British advance inland, and five of the eight Luftwaffe personnel sent from the nearby radar station also lost their lives.

Once the general alarm had been given at 0530 hours, however, that landings were being attempted all along the coast, German reaction was swift. The counter-attack against the Commandos was entrusted to Maj. von Blücher, who was in command of the 302nd Division's anti-tank and reconnaissance battalion. An infantry squadron mounted on bicycles, a company of the 570th Infantry Regiment and a company of the 302nd Division's engineer battalion in lorries were hurried towards the scene from their reserve areas inland. The counter-attack group was known as Blücher Force, and its speed in getting into action was delayed only by the fact that more than half of the bicycles being used collapsed or broke down under the weight of the laden infantrymen.

Once off the beach Capt. Geoffrey Osmond was unhappy to discover 'that the actual physical features of the countryside were nothing like the scale model we had been studying'. The task of the Commandos was to strike up the valley containing the hamlet of Petit Berneval, past the anti-aircraft position defending the Goebbels Battery and hook right to attack the battery itself from the rear. The first snag that Osmond encountered was that the road was overlooked by more houses than he had been led to believe, so he took his group, consisting of about 40 fighting troops, the demolition party and the medical section, over a hill to the rear of the houses.

Split up because of the German resistance and the nature of the terrain, the Commandos were never able to mount a concerted movement towards the battery. 'It was a shambles for a while, you didn't know what the score was,' Sgt Wally Dungate recalled. 'We did the best we could with what we had but we were no longer a fighting unit after that attack at sea. Half our gear was in the boats that hadn't arrived. We had been trained to a pitch for this but had no plans in case anything went wrong. It was like a boxer who has won five rounds and then gets a cut eye. All his efforts have gone down the drain. That's the sort of feeling we got.'

'We had been ashore quite a while and hadn't moved very far. I'll never forget it. We were in an orchard and the fruit was ripe and the blokes were all saying "Hey, look at this fruit, plenty of fruit here." I remember thinking, this is not very clever, it's too quiet.' We moved out on to a road and there was this tremendous clatter as they opened up on us. One man called Easterbrook got hit. When we undone his belt his stomach was in his trousers, he wasn't in very good nick at all.'

At 0700 hours, when the Commando had been ashore just under two hours, three of the landing craft which had been waiting offshore moved in to Yellow One to answer a white Very light signal for withdrawal. But when they beached, in a hail of rifle and machine-gun fire and with grenades being lobbed at them from the cliffs, they found only the naval communications party waiting to be taken off. After reporting that they had heard nothing from the Commandos, they were taken aboard LCP 157, which promptly stuck on the rocks exposed by the ebbing tide. When another landing craft, LCP 1, went to its assistance it too ran aground on rocks and steel stakes. The third vessel, LCP 85, went alongside LCP 157 and successfully removed both the crew and the beach party without casualties. As 157 was still stuck fast, it was set on fire and abandoned. LCP 1 had meanwhile managed to free itself and retired offshore. Half an hour later at 0730 hours, Lt Dennis Stephens, in charge of the landing craft flotilla, decided there was no chance of any more survivors and withdrew his remaining boats, leaving LCP 157 ablaze on the beach and LCPs 81, holed during the night battle and sinking, and 42, whose crew had been killed during the landing, abandoned offshore.

There were still plenty of survivors, however. At about the time the empty landing craft set off back to England, Capt. Geoffrey Osmond decided to pull back in face of increasingly heavy attacks from the cycle-borne reinforcements. 'Just before we started to withdraw we got shot up by machine-guns,' he said. 'Where it came from I don't know. Sam Corry, our doctor, got both his legs broken. I collected seven bullets in various places which smashed my right arm to bits.' As Pte Albert Moore recalled, 'We were the only people in the world who were fighting a war, it seemed. We could see and hear all these lorries heading towards us down the road from Dieppe.'

Most of the Commando losses were incurred during the withdrawal to the beach. German reinforcements had succeeded in covering the path leading down to the sea with a machine-gun. 'We had to lie in the grass, take our turn and dash across the path,' said Ron Grove. 'I was lucky. They just knocked the heel off one of my boots as I ran for it. Every one of my party got across but a couple of US Rangers came directly down the path. They hadn't a cat in hell's chance. All we heard was them screaming.' One Ranger, Lt Edwin Loustalot, was the first American soldier to be killed in Europe in the Second World War.

Since the only boats in sight offshore were derelict, the Commandos set about attempting to signal for assistance on a radio left behind by the naval beach party, but without success before it was shot up by the Germans. A Union Jack flag, intended to be hoisted above the captured battery as a signal to friendly aircraft, was pinned to the cliff face with bayonets in the hope that some of the vessels which could be seen passing would spot it.

Recognising the hopelessness of their predicament, one or two tried to swim to safety. Ron Grove recalled, 'Sgt Tim Connolly was sheltering in a cave with us. He stripped off, apart from a Mae West and tin hat. The tide by this time was fairly well out. There he was, a stocky little fellow, trotting down the beach naked with the Jerries on top potting at him and the bullets spurting all round him. He made it to the sea, swam out about 50 yards, then turned round. They shot at him for a while, then desisted since they could see he was coming back in. When he got back I asked him what went wrong. He said "It was too bloody cold" and got dressed again.

'Another fellow, a captain out of the Signals who was attached to us, swam out to one of the abandoned landing craft. But the foolish man never stripped off his uniform to start with, and those boats were very highsided and difficult to climb into. The last we heard of him he was shouting for help.'

As the remainder took shelter in caves and beneath outcrops of rock protecting them from the grenades being tossed down from the clifftop, resistance had become pointless, though there were some still determined on it. According to Ron Grove, 'There was a bunch of us, a sub-lieutenant, I forget his name, a very young fellow, and about twelve others, hiding in a cave. The officer wanted to defend this cave but it had a very wide mouth, no protection at all. He ordered a Bren gun to be set up and I said, "What are you going to do, sir?" He said "Defend the cave", so I told him "That's ridiculous, the Germans only need one mortar bomb in here. Why throw all these lives away?" It would have been sheer waste. He agreed, and that was that.'

Albert Moore remembered, 'There were only a few of us and by this time there were hundreds of Germans, lined up along the cliffs and moving on to the beach. One officer – we nicknamed him American Joe because he shouted to us in an American accent – said "Now then, fellas, the war is over for you. I am your friend. Come out and I'll guarantee no harm will come to you".'

Capt. Osmond made the decision to surrender: 'It was quite obvious that nobody was coming in to collect us, so when the Germans got about 20 yards away I made everybody pack up.'

The surviving Commandos were marched back to the clifftop. 'There were masses of Germans', said Wally Dungate. 'There must have been hundreds of them, all with their bicycles stacked up along the road.' By 1020 hours Blücher Force was able to report to von Rundstedt's Headquarters West that Berneval had been 'completely cleaned up'.

The episode cost No. 3 Commando 140 casualties. Of the 120 men who landed on Yellow One beach 37 were killed, 82 captured and only one, a lance-corporal named Sinclair, managed to escape by swimming out to a passing ship. Of the 23 landing craft which had carried the raiders across the Channel four turned back with engine trouble, 16 returned to Newhaven in various stages of damage and three were abandoned at Berneval.

The force's commanding officer, Durnford-Slater, finally reached the headquarters ship *Calpe* off Dieppe at 0645 hours to report to Gen. Roberts. 'I found him in a mood of the deepest depression,' said Durnford-Slater. That depression was deepened still further when the Commando colonel informed the Military Force Commander that his raiders had been scattered, after which he 'hung around for the rest of the day watching the spectacular air battle and feeling useless'.

It was not until they got back to Newhaven shortly before midnight that Wyburd and Durnford-Slater heard that landings had been made, after all, and Wyburd admitted later, 'I can but reproach and blame myself for not personally going in at any time during the day.... If at any time Col. Durnford-Slater and I had thought that a landing had taken place we would immediately have proceeded there.'

CHAPTER SIX
Orange Beach

'My task was fundamental: in and out – smash and grab.'
– Lord Lovat, 4 Commando

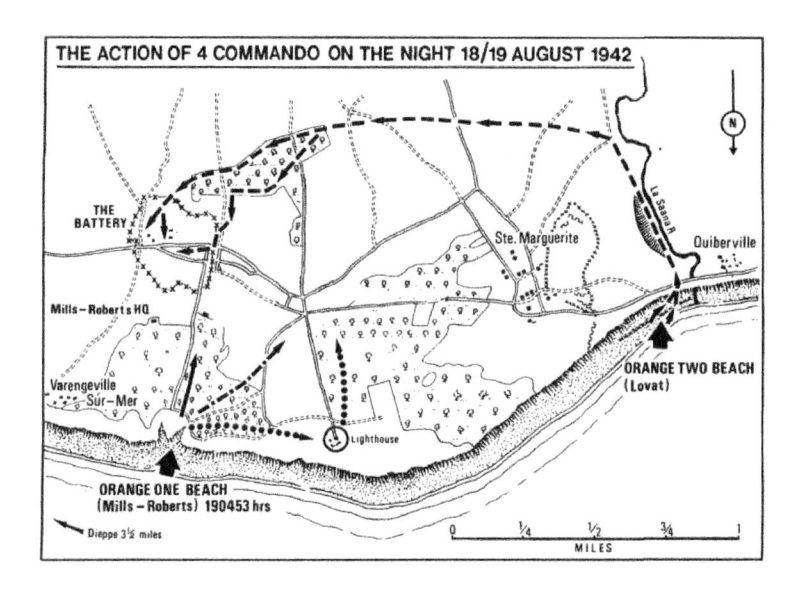

```
THE ACTION OF 4 COMMANDO ON THE NIGHT 18/19 AUGUST 1942
```

The other Commando group, No. 4 under Lt-Col. the Lord Lovat, was on the extreme right of the 'Jubilee' Force as the ships steamed towards Dieppe. The so-called 'Hess Battery' which they were to attack lay in wooded country behind Varengeville, a straggling village about four miles west of Dieppe made famous by Claude Monet, who painted seascapes there.

The battery was manned by No. 813 Army Artillery Troop, and though its official strength was 130 there were only 97 on duty on 19 August under their 48-year-old commanding officer, Capt. Schöler. The battery consisted of half a dozen 150 mm. guns mounted on revolving platforms in individual concrete pits 25 feet in diameter and five feet deep. These massive weapons, manufactured in 1936, could hurl a shell weighing 113 lb more than 13 miles, though their main task was to put down a barrage in the Channel in front of Dieppe. The guns were capable of firing one round a minute, but could double that rate for short spells when necessary.

The site was well protected by seven defensive points situated around a double apron barbed wire perimeter, each post manned by four men under a junior NCO. The battery's chief weaknesses were that it lay outside the Dieppe defensive strongpoint and its guns did not overlook the Channel. Instead, they were connected by cable to an observation post situated alongside the Pointe d'Ailly lighthouse, where a 77-strong naval contingent was stationed. Like their comrades in Dieppe itself, the garrison of 813 Battery had certain makeshift qualities. Their transportation was horse-drawn, and the problems of supply were underlined by the fact that some of the soldiers' uniforms were mended with sacking.

For his task Lovat had under his command a force of 252 men, which included five US Rangers, in addition to naval beach parties and a journalist, A. B. Austin of the *Daily Herald*.

The plan was that 88 men, led by Lovat's second-in-command Maj. Derek Mills-Roberts, should land at a tiny beach known as Orange One and move directly inland to engage the battery frontally, while Lovat's group of 164 would be put ashore two miles further west at Orange Two, just east of the River Saane and the seaside resort of Quiberville, move up the river bank for a mile or so, then swing left to come upon the battery's defences from the rear. If all went well, the Commando force would withdraw to the coast by the direct route by which Mills-Roberts had come and would be taken off Orange One beach.

After embarkation aboard *Prince Albert* at Southampton the Commandos were briefed by Mountbatten himself. One of the US Rangers, Cpl Franklin D. Koons, recalled, 'He struck me as a grand guy and very full of fight; he made us all laugh and we were very cheerful.'

During the smooth, incident-free crossing, Mills-Roberts introduced himself to the *Daily Herald* man, Austin, who would be landing at Orange One with his party. Mills-Roberts was impressed: 'He did not appear to be the type of reporter who would feed the reading public with "What the curly-headed sergeant had for breakfast", supplemented by a photograph of some half-wit with a parrot perched on his shoulder.'

At 0115 hours Mills-Roberts joined his fellow-officers in the ship's wardroom for an early breakfast, and thought them 'the usual depressed crowd that one finds before the start of a day's work' with everybody eating in preoccupied silence. His own mood was not lightened when a steward presented him with a mess bill for 13*s.* 4*d.* for his short stay aboard.

Soon afterwards the unit was assembled to check ammunition, explosives and fighting equipment. All items considered too heavy had been discarded. Ammunition was carried in special bandoliers made of light cloth rather than the standard webbing pouches. Knitted woollen hats were worn instead of steel helmets. Lovat and Mills-Roberts, old friends from Oxford University days, were in total agreement about the worthlessness of helmets on an operation calling for speed and mobility. Mills-Roberts considered that a steel helmet 'slows down a man like a grand piano, for it fetters him at his main point of balance', while Lovat's opinion was that 'tin hats, gas capes and all that paraphernalia would have meant that the poor chaps couldn't have broken out of a waddle'.

Members of F Troop, the demolition group, were heavily laden, however. Trooper George Cook recalled, 'I was carrying about a hundredweight of plastic explosives. It looked like sticks of shaving soap.' Another demolition expert, Sgt Bill Portman, went ashore with 85 lb of explosives in his back pack 'so I kept low when we landed, naturally'.

Just before moving to their boat stations, all ranks assembled for a pep talk by Lovat, who reminded them that they were 'the flower of the British Army' and impressed on them the vital nature of their mission. If the battery was not destroyed it would create havoc among the convoy off Dieppe. 'We were warned that casualties were expected to be heavy and that if a man got wounded he would be left behind,' said George Cook, who had celebrated his 21st birthday only two weeks previously. Cook would have grim cause to remember the warning later.

Lovat presented an engaging sight as he addressed his men. The only Commando not to have 'blacked up' for the landing, he was dressed for battle in his favourite sweater with his name etched across it, and a pair of corduroy slacks, donned for comfort, contrasted sharply with his battledress jacket. He carried his favourite sporting rifle, a Winchester repeater: 'It was a rifle I had done a lot of shooting with and I was dead accurate with it.'

At 0258 hours *Prince Albert* stopped seven miles from Pointe d'Ailly lighthouse and the Commandos were lowered overboard in seven assault landing craft 41 feet long and capable of doing ten knots fully laden. Not only were these boats bigger than the Eurekas in which 3 Commando had crossed the Channel but their steel sides ensured better protection.

While the landing craft were forming up Lt Peter Scott, the wildlife expert, who was in command of their accompanying vessel Steam Gunboat No. 9, appropriately named Grey Goose, noted with the sensitivity of the outdoors man 'A warm wind was blowing from the French coast, laden with the smell of hay-fields.' As Scott peered into the blackness he suddenly saw a light ahead: 'It flashed three times, then twenty seconds later it flashed three times again. The Germans had left their lighthouse burning to guide us. Then we *were* achieving surprise!'

The naval officer in charge of the landing, Lt-Cdr Hugh Mulleneux, led the seven landing craft towards France in two columns in Motor Gunboat 312, with Scott's SGB 9 following astern. Mulleneux reported no serious navigational difficulties during the approach 'thanks largely to the fact that Pointe d'Ailly showed for about five minutes every quarter of an hour and the harbour lights of Dieppe were kept gaily burning'. At 0350 hours, only three minutes after the night sky had been illuminated by the clash of Durnford-Slater's group with the German convoy, Lovat's force came desperately close to the same fate, Mulleneux having to alter course 'fairly drastically' to starboard to avoid three darkened vessels, an eastbound German convoy. 'At this time I couldn't help feeling rather naked whilst contemplating the extreme vulnerability of the flotilla,' he said. At 0430 hours, 20 minutes before zero hour, the group divided two miles off the coast. Mulleneux set off with Mills-Roberts's three landing craft to find the gap in the cliff above the tiny cove which constituted Orange One beach, while Lovat's four boats fanned out in line abreast for the run-in to the wider and more easily-recognised Orange Two at Quiberville, where the coastal cliffs drop down towards the mouth of the River Saane.

As he huddled in his landing craft with Lovat's group under his heavy pack of explosives, George Cook did not share Peter Scott's enthusiasm about the flashing lighthouse: 'I was amazed. I thought, blimey, they're waiting for us, silly is this, going in here.'

The Germans were not, in fact, waiting for the Commandos but just before they beached Lovat's boats were finally spotted. Star shells were sent up and tracer fire was opened on them. 'Our boats landed on a front fairly close together, each one about a cricket pitch apart on a beach about 150 yards wide,' said Lord Lovat. They were immediately raked by machine-guns and mortars firing on fixed lines on to the beach. One four-man section was wiped out by a mortar, and Capt. Gordon Webb was wounded in the right shoulder by a fragment. Though about a dozen men were hit in all, Lovat's Commandos were saved from heavier losses by two factors. First, as the landing craft pulled away having discharged their loads and busily laying smoke to cover their withdrawal, the defences raised their fire to shoot at the boats; and second, Lovat had ordered that nobody must lie down on the beach after landing, unless hit. He had told his officers to take the names of any Commandos sheltering on the beach and, if they survived the raid, they were threatened with being returned to the units from which they had come to join Lovat's Commando.

Lovat recalled that Orange Two was 'a nasty beach, quite a steep affair, and the wire on top of it in the half-light looked almost as high as a ceiling'. After the explosion of the first mortar shells in their midst, the Commandos needed no further galvanising or name-taking threats to get past the formidable barrier of wire, more than 15 feet deep. Instead of cutting or blowing up the obstacle, they made human carpets of volunteers wearing leather jerkins, threw heavy coconut matting over the wire and simply ran over the top of it. The first five men laying the matting were shot down, but their places were immediately taken by another half dozen.

'If we had hesitated on that beach, as some do when they get windy and flop down, we would have been in trouble,' said Lovat. 'When that happens with bad troops you've had it, you can't get them up again. But these men really tore the wire apart in a way which I can't believe was possible, looking back on it. They really rolled about in it and they went through like loose forwards following a rugger ball.'

Lt Donald Gilchrist's section was one of the first to get through the wire but the strain of negotiating it had proved too much for Gilchrist's battledress. As he ran off the beach his trousers, their buttons severed, fell down and he raced inland 'clutching my trousers in one hand, tommy gun in the other'. Despite his predicament Gilchrist had time to note that Lovat, his sporting rifle hung rakishly from the crook of his arm, looked as if he was out for a day's shooting on the moors. And Lovat himself was not too busy to miss the fact that Capt. Gordon Webb was carrying his rifle over his left shoulder. Unaware that Webb had been wounded in the right arm, Lovat briskly informed him that he was a disgrace and would be on a charge when they returned to England.

Trooper William Finney shinned up a telegraph pole in full view of German guns and cut the wires, severing the communications between the villages on either side of the River Saane, though the pole to which he was clinging was almost cut in half by machine-gun fire. This done, Lovat's men moved off at a fast trot in Indian file along the left bank of the river.

As Mills-Roberts's three landing craft followed Lt-Cdr Mulleneux's guide boat towards Orange One, the lighthouse continued to provide an excellent direction finder. 'Its beams swept across and over us and we felt like thieves in an alley when the policeman's torch shines,' Mills-Roberts wrote afterwards.

The *Herald* man, A. B. Austin, reported, 'As we nosed in under the Dieppe cliffs I heard a Commando whisper to his mate "Don't forget the other bastards is twice as scared as you." One question worried all of us in those last silent 20 minutes after the long cramped voyage in the starlight. Would the Germans be ready for us? The thought of it made me hang, in my rising funk, on to the thoughts that the "other bastards" were twice as scared as I. A sergeant crouching in front of me kept up a whispered running commentary: "About 500 yards now ... see the cliffs? ... There's the crack we want.... Look at the Jerry tracer bullets. Don't think they're firing at us though ... hundred yards now ... fifty".'

Suddenly the Pointe d'Ailly light was doused as fighter-bombers roared in to attack the Hess Battery, but by now Mulleneux had spotted his destination and he delivered the Commandos to a dry, unopposed landing exactly in the right spot and, at 0453 hours, only three minutes behind schedule.

There were two clefts in what Austin described as 'the cold-looking, unscaleable, chalk-white cliffs of Orange One'. Lt David Style took a small group up the left-hand opening but after 35 yards could make no further progress because it was choked with heavy wire. While Style was exploring, the rest of the Commandos waited impatiently under the lee of the cliff as the sky grew gradually lighter. The second cleft, which ended in an almost vertical staircase for holiday bathers, was about 20 feet wide and behind it a long gully ran towards the woods which sheltered the shuttered villas of the seaside community of Vasterival-sur-Mer. Style decided to blow the wire blocking this exit with Bangalore torpedoes and in order to do so had to lie only a few feet from the explosive devices. Mills-Roberts had given permission for the use of the explosives: 'I realised it was likely to sacrifice surprise but progress otherwise was impossible and time was paramount.'

As the wire was being blown, both A. B. Austin and the Commandos' intelligence officer, Lt Tony Smith, were having similar thoughts about the precariousness of their position. The *Herald* man wrote afterwards, 'Had the Germans prepared their defences properly we would not have had a chance. One platoon with a machine-gun could have held the beach against a fair-sized army,' while Smith commented, 'I could not help thinking that had there been anyone at the top of the cliff with a supply of grenades he could have done us all in.'

Even the noise caused by clearing the wire did not bring bullets down on the heads of Mills-Roberts's group, however, and two sections, led by Lt Style and Capt. Robert Dawson, moved up the gully and began to search the villas of Vasterival. They were followed by the mortar section and Mills-Roberts with his headquarters group. Two of Style's men returned from one of the decrepit houses escorting a barefoot old man wearing a nightshirt. 'I felt sorry for the poor old chap,' Mills-Roberts recalled. 'How could he preserve his dignity in such a garment?' After explaining gently that they were British troops and not Germans, Mills-Roberts had the man taken back to his house. On the verandah stood a young girl, who asked 'Are you going to shoot Papa?'

A patrol was sent to cut the cable linking the battery with the lighthouse and gunnery observation post. On the way they met and questioned a woman who told them she was a gardener at the lighthouse. Lt Tony Smith was not convinced. 'It was possible that she was the local prostitute and that her duties at the lighthouse extended beyond the garden. She appeared very frightened, both of our troops and lest the Germans should take reprisals if she helped us.'

By now it was 0540 hours and, despite the delay in the gully, Mills-Roberts was well on schedule at this stage since he did not need to be in position to open fire on the battery until 0615, fifteen minutes before Lovat's group was due to attack from the rear with the bayonet. Suddenly the early morning silence was shattered by a tremendous noise. The battery had opened fire on the vessels off Dieppe, and when Mills-Roberts received reports from his observers at the foot of the cliffs that some shells were falling close to the British shipping he decided that quick action was called for. Abandoning all attempts at stealth he hurried his force through waist-high undergrowth in the woods and towards the battery, 'crashing ahead like a herd of elephants'. Soon they could hear the words of command clearly as the Germans fired a salvo.

As Mills-Roberts and his men broke clear of the woods they dropped to the ground. Ahead of them was the perimeter wire and behind that, at a distance of some 170 yards, the huge barrels of the battery. To Mills-Roberts's right, on the edge of the wood, stood a two-storey barn. Taking two snipers with him, he worked his way round to the barn and, from the upper storey was presented with a clear view of the six guns and the crews working them.

The first sniper's bullet was to be the signal for all-out fire to be opened on the Germans and Mills-Roberts gave the order to proceed: 'The marksman settled himself on a table, taking careful aim. These Bisley chaps are not to be hurried.... At last the rifle cracked. It was a bullseye and one of the Master Race took a toss into the gunpit. His comrades looked shocked and surprised – I could see it all through my glasses. It seemed rather like shooting one of the members of a church congregation from the organ loft.'

The Germans reacted quickly. A flak tower on stilts sprayed the woods with tracer, and mortars caused casualties among the Commandos around the perimeter wire. The flak tower was silenced by an anti-tank rifle and soon the raiders brought into action their own 2 in. mortar, operated by Troop Sgt-Major Jimmy Dunning with spectacular results. 'The first shot fell a bit to the left,' said Dunning, 'so we adjusted the angle and the second one went into the middle of the battery. We kept it at that angle.' The third shot struck a stack of cordite which ignited with a mighty explosion. 'The screams and cries of the wounded Germans could be plainly heard and the battery never fired again,' Mills-Roberts reported.

A. B. Austin of the *Herald* had been busying himself helping to ferry mortar shells and messages between the beach and cliff top ('Even if you are not allowed to carry arms there is always plenty to do in a modern battle,' he explained to his readers). He described the sound of the cordite igniting as 'the father and mother of all explosions' and ducked involuntarily. 'Presently', Austin reported, 'Mills-Roberts came back through the trees grinning. "We've got their ammunition dump. Mortar shell, bang on top of it. Bloody fools, they'd got their ammunition all in one lot".' A few moments later Austin was scurrying down to the beach with another message for transmission. It read 'Battery demolished'.

Though the battery had not, in fact, been demolished at that stage it was effectively silenced. Gleefully, the Commandos sniped at the battery crews frantically trying to extinguish the fire started by the explosion. The most daring was L/Cpl Dick Mann who, his hands and face painted green, crawled forward over open ground with a telescopic rifle and sniped at the crews from a fully exposed position.

Franklin Koons, the US Ranger corporal, was getting his first taste of action from the barn: 'I found a splendid spot for sniping, just over the manger, and I fired through a slit in the brick wall. I fired quite a number of rounds on stray Jerries and I am pretty sure I got one of them.' Despite his lack of certainty, Koons is popularly credited with being the first American Soldier to kill a German in the Second World War.

Though pinned down by the Commandos' fire, the Germans replied energetically with mortar shelling of their own. Mills-Roberts himself had a narrow escape when one bomb hit a tree, bringing down a large branch at his side, and a medical orderly was killed as he went to tend a wounded soldier. By now Mills-Roberts, who had engaged the battery earlier than the planned time, admitted that he was 'desperately anxious' to know how Lovat's flanking move was coming along. In the event of something going wrong with Lovat's landing, the job of assaulting the battery at 0630 hours would fall on his group. Eventually, as the German mortaring grew heavier, he was told that contact had been established with Lovat so, at 0625 hours as arranged, Mills-Roberts's mortars deluged the battery area with smoke. Three minutes later, right on schedule, Spitfires poured cannon shells into the battery and at 0630 hours three white Very lights hanging in the air indicated that Lovat was ready to make his move. Mills-Roberts's job was done. He withdrew his force to a defensive perimeter around the gully leading to Orange One beach to await the arrival of Lovat.

As Lovat's men moved inland at the double they left behind their wounded on the beach in care of a medical orderly, James Pasquale. 'A few had been hit and a couple were dead on the wire,' he said. 'The numbers one and two on the mortar were kneeling ready to fire and had been killed in that position. I've never seen anything like it. There was a man named Mercer with his eye hanging out and of course he was in a terrible state, so I stayed with him. It had got light by this time and I spotted another chap further along the beach. As I walked towards him someone started firing at us, so I crawled over the shingle towards him, but he had just been knocked unconscious and shocked.'

The shocked Commando was L/Cpl P. Flynn, Lovat's only signaller. Realising that his presence was vital, the dazed Flynn chased after the main group and caught up with them as they were preparing to attack the battery, just in time to get off a signal to the worried Mills-Roberts.

Less than half an hour after landing, Lovat's force had penetrated more than a mile inland, through occasionally boggy going, along the left bank of the Saane. It was testimony to the efficiency of their training methods. 'One of the remarkable things was the speed at which we got around, considering that we might have run into trouble and didn't,' said Lovat. 'Although we went through German infantry on both sides we weren't even shot at once we had left the beach. We ran the whole damned way, just stopping occasionally to regroup but nobody go out of breath and we didn't have to wait for laggards. These chaps were trained like athletes to run the course and, my word, they did.'

George Cook recalled that as they passed a small house near the river a woman emerged. 'She was shouting, *bonjour, bonjour* and waving a bottle of wine. I would have loved a drink but we had no time.'

As they neared the battery defences a group of Commandos under Capt. Roger Pettiward came across some German artillerymen who had been billeted out at a farm and were in the act of climbing into a lorry to be driven back to the battery. Many of them were unarmed. As Lovat recalled, 'There is no finer target at point blank range than troops in or out of lorries before they have shaken into any fighting formation. They were liquidated and we moved on to take up our final position.'

Gordon Webb recalled that the defenders 'were all looking the other way' as Lovat's group formed up in an orchard at the edge of woods near the perimeter wire. Webb gave the order to fire at a flak tower and Lt Donald Gilchrist said, 'We watched amazed as a German soldier toppled over the edge and slowly fell to the ground some eighty feet below, like an Indian from a cliff in a Western picture.'

George Cook and Sgt George Horne then moved forward to cut the wire and were fired at. 'I was against a tree and I could see little bits of it flying off,' said Cook. 'Then I heard Horne go "Uh" and he fell on his side. I cut the wire, went over to him and rolled him over. He had gone very white and I thought he was dead. So I nipped back to report to Capt. Pat Porteous that Horne had been killed. The next thing I knew I was hit too.

'It might sound daft but I actually felt nothing. It was just as though somebody had shone a big light straight in my eyes. I could feel myself falling. Then I knew no more.'

As the Commandos advanced through the orchard Capt. Pettiward was killed by a grenade. Sgt Bill Portman, still carrying his pack of high explosives, saw another grenade land just in front of him and when it went off a fragment lodged in the skin below his eye. 'I pulled it out and looked for the guy who had thrown it,' said Portman. 'Like a fool I was looking towards the gunpits about 300 yards away. My own common sense should have told me nobody could throw a grenade that far. Then a second one was thrown. It exploded in a tree behind me and the pieces went through my pack of explosives, detonators, charges, everything. I could feel the blood from the splinters running down my bottom. If it had hit one of the charges I would have just been a hole in the ground.

'Then I saw the bloke who had thrown it. His head was poking up out of the ground eight to ten yards away. I pulled one off at him with my rifle. I was a marksmen, a pretty good shot, and I got him plumb centre. I reloaded, pulled out my bayonet and started to walk towards him. When I got there I saw there were two of them, in a dog-leg slit trench. The one I had shot had half his head blown off, but the other one was looking the other way, his rifle poking through the bushes. He hadn't noticed his pal was dead. He turned and saw me at the same time as I noticed him. I can see his face now, turning. I stabbed him in the neck with my bayonet, then I was so scared I shot him about three times to make sure.'

As Lovat fired his Very pistol to signal the start of the assault, the Commandos fixed bayonets and charged through the smoke laid by Mills-Roberts's group. 'It was a stupendous charge which went in, in many cases, over open ground swept by machine-gun fire,' said Lovat.

Gordon Webb, who participated in the charge despite his arm wound, using a revolver in his left hand, recalled 'We were asphyxiated by our own bloody smoke and couldn't see a thing. Fifty of us lined up abreast and went forward, disposing of Germans as we came across them. I only remember one casualty. This German came out of a bunker, shot him down and started kicking him in the head. Everyone opened fire on that bugger and he was cut in half. Then we came across a dozen or fifteen Germans all lying in firing positions, all facing the other way. Several of them hadn't even had time to put their trousers on.'

Bill Portman, explosives still on his back, was among the first to reach one of the gun pits. 'There were two Germans still in there, so we sorted them out, bayoneted them.' There were numerous acts of gallantry in those furious few seconds of the bayonet charge. Sgt-Major Bill Stockdale, part of his foot blown away by a grenade, carried on firing from a sitting position. Capt. Pat Porteous was wounded at close range, the bullet passing through the palm of his hand and lodging in his upper arm. Porteous grappled with the German who had shot him, and disarmed and bayoneted him. 'We got to the guns to find a scene of terrible desolation,' Porteous said. 'The first gun I reached was the one in which the mortar had landed and there were bodies all over the place. It was an awful shambles. Then we swung left towards the other guns and I was hit in the thigh and unable to finish the final assault.'

Porteous's modest version of what happened did not match the descriptions of those who witnessed what the *London Gazette* called his 'most gallant conduct, brilliant leadership and devotion to duty' when Porteous was awarded the Victoria Cross for his part in the assault.

The citation told how Porteous 'without hesitation and in the face of a withering fire' had rallied a group of Commandos who were leaderless. Though already wounded himself, he led the charge which carried a gun pit at the point of the bayonet, when he was severely wounded for the second time. 'Though shot through the side he continued to the final objective where he eventually collapsed from loss of blood.'

'The morale of the enemy was good' reported Lt Tony Smith. 'They fought well and their discipline was good, at any rate so long as they were fighting from within a building. Once in the open they were inclined to run.' The German commanding officer, Capt. Schöler, who had been sniping at the Commandos from the window of his battery office, was left for dead when Tpr Dennis kicked in the door, sprayed him with a tommy gun and grabbed all the official papers he could find. 'I couldn't take him prisoner,' Dennis explained. 'It was him or me.' Though severely wounded, Schöler survived the experience. In the battery office Gordon Webb helped himself to a pair of Luger pistols, confessing later he was a little disappointed with the pickings. 'I did much better on the Lofoten Raid, got some fox furs there.'

As the Commandos paused in their moment of triumph a flight of Messerschmitts appeared over the battery. Lovat raised a hand and waved at them. Though he termed it 'a debonair, wholly half-witted gesture', it worked. The Germans were deceived. 'Looking back, I suppose it was the right thing to do,' he said. A Union Jack was then spread on the ground, as planned, in case Allied aircraft attempted to attack the battery, and the Commando dead were laid alongside the flag. Those wounded who could be safely evacuated were loaded on to doors which had been converted into makeshift stretchers and carried back towards the evacuation beach, Orange One. Four Germans who had been taken prisoner were pressed into service as bearers, one of them complaining bitterly that he had been excused marching because his feet had been frostbitten on the Russian front. An indication of the surprise achieved was that one of the captured men was in shirt sleeves and braces and was wearing one carpet slipper.

Three more wounded Germans had been made prisoner and placed alongside a small cottage. 'I went and got a pan of water because one of them had been hit in the guts,' said Bill Portman. 'Then I had to blow up an ammunition dump near the cottage. Unfortunately I blew the bloody house down as well and a wall fell on those three poor sods.'

Next Portman prepared to destroy the guns. 'First we had to hump Capt. Porteous out of a gun pit to that we could blow the charge. The time charges were supposed to be for two minutes but to speed things up we cut it down to a minute. When they went off they split the gun barrels like bananas.' As the Commandos pulled back to the beach a pall of smoke hung over the shattered battery of Varengeville.

During their withdrawal they came under increasingly accurate sniper fire from those Germans in the area who had survived the attack and several men were hit. 'For their songs and their snipers the German army get full marks' is Lord Lovat's opinion. Although two hours had passed since the Commandos landed the German garrisons in the nearby villages which could have inflicted severe damage on the raiders, were still uncertain what was going on. A small patrol sent out from Ste Marguerite, about a mile away, was ambushed and destroyed. As Lovat described it, the Commando section concerned 'let the patrol come through and them shot 'em up the arse'. An elderly Frenchwoman who had witnessed the ambush was so impressed by their efficiency that she presented each of them with a new-laid egg.

As the Commandos filed past the villas of Vasterival and down the steep gully towards the beach, the elderly Frenchman who had earlier appeared in his nightshirt was now resplendently dressed in a formal black morning coat and striped trousers to say goodbye, and offered Mills-Roberts a glass of wine.

On the beach A. B. Austin was helping to pass ammunition for the 3 in. mortar to shell machine-guns firing on the withdrawal area. 'I looked up to find Lord Lovat sitting against a rock beside me. He was bubbling with happiness. "By God, we did the job all right," he said. "Went straight in with the bayonet, cut them to shreds. Glad I wasn't in that battery. But they fought hard." As the enemy kept firing Lovat said "Getting a bit hot. I'm going aboard" and he strolled out into the sea up to his knees, following the long lines of men scrambling into the landing craft. He yelled to the nearest craft some way out, "Come in here, why should I get my knees wet?" But it was too shallow now that the tide had fallen and we had to wade out.'

Because of the tide the German prisoners carrying the wounded Porteous were forced to wade out up to their necks and Porteous remembered 'they needed a little encouragement with the bayonet'.

As the Commandos drew away from the beach under a smokescreen, their task completed in spectacularly successful fashion, Lovat sent a signal to Mountbatten informing him of the battery's destruction. It ended 'Every one of gun crews finished by bayonet. OK by you?'

This dramatic announcement was not strictly true. Within the battery perimeter the Germans had lost 28 dead, 33 wounded and four prisoners, though Lovat's estimate of a further 30 to 35 killed in ambushes outside the battery is probably not far from the mark.

Losses among No. 4 Commando totalled 45 – two officers and ten other ranks killed, three officers and 17 other ranks wounded, and 13 men left behind in France and posted as missing. Twelve of the 20 wounded were back on duty within two months.

Though they managed to bring back most of those wounded during the assault on the battery itself, Lovat's men had to leave behind the Commandos injured during the Orange Two landing and the approach to the battery. The medical orderly, James Pasquale, though himself unhurt, stayed with the wounded on the beach and was taken prisoner. So too were George Horne and George Cook, shot before the bayonet charge on the battery began. Cook, who had been hit in the jaw and shoulder and passed out, recalled, 'When I came round I tried to move and couldn't. I had had my chin shot off. I was covered in blood and there were thousands of flies around me. I could hear all these flies and I was looking right up into the sun.

'I thought I would try to hide under a hedge but I just couldn't move. While I was debating what to do and wondering what the hell had happened three Germans came along the path. One of them stuck a bayonet at the side of my throat. Then they went through my pockets, took my watch, cigarettes, money and ammunition off me. I said to one of them "Can I have a drink?" One who spoke English said yes and shouted to two women nearby. One was youngish and the other was right old. The old one sat down and put my head on her knee and the young one came back with a cup and tried to give me a drink. I couldn't manage it, so she ran off and came back again with a beautiful red glass with a bit of white moulding round it, an old Victorian-type glass. She had a spoon with her, and kept dipping the spoon into the glass and tipping it down my throat. It was wine. All the time the old woman was crying.

'Then I knew no more until I came to in a hospital in Paris. They had fixed up my jaw with a bone graft from my thigh. The bullet had gone through my shoulder, smashed everything on the way, so I was in a plaster jacket and my arm was up in the air, like a Hitler salute.'

George Horne, left for dead by his comrades with a chest wound, also owed his life to German doctors, though he wondered whether he was being preserved for a worse fate. Horne, a career soldier who had served in India before the war, had dodged church parades by pretending he was Jewish, and this was entered as his religion on his documents taken by the Germans.

The boats carrying No. 4 Commando approached *Calpe* off Dieppe to enable Lovat to report personally to Roberts and to transfer the more seriously wounded to the ship. 'We put seven or eight of them aboard *Calpe*, which was a mistake because she was full of wounded already and was very lucky not to be sunk,' said Lovat. 'We then circled the ship, taking avoiding action for the Luftwaffe were starting to buzz, waiting for General Roberts to give further orders but there was no sign of him. After what seemed an interminable delay – but probably was no more than ten minutes – we were told by an unidentified and hesitant staff officer on the loud hailers "that we might as well go home". A bad order of which I took full advantage.'

The journey passed quietly. 'All through the afternoon I watched fighters scribbling their quarrels across the sky,' reported A. B. Austin. 'After many hours, even watching one of the most significant air battles of the war palled and we huddled slackly down in the boat, dead tired, filthy-looking, ragged, happy men – happy because we knew the Commandos had made the Battle of Dieppe possible.'

They got back to Newhaven about 1600 hours to be met by anxious service personnel, curious civilians and journalists thirsty for news of the great battle across the Channel. The *Daily Sketch* correspondent reported: 'They may have been tired but they sang all the time.... On their faces were the remains of black, green or yellow paint. All wore Balaclava hats. One man walked barefooted carrying his boots in his hands. There was little delay while the men were loaded into lorries and coaches, but it was long enough for some of the cottagers to run indoors and reappear with cups of tea, matches and cigarettes. One coach went off so quickly that a Commando had no time to return a cup. The woman looked glum for a little while, then cheerfully said "Well, he's worth it".'

Instead of having his arm wound treated locally, Capt. Gordon Webb, a Scotsman, determined to travel all the way to Victoria Infirmary in Glasgow, where he had been well looked after when injured by a faulty grenade during training. 'I got to London, bought an *Evening News* and there was my picture all over the front page' he said. 'While waiting for the train to Scotland I got a bit tight in the station buffet. Nobody there would let me buy.'

While most of his force spent the night at a transit camp near Newhaven, Lovat was taken by car to London to report to Mountbatten. Late that night the porter at the Guards Club had to be roused to let the Commando chief in. 'The club was full,' Lovat said. 'I was filthy and without a penny; there could be no admission elsewhere. So I went in. There were bathrooms and hot water; the old servant got out a new cake of soap – a wartime luxury – that did not lather and, shaking his head, sorrowfully removed various garments to clean and dry them. I fell asleep in the bath, then spent the night wrapped in towels in the library.... It had been a disturbing day.'

The headquarters of the German 302nd Division did not learn until mid-morning that 813 Battery had been destroyed 'by men with blackened faces'. So worried was von Rundstedt, the C.-in-C. West, by the Commandos' success that he pressed for all 215 coastal batteries along the Atlantic Wall to be better protected by infantry, a task which would have occupied a dozen divisions.

So highly did the War Office regard Lovat's raid ('A classic example of the use of well-trained infantry, thoroughness in training, planning and execution') that a special booklet was prepared for distribution to other units as a model.

Lovat learned later that the Gestapo had put him on their 'most wanted men' list, with a price of 100,000 Deutschmarks on his head, dead or alive. He confessed he was 'really quite flattered'.

CHAPTER SEVEN
Blue Beach

'It was only when you got on to the beach and came out of the smoke ... that you realised you had landed in Hell.'

– Jack Poolton

Ill-fortune dogged the Royal Regiment of Canada for the length of its involvement with the Dieppe Raid. Bungled exercises, accidents and enemy air attacks all helped to induce the feeling among some of the Royals that they were fated, and the task allotted to them in Operation 'Jubilee' could only have strengthened that opinion.

The Royal Regiment was to carry out the inner flank attack a mile to the east of Dieppe, landing between No. 3 Commando at Berneval and the main assault on the port itself. Its target was the village of Puys and the codename of the destination was Blue Beach. Puys itself is situated a little way inland from the sea front, sheltered from the Channel weather by the cliffs and gullies in which the houses huddle. It had been the home of Alexandre Dumas and in the 1870s Lord Salisbury built a holiday house there which he visited regularly for 23 years.

The beach at Puys, the first break in the formidable cliff barrier to the east of Dieppe, is short, narrow, dominated by the cliffs and overlooked by the houses leading up the steep gully from the beach. It is no more than 250 yards long and at high tide, when the Royals were to land, there was only 50 yards of pebbly beach between the water's edge and a sea wall 12 feet high which in peace-time protected the gully from erosion and in war-time, with multiple layers of barbed wire along the top, also constituted a formidable barrier. Well-sited pillboxes and defence points covered the beach and its approaches and, as the Royal Regiment's official history points out, 'It would have been difficult to discover anywhere on the coast of Europe a less favourable area for an assault landing.'

After storming the beach and gaining the clifftop, the Royals were to swing right to overrun from the rear the strongpoints on the East headland overlooking Dieppe's main beach. Other targets were assigned: to deal with an anti-aircraft battery in the area, destroy a German barracks at a former holiday camp known as Les Glycines, and to capture the four-gun heavy battery situated behind Puys and code-named Rommel by the raid's planners. Once taken, these guns would be turned against the Germans if possible, or destroyed. And if these duties were not enough to cope with, the plan then called for the Royals to provide support for a group of engineers who would move into Dieppe and blow up the gasworks.

If the East and West headlands overlooking Dieppe were not captured or silenced, 'Jubilee' was certain to fail. Yet the planners' assessment of the Royal Regiment's chances was highly optimistic and, worse, quite inflexible. Reliance on surprise was almost total and the plan made no alternative provision for what in fact was to happen, that the Blue Beach force would be pinned down and unable to carry out any of its tasks.

To undertake this formidable list of assignments, the Royals' newly-appointed commanding officer, Lt-Col. Douglas Catto, possessed an attacking strength of 554 (26 officers and 528 other ranks), among them his brother, Capt. Jack Catto. The total included detachments of Royal Canadian Artillery, who would take over any captured guns and also dismantle and bring back new German anti-aircraft weapons, and a company of the Black Watch of Canada, whose role was flank protection of the Royals against counter-attack.

Since the Royals had suffered more than any other regiment during exercise landings from being put ashore late and at the wrong points, Col. Catto favoured abandoning the hope of surprise in exchange for an obliterating bombardment of Blue Beach and its defences. Aerial reconnaissance pictures had not shown up any wire on the Puys sea wall and Gen. Roberts told Catto that since there was no wire on the beach a bombardment was not necessary. Catto, a First World War artilleryman, said he had never known a German defensive position to be without wire. He was coldly informed by Roberts that if he was afraid someone else would be found to lead the Royals.

Just before 0300 hours the Royal Regiment boarded the boats being lowered from *Queen Emma*, *Princess Astrid* and *Duke of Wellington*. They were two minutes ahead of schedule at this point but things soon went disastrously wrong. The landing craft were supposed to form up behind a motor gunboat to be led into Blue Beach ten miles away but there was confusion in the darkness and the boats from *Princess Astrid* took up station behind another gunboat. By the time the mistake had been sorted out 15 precious minutes had been lost and the combined flotilla did not move away until 0325 hours. In an effort to make up the lost time and get the troops ashore before first light, the naval officer in charge of the landing, Lt-Cdr Harold Goulding, was forced to proceed faster than intended. Two large mechanised landing craft (LCMs) each carrying a hundred men, and four smaller boats from *Queen Emma* were soon left hopelessly behind and within half an hour had lost contact with the guide boat.

Goulding might have made up some of those lost minutes if he had navigated directly for Puys but, perhaps conscious of the Royals' previous unfortunate experiences in exercise landings, he was worried about missing Blue Beach in the dark. Accordingly, he settled for the safer method of covering two legs of a triangle, heading for the harbour lights of Dieppe and then turning to port to find Puys. And so, their landing plans already a shambles, the Royals straggled towards their doom.

The efficiency and good fortune of Capt. Richard Schnösenberg in selecting the night of 18–19 August for the weekly stand-to alarm along the defence sector he commanded from the east mole of Dieppe harbour to Puys contributed to the extent of the disaster which befell the Royals. Shortly before the defenders were due to stand down from their routine watch, Schnösenberg was informed about the shooting out at sea. 'My adjutant reported that it was heavier than usual. I knew he wouldn't disturb me for nothing. Most of my soldiers were already at their posts anyway and it was misty at sea, so I ordered the alert. This was the decisive command. The East headland was completely prepared.'

The defences of Puys itself were in charge of Lt Willi Weber and some 60 men, a small group armed with nothing heavier than mortars and machine-guns but virtually impregnable behind the concrete of their pill-boxes and emplacements. An indication of their strength was that, although reinforcements were available nearby, they were never needed on 19 August.

As the landing craft following Lt.-Cdr Goulding's gunboat approached the harbour mole of Dieppe a recognition signal winked out at them. When it went unanswered searchlights were turned on the landing craft and they came under increasingly heavy fire as they approached Blue Beach. The nine landing craft which comprised the first wave touched down at 0507 hours, 17 minutes late and two minutes after sunrise. Bullets aimed downwards into the boats as they neared the shore had already caused several casualties but it was not until the ramps went down that the full fury of the German fire struck the Royals. Though the shelter of the sea wall and cliffs was only a few yards away only a few men got that far.

As the ramp dropped in his boat L/Cpl Leslie Ellis saw he was opposite a flight of steps in the sea wall. He leapt out, getting no more than his feet wet, sprinted for the wall and crouched down waiting for the others in his boat to join him. As he looked round he saw them being cut down by machine-gun fire.

Bill McLennan, a stretcher bearer, also reached the wall unhurt, but a mortar bomb then knocked him over. When he came to, a headless corpse was lying on top of him. As he moved the body, a machine-gun ripped his left hand to shreds. 'There was nothing I could do except stay under the wall and help the others around me,' he said. That help consisted of treating injured men despite the severe pain of his own wound.

Pte Leonard Keto was not so lucky as Leslie Ellis. 'I was right up at the front when our ramp went down. I leapt into the water and sank up to my chest. Holy Jesus, that water was cold. I waded ashore, holding my rifle clear, and ran for the shelter of the wall. I didn't have time to look around, I just wanted to get out there as quick as I could. About ten feet from the wall I got hit by shrapnel, on my chin and right between the eyes, but I kept going. We couldn't do nothing. I never even had a chance to fire my rifle. I just threw myself to the ground and kept my head down. All I was thinking about was staying safe.'

Such was the severity of the Germans' fire and the shock of seeing their comrades cut to pieces that some of the Royals were too demoralised to leave their landing craft and had to be ordered out at gunpoint by the boat officers. This contentious issue still angers the members of a regiment which suffered terribly at Dieppe, and Maj. Brian McCool has asserted, 'If the Navy boys had tried to pull a gun on anybody from my regiment, they would have chucked a grenade at them.' Lt-Cdr Goulding reported, however, that in his boat Maj. George Scholfield and one or two others left the craft promptly but 'the remainder had to be urged'.

An inquiry, of which no report was ever forwarded officially, was held at Portsmouth three days after Dieppe into the allegations of troops being forced ashore at gunpoint. Though several naval officers testified that behaviour under appalling conditions was good, others referred to troops 'hanging back'. The Canadian Army historian, Col. Charles Stacey, came to the conclusion that 'although there were definite instances of reluctance to land, this attitude appeared only in certain craft and was assuredly very far from universal.'

As the remnants of the decimated first wave hugged the sea wall and cliff face to escape the murderous rain of bullets and bombs, the second wave, consisting perforce of the two large LCMs and four smaller landing craft which had lagged behind the main wave, finally drew near to Blue Beach at 0530 hours. Already late, they had been further delayed because they found themselves heading for the cliffs to the west, rather than the east, of Dieppe and had to retrace their path. The war correspondent, Ross Munro, was in one of the LCMs and wrote of the run into Blue Beach, 'We kept our heads down behind the steel bulwark but our craft was so crowded that even to crouch was crowding someone beside you. I sat on a cartful of 3-inch mortar bombs.'

For some time, there was an awful fascination about the firing ashore. Pte Jack Poolton said, 'My God, talk about a display of fireworks, the tracer was going everywhere. It was a beautiful sight. I thought, who's getting it, our fellows or them? I was in Col. Catto's boat and I remember this naval officer saying to the colonel after seeing the tracer, "You'd better get the rest of your men out of here, something's gone wrong." Catto told him "I can't. Half of my men have gone in there, I've got to take the rest in".'

Ross Munro, who was to term the next twenty minutes 'the grimmest of my life' described what happened when the ramp was lowered on his LCM and the first troops attempted to land: 'They plunged into about two feet of water and machine-gun bullets laced into them. Bodies piled up on the ramp. Some staggered to the beach and fell. Bullets were splattering into the boat itself, killing and wounding our men.

'Looking out the open bow over the bodies on the ramp I saw the slope leading a short way to a stone wall littered with Royal casualties. There must have been sixty or seventy of them.... They had been cut down before they had a chance to fire a shot.... On no other front have I witnessed such carnage. It was brutal and terrible and shocked you almost to insensibility to see the piles of dead and feel the hopelessness of the attack at this point.

'There was one young lad crouching six feet away from me. He had made several vain attempts to rush down the ramp to the beach but each time a hail of fire had driven him back. He had been wounded in the arm but was determined to try again. He lunged forward and a streak of red-white tracer slashed through his stomach. I'll never forget his anguished cry as he collapsed on the blood-soaked deck: "Christ, we gotta beat them, we gotta beat them." He was dead in a few minutes.'

A blanket of smoke laid over Puys by Hurricanes gave temporary cover as the second wave went in but the casualties were still horrendous. As Jack Poolton pointed out, 'They didn't even have to take aim. A blind man could have got a few that day.'

In their anxiety to get away from the hell of Blue Beach some of the landing craft were spilling their loads early or backing away from the shore before all the soldiers had disembarked. Poolton, carrying a 2 in. mortar and a haversack containing 12 mortar bombs on his back, went into about eight feet of water and sank like a stone. As he stood on the bottom the landing craft, still going into the beach, rubbed over the top of his steel helmet. 'I don't know whether you would call this dedication or bloody stupidity, but I had dropped the mortar when I hit the water. There was no way I was going ashore without it, so I grovelled around until I found it. By the time I started to make my way in, with my head out of the water, the boat was going back out, while the rest of the chaps were still jumping out of it.

'It was only when you got on to the beach and came out of the smoke that you saw the carnage and realised you had landed in hell. The first wave were two or three deep against the wall, wounded and dead and a few still living.' Still staggering beneath the weight of his mortar, Poolton reached the sea wall, only to discover that immersion in the salt water had rendered the weapon useless.

When another landing craft dropped its ramp about 25 yards short of the beach, Sgt Johnny Carroll led his mortar detachment out into water which was well over their heads. Ptes Al McDonald and R. D. Jones went off the ramp carrying a mortar between them. 'Splash, we were in deep water,' said McDonald. 'There went our mortar. Then I saw Johnny Carroll lying on the beach. He had his hands clasped over his abdomen and his entrails were hanging out over his hands. I didn't see how a man could possibly live in that condition.' But Carroll was pulled on to the landing craft by Jones before it backed away. The two men got back to England, and Carroll lived to fight again on D-Day.

'I just floundered ashore and started firing my rifle,' said McDonald. 'I think I got four rounds away before I was stopped. I was hit three times, left arm, right hand and right leg. So I lay there for about 20 minutes, getting weaker and weaker, and I thought, Christ I've got to get out of here. So I pulled myself on to my feet and started to head for the wall. My left arm was pulling me down and I was dragging my right leg. I didn't get another scratch crossing that beach. I've always said that I was staggering so damned much that every time one came my way I was moving out of the road.'

Pte Ron Beal recalled, 'I don't think a man in my platoon had a dry landing. I went into water up to my waist, waded ashore and got about five feet up the beach when I fell flat on my face. I couldn't see a thing because of the smoke and I still don't know whether I tripped over a body or what. The next thing I knew everything was clear and it was a sight of absolute carnage.

'I knew that the shortest distance between two points is a straight line and I got up and ran like a bloody rabbit for the wall. When I got there I was carrying a rifle and a medical kit. I threw away the rifle and went to work with the medical kit, but as fast as I was patching 'em up they were getting hit again.'

Sgt Charles Surphlis still isn't sure how he reached the wall safely – 'soaking wet, slipping and sliding over the pebbles' – when most of his platoon did not. The thing that Pte Harold Price remembered was not the German bullets but the sheer physical size of the task facing him as he waded ashore. 'I took one look and saw the wall and the steepness of the beach, it seemed to me like a bloody mountain. We had never trained on anything like that. Nobody had ever mentioned anything about barbed wire and when we got there, there was this concertina wire on top of the wall. That was some obstacle.'

At least Pte Bill Stevens had a dry landing. 'Being a Bren gunner I was one of the first three off. The other two, Elmer Post and Russell Brown, were on my left and they took practically all the bullets from a machine-gun firing from a house up on the left. But I still got a few of them in the cheeks of my arse and that gave me a little more oomph to get to the cliff.

'I got up there and I was lucky, there was a little indentation in the cliff and the only part of me that was sticking out was a little bit of my feet. I had some brand new gaiters on and they were very loose. I felt a burning sensation, and when I took a look what did I see but my bloody gaiter going round with machine-gun bullets cutting right across it.'

As the survivors of the second wave hugged the sea wall and cliffs, an officer who had landed with the first wave screamed 'It's hopeless, get back to the boats if you can.' Pte J. Creer needed no further urging, but as he got to the water's edge the landing craft he was making for began to pull off. Undeterred, Creer plunged after it, was picked up unhurt and later put aboard a destroyer 'where I went through another seven hours of hell, being dive-bombed and machine-gunned'.

Most of the Royals who managed to get back to England did so aboard the LCM in which Ross Munro had witnessed, and was to describe so graphically, the slaughter at Blue Beach. Most of the hundred men in the crowded boat had landed 'and been cut down in front of our eyes' wrote Munro. Capt. Jack Anderson, emptying his Sten gun at pillboxes while waiting to get ashore, was hit in the head and sprawled across Munro's knees. Next to Anderson a naval rating lay dying, his throat ripped open.

The loss of Anderson caused hesitation among some of the soldiers still aboard 'and they had to be forcibly made to disembark' reported the ship's commanding officer, Lt Ernest Cook. Unable to get to the ramp because of the dead and injured sprawled inside and a knot of men plucking up the nerve to hurl themselves into the German fire, Cpl Fred Ruggles decided to open fire on the pillboxes with his antitank rifle: 'I heard the sailors yelling for the men to get off,' he said. 'I don't know what was happening in front of us but we were unable to move at all, so I concentrated on firing.' Ruggles was joined by Pte James Murphy with a Bren gun and together they turned their attention on a large white two-storeyed house to the left of the beach from which much of the damage was being done to the Royal Regiment. 'I think each floor had six windows,' Murphy remembered. 'I fired into each of them. By the time I would get to the sixth window the first one would open up again.'

The Naval Beachmaster for Blue Beach was in the LCM and, deciding that further sacrifice was pointless, he gave the order to withdraw. 'The hand of God must have been on that boat,' wrote Munro, 'for we were nosed up hard and yet when the engines were reversed it slid back into deep water as if it had been pulled by something out to sea ... and slowly, ponderously swung around. There was an opening at the stern and through it I got my last look at the grimmest beach of the Dieppe raid. It was khaki-coloured with the bodies of boys from Central Ontario.'

Still intent on fulfilling orders to the best of his ability, the wounded Capt. Anderson instructed Ruggles to try to contact other Canadian forces at Red Beach, immediately in front of Dieppe, but as they approached the harbour mole they again came under heavy machine-gun fire and withdrew. The more badly wounded were off-loaded to a destroyer and the rest sensibly decided to call it a day.

The futility of Blue Beach was not yet ended, however. At 0545 hours, ten minutes after the second wave had sailed in to its doom, a third wave prepared to touch down. This group, under a Royal Regiment officer, Capt. Raymond Hicks, was known as Edward Force and comprised the contingent of the Black Watch of Canada and the artillerymen who were to operate any captured guns against the enemy. It had been arranged that Edward Force would land when requested to do so, but when no signal was received a joint decision was taken by Capt. Hicks and the senior naval officer, Lt Jack Koyl of the Royal Canadian Navy, to go in anyway. At Hicks's request, the five landing craft were put ashore under the cliffs at the far western end of the beach, nearest to Dieppe and away from the most severe German fire.

'There was no sense of foreboding, people were lighthearted enough in our landing craft, even though it was bright daylight by the time we got there,' said Pte Reg Hall. 'They opened up on us about a hundred yards from shore, mainly machine-guns. I happened to be near the front. Bullets were going in over my head and I heard someone say "I've been hit, bugger it, I've been hit."

'It was quite a good landing, actually. The water was only just above our ankles. We just had to dash 50 or 60 yards to the cliff.' Although he stands 6 ft 2in., Hall was not hit as he raced for cover. According to Lt Mark Mather casualties were few on landing: 'I was right beside Lt Jack Colson when he got his – a burst right through the eyes and head. Except for poor Jack the Black Watch didn't lose a man, though we had a few wounded.'

As he ran out of his landing craft Pte Albert O'Toole stumbled on the ramp and wrenched his ankle badly. Since he could only hobble, O'Toole was dragged back inside and was the only one of the group who actually landed to get back to England.

Although more or less intact, the Black Watch group was prevented by the very cliffs which afforded protection, from offering any assistance to the remnants of the Royals. 'We couldn't move,' said Reg Hall. 'We didn't get any offensive work done at all. For every bullet we fired towards the top of the cliff a hail of machine-gun bullets came back. The Germans were lobbing hand grenades and mortars down on to us and every time a mortar bomb landed it turned the beach stones into shrapnel. There was no point in creating further havoc for our wounded comrades, so we stopped firing. There was nothing we could do, we didn't have a chance.'

When he landed with the second wave Capt. George Alleyne Browne, a former announcer with the Canadian Broadcasting Company whose role at Blue Beach was forward artillery observation officer, sent off a message 'Doug touched down 0535'. Doug the first name of the Royals' commanding officer, Col. Catto, was the designated codename. Browne had with him a party of three naval ratings instructed to maintain contact with the destroyer *Garth* patrolling offshore. This contact between Browne and *Garth* constituted the single tenuous link between ship and shore, since the Royals' own main signalling set, and its operators, was speedily put out of action. The set, saturated on landing when the signaller carrying it was shot, would not function and Jack Poolton witnessed the bravery of a signals officer as he sacrificed his life trying to get off news of the landing at Blue Beach: 'He was a young-fair-haired guy, John Fostan. We used to call him The Button. He was only around 18. When I saw him he was sitting cross-legged out in the open trying to talk with the destroyer, cool as a cucumber. He really amazed me, he just sat there, talking away. Then he got it. That was it.'

Though contact was maintained with *Garth* for more than two hours, the news of the disaster which had overtaken the Royal

Regiment was a long time reaching Gen. Roberts. *Calpe*'s intelligence log noted at 0550 hours, 'No word from Doug' and in fact the first signal Roberts received, at 0620, told him quite erroneously 'Royal Regiment not landed'.

There were many acts of bravery like Fostan's and most of them were just as futile as the Royal Regiment tried to fight its way off Blue Beach. Sgt Ewart Peaks and three men of his crew set up a 3 in. mortar out in the open under cover of the brief smoke screen. Pte M. Hamilton reported, 'They didn't get more than three bombs away when Heinie found them with his machine-gun and they were cut to pieces.'

'A lot of us never had a chance to do anything on the beach but there was no lack of brave acts,' said Jack Poolton. 'I can remember a foreign guy we called Big Mike who went in firing his anti-tank gun from the hip, knocking chunks out of a pillbox. He lost a leg. I saw men crawl up one after the other and try to get a grenade into that pillbox. They were stacked in front of it where they had tried.'

Lt John Woodhouse, though wounded, called for volunteers to help him subdue the pillbox causing the heaviest casualties. 'The last I saw of him he was walking right at the pillbox firing a Bren gun,' said Sgt John Legate. 'That Mr Woodhouse took no end of risks.' Woodhouse was killed, as was Lt William Wedd, who managed to silence the strongpoint. When a hole was finally forced in the sea wall wire, Wedd crawled through and ran at the pillbox carrying a grenade. Though hit repeatedly, he thrust the grenade through the firing slit and put the gun out of action. His body, riddled with bullets, was later picked up in front of the pillbox.

Others were too hurt or too busy trying to stay alive to achieve anything. Bill Stevens was still huddled in the cliff crevice attempting to keep out of the enfilading machine-gun fire. 'Bill McCluskey, a stretcher bearer, got shot and fell on top of my left leg, and shortly after that one of their mortars exploded on his helmet, taking out a huge chunk of my right leg and blowing my pants off. That's where I stayed until the end, I didn't have too much damned choice. Then they started throwing stick grenades down on us and every time one dropped near me I picked it up and threw it further away.

'A guy called Frenchy Lacome who was nearby got McCluskey's medical kit and gave me all the morphine in it. I was delirious, coming to and passing out again, but the one thing I'll always remember was seeing all these dead men lying at the edge of the water. The tide was washing up and going out and the water was blood red. Bodies were rolling in and out with the tide and the Germans were firing at them all day long because they thought they were alive.'

Stevens was wounded in 23 places and as late as 1977 he failed the security gate check at Calgary airport. 'The buzzer sounded every time I walked through. It was the shrapnel still in my backside.'

The Royals' medical officer, Capt. Reginald Robert Laird, known as 'Pinky', continued to treat the casualties although terribly wounded himself. 'The lanyard from his revolver was hanging through the inside of his thigh and out through the other side, yet he still did his job,' said Al McDonald. Laird later had the leg amputated in captivity.

Incredibly, a small group of Royals, led by Col. Catto himself, managed to get off the western end of the beach and on to the cliff top. As they went about the laborious task of opening a gap in the wire with cutters while exposed to the German guns, Lt Bob Stewart climbed the sea wall to provide what protection he could. 'There he was, standing on top of the wall with a bloody Bren gun, just letting go,' said Bill Stevens. 'How the hell he didn't get picked off I don't know.'

'Stewart kept hollerin' for more ammunition, so I started running around picking up Bren magazines and throwing them up to him,' said Harold Price. 'When I couldn't find any more I heaved him a tommy gun and ammunition for that. He must have been out of his mind with rage because he couldn't remember any of it afterwards. I remember him getting hit in the legs but still standing up, cursing and swearing.'

Eventually Stewart collapsed, one leg badly smashed, but Catto had managed to get a group of twenty-two off the beach, which included Lt Sterling Ryerson, grandson of the founder of the Canadian Red Cross, and Capt. Browne, the artillery observation officer. Not wanting to lose touch with the Royals' commanding officer, Browne left his one remaining signaller in the middle of a message to *Garth* and dashed after Catto, ordering the telegraphist to follow as soon as he could.

Catto's group had been able to get through because a machine-gun covering that section of the sea wall jammed, but another one was quickly brought into action. Jack Poolton was attempting to follow Catto at the time. 'I got right to the top. One fellow was going over and I was right behind him when he received a direct hit. He fell back and knocked the lot of us down, because we were all using each other's heads for leverage.' Now it was again impossible for anyone else to get through, 'or for us to go back' as Browne noted. 'The commanding officer was thus cut off from his battalion and I was cut off from my link to the destroyer.'

Messages were still being received from the beach signaller by *Garth*, however. Minutes after Catto's party had got off the beach the destroyer was asked to lay down fire on the German defences, but her shells only caused more misery to the Royal Regiment, knocking down huge chunks of cliff on to the survivors huddled below, and soon *Garth* was driven off by shore batteries.

When they reached the top of the cliff, Catto sent Lt Ryerson along the road which led into Puys and he returned to report that a strong German patrol was moving out of the village towards them. Sgt Edward Coles came back from the cliff edge to report that there was no response to his shouts to the beach, so Catto decided to work his way west towards Dieppe in the hope of meeting up with the Essex Scottish as planned on the East headland. There was no sign of friendly forces and eventually the Canadians were forced to take refuge in a small wood a short distance from a six-gun anti-aircraft battery which had been one of the Royals' objectives. Outnumbered and encircled, Catto could only listen as the morning passed to the dwindling sounds of gunfire from Blue Beach.

Only one member of the Royal Regiment managed to cross the sea wall and get back to England. He was L/Cpl Leslie Ellis, who had landed with the first wave opposite steps in the wall which were blocked with thick wire. Eventually he was joined by two officers, Lt William Patterson and Capt. George Sinclair, his company commander, who had with him a soldier armed with a Sten gun. When Patterson attempted to thrust a Bangalore torpedo under the wire he was hit and the equipment he was carrying caught alight, setting him on fire. 'He was last seen smothered in flames near the wall,' said the official report of the action. Capt. Sinclair then managed to blow a gap in the wire at the head of the steps, looked over the wall and invited Ellis to 'come on over'. Ellis pushed past him and sprinted to the cover of a scrub-filled depression, but when Sinclair and three soldiers tried to follow they were spotted and shot down, leaving Ellis alone.

Ellis worked his way towards a house at the top of the gully leading from the beach, threw a grenade into one of the back rooms and went in. The room was empty but inside he found cartridge cases still warm. As he moved upstairs to explore further, *Garth* began to shell the building so he left by the back window.

As the lone Royal cautiously explored the area behind the beach he came across a pillbox and three weapon pits, all empty. When he fired a few shots into the village of Puys, where he could see no sign of movement, Ellis received in return a bullet which creased his helmet. He had now spent an hour or so above the beach and had still not seen a German soldier, an experience shared by the rest of his battalion, which had been decimated by an invisible enemy. As Sgt Charles Surphlis recalled, 'Until we surrendered I never saw so much as a helmet.'

Ellis decided to make his way back to the beach. Moving down the cliff he came across a wounded Canadian, probably from the group which had attempted to follow him. He dragged the man as far as the sea wall barricade but in cutting the wire he detonated a booby trap, killing the wounded man and slightly injuring himself in the face, right hand and left foot, and puncturing one of his eardrums.

Ellis vaulted the wire on to the beach. As he scrambled to his feet he saw a landing craft putting in to shore in front of him. Soon after 0700 hours the lone signaller still in touch with the ships had put out a message asking for vessels to evacuate the survivors of Blue Beach. Only one landing craft responded to the call.

Pte. H. E. Wright, who had been knocked unconscious by mortar bomb shrapnel which pierced his steel helmet, came round to see a crowd endeavouring to reach the boat 'according to their state of disability'. He staggered towards it. 'Halfway down the beach one of my chums, Norman Orpen, was lying with a bullet through each leg and one hand practically blown off. I managed to drag him to the landing craft and heave him aboard.'

The boat was so besieged by men trying to get away that it stuck fast on the shore and the crew were forced to beat off further would-be boarders with boat hooks. The boat was so crammed with wounded that the ramp could not be raised and when the engines would not start those still in the water around the landing craft pushed it off the beach and out to sea, grenades and mortars exploding among them and causing more dreadful casualties.

Water began to pour into the overloaded boat through the open ramp door, over which desperate soldiers were still trying to pull themselves aboard, and Sgt John Legate recalled, 'The skipper yelled at them to let go or the boat would sink, but they wouldn't listen.' Eventually the inrush of water, the weight of men clinging to her sides and several near misses from mortar bombs capsized the vessel.

'Realising it was now every man for himself many of us swam out to sea but mortar bombs and snipers picked us off until there were only five or six of us,' said Wright. 'After getting fairly well out of range I stripped off my uniform and boots and, coming close to Sgt Legate, we swam together.'

Leslie Ellis had wisely decided not to risk getting into the landing craft. Nevertheless he made up his mind to swim for it and, taking off his boots and equipment, he sprinted for the water. As he began to put some distance between himself and the shore a bullet struck the water alongside his nose. Ellis threw up his arms and sank, pretending to be hit, and when he surfaced again no further fire was directed at him.

After the horrors of the landing craft few other Royals cared to risk the water. One of those who did fancy his chances was the wounded medical orderly, Bill McLennan. After exhausting his supplies treating the injured with his one good hand, McLennan decided to make a run for it. First inflating his Mae West to make sure it wasn't punctured, he made for the water and floated among the living and dead until he was dragged on to a landing craft and eventually put aboard the Polish destroyer *Slazak*, where he alternated between treating more wounded and pushing shells up a chute to one of the ship's guns. McLennan may well have been the escaper seen by Al McDonald as he crouched, wounded in arm and legs, by the wall: 'I remember a feller swimming away from the shore. He had his Mae West on. Some bugger with a machine-gun opened up on him and you would see the water spurting all around him and he would stop kicking. I figured, well the poor bugger's caught it. As soon as the fire switched away from him you would see the splash as he started kicking again, going like hell. More bullets, and he'd stop kicking. The last time I saw him he was just about out of sight and still going. I don't know who he was but I hope to God he got home.'

After swimming from the capsized landing craft Legate towed the exhausted Wright along by the tapes of his Mae West. 'We were swimming around for hours,' said Legate. 'There was such a smokescreen around us that the other boats couldn't see us in the water. Then I spotted a rowing boat about half a mile away and swam for it.' Legate pulled Wright aboard after him.

Ellis was nearing exhaustion when he came across the floating bodies of two soldiers, both shot neatly through the head by snipers, so he removed their lifebelts. Soon afterwards Legate, manoeuvring his rowing boat with the single canoe paddle he found in it, picked up Ellis and another survivor of the landing craft disaster, Sgt Ernest Thirgood, who was also wounded. Thirgood, the regiment's best shot and leading runner, had been runner-up in a regimental swimming competition, a skill which saved his life.

Soon afterwards the little boat was spotted by a naval vessel. 'The medical officer looked after the wounded I had picked up and the sailors made me as comfortable as they could,' said Legate. 'They took all my clothes off me and put me to bed with six blankets, two hot water bottles and a big shot of rum.'

A further handful of Royals managed to get away from Blue Beach, all from the capsized landing craft. Capt. Jack Catto, the commanding officer's brother, who had had one eye shot out, spent four hours in the water before being rescued by a flak landing craft. As he was hauled aboard, Catto told his rescuers, 'Don't hurry me boys.'

Pte Ed Simpson was one of those who continued to cling to the upturned keel of the landing craft. 'We were only about a hundred yards from the beach and were still being blasted by fire, slowly being picked off by snipers on the cliff.' An artilleryman, Gunner Henry Rowe, said 'If anybody moved the slightest bit, the move was rewarded with a sniper's bullet. The chap clinging next to me was hit three times immediately after moving from the pain of his wounds.'

Gradually the numbers hanging on to the boat were reduced to eight. Then through the offshore smoke appeared two wooden Eureka landing craft. They belonged to the group which had ferried the Cameron Highlanders across the Channel and, after landing their troops at Pourville, had been ordered to Berneval to collect any Commandos still on Yellow Beach. By mistake they approached Blue Beach and spotted men clinging to what appeared at first to be a raft.

As the boats drew closer they came under heavy fire. A Canadian naval officer, Sub-Lt John Boak, manoeuvred his craft alongside with trailing ropes and urged the soliders to jump. Ed Simpson recalled, 'The boat only slowed down and a rope was grasped by four of us, myself, Armstrong, Wallace and Roberts. The boat swung out to sea at top speed and a mile or so out Armstrong let go. I clambered on board unassisted and helped the seamen to bring Roberts and Wallace on the deck.'

Though the second rescue boat bravely ignored the hail of bullets to stop and pluck the rest of the men from the upturned landing craft it was a costly business. The commanding officer, Sub-Lt Ben Franklin, was wounded and two of his crew killed.

What was left of the Royal Regiment surrendered at 0830 hours and five minutes later the 571st Regiment's headquarters reported to 302nd Division, 'Puys firmly in our hands. Enemy has lost about five hundred men prisoners and dead.' The figure, quickly put together, was tragically accurate.

'Although there was the odd German who was vicious most of them were pretty reasonable,' said Charles Surphlis. 'Generally speaking, as they rounded us up they were quite helpful and detailed guys who were fit to look after the wounded.'

Capt. Richard Schnösenberg went down to the beach a few minutes after the surrender to supervise the evacuation of prisoners. 'There was a sergeant, only lightly wounded, who was carrying a belt of four hand grenades,' said Schnösenberg. 'We weren't sure what he intended to do with them, so he was told to raise his arms but he refused. When he got to the top of the wall I gave a sign to the soldier covering him not to do anything, I wanted to see what was going to happen. It was very impressive. He stood there, then turned around and saluted his dead comrades. Then he raised his arms in surrender, and he wept.'

In common with the other Royals led away to captivity, Jack Poolton still nurses the bitterness of the waste on Blue Beach. 'If we had only had a 40–60 chance we could have given Jerry a bloody good run for his money.' Another survivor said, 'I shall always remember, after the surrender, the faces of the prisoners sitting on the beach among our dead, crying. We felt robbed, robbed of the chance to fight and show what we could do. We had the right kind of men and equipment to put up one hell of a fight, but we were not given the chance to land as an organised unit but as a confused, bewildered bunch of men seeking shelter and defending our lives as best we could. Such it was on the beach where the Royal Regiment landed – a massacre, a bloody mess.'

Col. Catto's party, still hiding in the clifftop wood, heard the captured survivors being marched past. There was little for them to do but admire the resilience of the 88 mm. gun battery nearby. 'It was low-level bombed at least four times and machine-gunned oftener,' said Capt. Browne, 'and each time the guns were back in action within a matter of a few seconds, firing upon the departing aircraft.

'Catto decided we should all wait until the operation had run its scheduled time, for now all were quite trapped, and if nothing had improved the situation by then we should surrender. The situation did not improve and we surrendered at 1620 hours to an officer who wore Luftwaffe wings on his steel helmet.'

Afterwards Schnösenberg inspected the captured Royals. 'I will never forget the signs of shock engraved on the faces of the prisoners when they realised that the whole battalion had disappeared. But they were bound to be wiped out, they had no chance of getting away. I will never be able to understand how anyone could give such an order as this raid.

'I had a long chat with Catto afterwards, discussing the tragedy of his regiment. Because they were only prepared for one course of action they were terribly defeated. I never ever had to witness anything as terrible as that day at Puys, not even in Russia,' said Schnösenberg. 'Col. Catto was very brave. He should have got a Victoria Cross. He was in a completely hopeless situation, following orders that had no chance of succeeding.

'Catto and I shook hands before he was marched away. I wished him a safe captivity and he wished me a safe war. This was the last noble and fair gesture that happened to me in the war.'

Of the 26 officers and 528 other ranks who went into Blue Beach, only two officers and 63 other ranks got back to England. Both officers, Capt. Jack Anderson and Capt. Jack Catto, were wounded; 31 of the other survivors were also wounded and two subsequently died. Half of those who returned had never set foot in France, being in the LCM which pulled away from the beach before landing all its men.

Eight officers and 201 other ranks were killed at Puys, a further two officers and 16 men were to die in captivity, and of the remaining 262 who became prisoners of war, eight officers and 95 other ranks had been wounded.

The Royal Regiment suffered the highest number of fatal casualties of any unit taking part in the operation, and the official report commented, 'There can be few, if any, cases in the history of the Canadian Army of units suffering a larger proportion of fatal casualties in half a day's fighting.'

In addition to the losses in men, six heavy and 16 light mortars, four machine-guns, 62 sub machine-guns, 12 anti-tank rifles, 304 rifles, two Union Jacks and a large amount of explosives and other equipment fell into German hands.

Losses among the defenders of Puys amounted to two dead and nine wounded. After the surrender a Canadian officer told Lt Willi Weber, in command at Puys, 'I congratulate you on your soldiers, sir.'

A monument to the Royal Regiment now stands at Puys with the following inscription:

> On this beach officers and men of the Royal
> Regiment of Canada
> died at dawn, 19 August 1942, striving to reach the heights beyond.
> *You who are alive on this beach*
> *Remember that these men died far from home*
> *That others, here and everywhere, might freely*
> *Enjoy life in God's mercy.*

The monument overlooks the beach. Immediately alongside it still looms the pillbox which took so many Canadian lives that day.

CHAPTER EIGHT
Green Beach

'We were very glad to go, we were delighted. We were up against a very difficult situation and we didn't win, but to hell with this business of saying the generals done us dirt.'
— Cecil Merritt VC, South Saskatchewan Regiment

The western inner flank landing carried out at Pourville (or Green Beach as it was known in the attack plan) by the South Saskatchewan Regiment was, initially at least, as successful as that at Blue Beach was disastrous. The main reasons for this were that the Saskatchewans were delivered punctually and that the Germans had chosen not to turn Pourville itself into a strongpoint.

Situated in the indentation at the mouth of the River Scie, Pourville consisted of a straggle of houses and shops along a roadway which was in effect little more than a dyke separating the waters of the Channel from the valley behind, which had been flooded as anti-tank protection by the damning of the river mouth. The road spiralled down into Pourville from the heights of Dieppe's West headland and at the far end of the village it passed between the village church and the Hotel de la Terrasse before mounting the western slopes and dividing. One branch led inland to the village of Petit Appeville, the other climbed to Varengeville, Lord Lovat's target.

Since the only reason for invaders to land at Pourville would be to attack Dieppe, the Germans had sensibly concentrated their defence points on the headland, a fortified zone which dominated not only Dieppe and its harbour but also Pourville, its valley and the bridge over the Scie which carried the road towards Dieppe.

A golf course, the fourth oldest in France, lay behind the cliffs, pillboxes sited among the bunkers. Here too were the fortified farm, Quatre Vents, the headquarters of the 571st Regiment, a heavy flak battery and a radar station. In contrast, the heights to the west of

Pourville were guarded only by a small infantry detachment, though the largest and most imposing of the homes on this slope, La Maison Blanche, was used as a billet and a mess by the officers in the area. The Hotel de la Terrasse housed the German foremen and the more important foreign technicians of the Organisation Todt, the labour force charged with the construction of Hitler's Atlantic Wall, which had about 400 workers in Pourville at the time of the raid.

The South Saskatchewans' recently-appointed commanding officer, Lt-Col. Cecil Merritt, embarked 25 officers and 498 other ranks aboard the troopships *Invicta* and *Princess Beatrix*, a total reduced by the explosion of a grenade which wounded 17 men among Lt Leonard Kempton's platoon on *Invicta* during the crossing. Zero hour for the landing was 0450 hours. The Saskatchewans' initial task was to secure Pourville and its beach so that a second landing, half an hour later, of the Cameron Highlanders could advance through this bridgehead and strike inland to attack the airfield at St Aubin and what was wrongly thought to be the enemy divisional headquarters at Arques-la-Bataille. Both the Saskatchewans and the Camerons would then link up with the Calgary Tanks near the aerodrome and eventually evacuate through Dieppe itself.

To establish this bridgehead, each of the Saskatchewans' four companies was allotted a specific objective; 'B' Company was to land to the west of the River Scie's mouth and clear the village; 'C' Company would tackle the lightly-defended western slopes above Pourville, and to 'A' and 'D' Companies fell the formidable task of subduing the fortifications on the headland east of Pourville with nothing heavier than mortars, before overrunning Dieppe's West headland and its defences from the rear.

A special platoon under Lt Leslie England was assigned to assist in the capture of the radar station on this headland and to give cover to a signals expert and his bodyguard ordered to removed sections of the equipment wanted by British scientists who were desperately seeking information about the Germans' more sophisticated system. The radar man, RAF Flt-Sgt Jack Nissenthal, contributed one of the more bizarre episodes of the Dieppe Raid. Nissenthal, from the East End of London and the son of an immigrant Polish tailor, went ashore wearing an Army uniform without identification and the orders for the raid emphasised '*under no circumstances must he fall into enemy hands*'. His armed escort of ten specially-chosen marksmen were to kill Nissenthal if he was in danger of being made prisoner. Nissenthal himself was also issued with a cyanide pill to prevent the possibility of his giving away British radar secrets under Gestapo interrogation.

Sailing into Green Beach with the South Saskatchewans was Wallace Reyburn of the *Montreal Standard*. He recalled the final moments aboard his landing craft: 'The first streaks of dawn were starting to appear as we came near to the shore.... Most of us were down like sprinters ready for the hundred yards dash. I rested on one knee until it got sore and then transferred to the other. I adjusted my tin hat with superfluous frequency.'

The regimental adjutant, Lt George 'Buck' Buchanan, said 'As our small boats crept into the shore we could see lights shining in some windows and smoke curling from a few chimneys. We thought how peaceful it was and how soon we would disturb this quiet seaside town by rifle and gunfire.'

The South Saskatchewans achieved total surprise. Not a shot was fired as the ramps went down and the prairie soldiers poured ashore, sounding as one of them said, 'like a herd of elephants charging across a field of walnuts.' Wallace Reyburn remembered, 'There was some humour in the landing, in the noise we made. One guy said "If there are a couple of lovers on the beach they're in for one hell of a shock." That was symbolic of how peaceful it was.'

At last the German gunners on the headland east of Pourville were alerted by the noise of the landing craft reversing off the beach and opened fire along fixed lines in the half-light. But by then the raiders had hacked an opening through barbed wire on top of the low sea wall and others had found a spot free of wire. 'We seemed to be lying under the sea wall for ages,' said Reyburn. 'Suddenly a call came from farther down the line that they'd found an easy way to get up. We filed along and came to a place where there wasn't any barbed wire at all ... with Battalion Headquarters I crossed the wide promenade and we established ourselves in a garage.'

Everyone was in high humour at the ease of the landing, and Lt Buck Buchanan recalled, 'There was many a wisecrack like "Nice place for a 48-hour leave".' Much of the elation vanished when it was realised that many of the South Saskatchewans had been put ashore in the wrong place. Most of 'A' and 'D' companies, whose tasks lay to the east of Pourville, were landed west of the River Scie's exit into the sea, which meant they would have to cross the exposed bridge over the tiny river against a now thoroughly-alerted enemy or find some way through the flooded fields inland.

Pourville itself was quickly cleared of the few Germans it contained. They put up little resistance and most were made prisoner. 'They were scruffy stuff when we picked them up,' said Reyburn, 'Pioneer Corps types, like Dad's Army. Poles and people like that. They had no interest in fighting. The real stuff came later.'

The Polish private, Otto Samulewitsch, one of the few members of the German Army brought back to England, was among those taken at Pourville. Samulewitsch had gone to bed at the normal time of 2200 hours noting that 'there was no exceptional vigilance'. He was roused about 0500 and ordered to report the state of alarm to a nearby platoon. Half an hour later he was wounded in the shoulder near the River Scie. Asked by his interrogators to explain the time lag he said 'I wasn't hurrying myself'. Soon afterwards Samulewitsch, who had been wounded a second time by a bomb splinter, was picked up by the Saskatchewans suffering from shock and according to his questioners 'rather bewildered as to whether he is our enemy or not'.

The medical officer, Capt. Frank Hayter, set up his regimental aid post alongside Merritt's temporary headquarters in the garage. His first patient was a German medical orderly whose arm had been almost severed by a grenade explosion when he was spotted sniping from the window of a house. While Hayter was still treating the prisoner, Merritt was forced to move his headquarters because of the accuracy of German fire. Quickly intercepting messages being put out from the Canadians' signal sets, the Germans were able to pinpoint the headquarters with a radio direction finder and lay down a devastating fire. When Merritt's signallers attempted to send messages from a tiny square a mortar bomb landed in it within minutes, killing and wounding several German prisoners as well as Canadians.

'I was lying down at the time but the force of the explosion sent me flying,' said Wallace Reyburn. 'Out of the corner of my eye I caught a glimpse of a young officer who was standing up with his back to the explosion. Spurts of blood shot out from the front of his neck and shoulder as the shell splinters went right through him. He toppled forward into the arms of a companion.' Reyburn himself was wounded: 'I felt what seemed to be pebbles hitting my back, like little stones thrown up from a motor car wheel. I didn't think anything more about it until later, when my shirt and trousers began to feel damp. It was blood.'

The Regimental Sergeant-Major, Roger Strumm, a First World War soldier whose thunderous voice was renowned across the parade grounds of Canada, was also hit by the mortar bomb, suffering a serious leg injury. Strumm had gone through the 1914–18 war unwounded and he was one of those careful Canadians who carried a steel mirror in the battledress pocket over his heart. The precaution saved his life. A large dent made by another splinter was later found in the mirror. Though in considerable pain, Strumm continued to shout encouragement and orders, and insisted on other casualties being treated first. Col. Merritt, who considered Strumm 'a great man', spared a moment to kneel by the RSM's stretcher. 'I'm very sorry to see you hit, Mr Strumm,' said Merritt and Strumm replied with a huge smile, 'They told me I was too old to get into action but I fooled 'em.' Because of the severity of mortar and sniper fire Strumm and other stretcher cases were moved to the beach and placed in the shelter of the sea wall to await evacuation.

In clearing the western end of Pourville and moving against the heights beyond, 'C' Company encountered little resistance at first. Grenades and incendiaries were tossed into cottages and buildings suspected of containing Germans and Pte Ernest Clark reported, 'Several Frenchmen came out of one building. They were dressed in blue denim shirts and trousers and some carried what appeared to be lunches. They were rather panicky and ran gibbering and waving their hands above their heads.'

Next, the hotel housing the Todt Organisation was cleared. Two Germans attempting to bar the hotel door were killed and an unsuccessful attempt was made to burn down the building. Pte William Haggard reported, 'A considerable time was lost getting the foreign workers out of the hotel because they were very frightened.' Some of 'C' Company then moved up to La Maison Blanche, which conveniently carried a board beside its impressive double gates announcing that it housed German officers. Some of them, who had slept late and heavily after a party, were surprised and killed in their beds and five Frenchwomen who had spent the night in the house were rounded up, sobbing with fear, in their underwear. Machine-guns, a mortar and ammunition found in the house were destroyed.

One platoon, led by Sgt Harry Long, moved towards the top of the western hill but on the first rise Long was wounded and the Bren gunner beside him killed. Deprived of leadership, the group hesitated and some of the men sat down. 'A sergeant then took command but he was uncertain what to do and we wasted precious time,' reported Cpl Guy Berthelot. 'I thought if we didn't do something very soon we would all be dead, as we were in a pretty compact bunch and could have been wiped out by a mortar.' So Berthelot and Pte William Haggard virtually took over the platoon to organise an encircling movement against slit trenches on the edge of a wood containing four machine-guns which were pinning down the advance.

While Berthelot gave covering fire with his Bren gun from the corner of a house, Haggard led a group along a sunken road between the slit trenches, exchanging shots with the defenders and bravely moving out into the open to attract and pinpoint the German fire. 'Haggard then called me over,' said Berthelot. 'When I got there the sergeant was in the deepest part of the road, hollering at the boys to charge the Germans. No one wanted to start out, so I took my Bren, shooting from the hip and advanced, firing almost directly into the trenches as I went along. Soon after I started, up comes Cpl Scotty Mathieson from the opposite side, firing his tommy gun from the hip. A few of the boys then dashed in and threw hand grenades into the pits.'

As soon as the Germans realised they were surrounded, they surrendered. Twelve prisoners were taken and the other occupants of the trenches killed. Haggard's comment 'the enemy gave in easily when it came to close-quarter fighting,' was borne out by other Saskatchewans. Pte Ernest Clark remembered the prisoners as 'rather snivelling, although several of the larger, sullen-looking creatures still had that arrogant look which made me want to pull the trigger'.

Haggard marched the prisoners back to battalion headquarters, by now set up in an orchard, and on the way five more Germans surrendered. The wounded Sgt Long was also carted back into Pourville in a borrowed wheelbarrow.

Though all the objectives on the western slope above Pourville had been secured fairly easily, thanks to the fortitude of such as Haggard and Berthelot, progress was a good deal less encouraging in the sectors more important to the success of the Green Beach attack. The special platoon attempting to get Flt-Sgt Jack Nissenthal into the radar station was the only section to land east of the River Scie, thus avoiding the need to cross the exposed bridge, but the group ran into problems as soon as they moved towards the higher ground east of the village and their leader, Lt Leslie England, was wounded.

Those attempting to cross the bridge to join the special platoon were delayed by a pillbox as soon as they got over the sea wall. While they took cover behind a road block, Pte Charlie Sawden volunteered to attack it 'if somebody will just hold my rifle'. A smoke bomb was thrown and Sawden, a grenade in each hand, moved forward. Pte Vaughn Storey said, 'Charlie nonchalantly strolled up to the pillbox and tossed in the grenades, wiping it out and killing four Jerries.' Sawden later had his leg smashed by a bullet. A rough splint was fashioned out of bayonets and he was carried back to the beach, where he was killed during the evacuation.

Since the approaches to the bridge were wired, the Saskatchewans were forced into a bottleneck as they attempted to cross. Though the early groups dashed across with few casualites, machine-gun fire soon pinned down the others, who took shelter behind houses near the bridge. 'They were mortaring us but we were quite safe because the streets were narrow and they couldn't get enough trajectory,' said Wallace Reyburn, who had carried his notebook in the very centre of the action. 'We were held up and there was nothing I could do, so I thought the best thing would be to talk to the fellows who had been injured. One of them got me to take out a picture of his girl friend and he was looking at it, being pretty unhappy, when along came this soldier, strolling down the middle of the street, his tin hat on his arm. It was Merritt.'

When he heard that the advance towards the fortified headland had been halted at the bridge, Merritt left his headquarters and went to see for himself. What happened next was to earn Charles Cecil Ingersoll Merritt Canada's first Victoria Cross of the war for what the official citation called 'matchless gallantry and inspiring leadership'.

The bridge was dominated by what Reyburn termed 'a concrete fort' looking down from high ground straight ahead and soon the crossing was piled with Canadian bodies. Lt Buck Buchanan reported, 'Col. Merritt saw the situation and, twirling his tin hat, for all the world like a boy with his school books, sauntered across the bridge, calling back "Come come on boys, they can't hit a thing. Come on, let's go and get 'em." And they did.' Capt. H. B. Carswell of the Royal Canadian Artillery, who was with the South Saskatchewans as forward observation officer for the destroyer *Albrighton* which was to deliver supporting fire, watched Merritt cross the bridge 'on many occasions', returning to escort further groups over and telling them, 'See, there is no danger here.' Carswell added, 'The men followed him splendidly but were shot down time after time.'

Merrit remains modest and unforthcoming about the incident. 'These stories get puffed up a bit,' he insists. 'How does one know why one behaves that way? But we had to get across that bridge or we were going to get nowhere. I had a responsibility, so I got out there and I guess I gave 'em a bit of a lead.'

Wallace Reyburn, who witnessed Merritt's astonishing performance, said 'I asked him afterwards how he did it and he said "I don't know, I was guided by God." All he had was a scratch on his nose at the end, and not through enemy action. He tripped and fell. Amazing.'

Although now across the bridge in greater strength, the Saskatchewans were still suffering from a pillbox along the road. Merritt was equal to this crisis, too, as Sgt Pat McBride recounted: 'The colonel said "We must get ahead lads, who's coming with me?" I replied "We are all going with you." He said, "Good lads, let's go," and we ran up the road with Col. Merritt leading, disregarding all danger.'

Smoke bombs were thrown at the pillbox and, under covering fire, Merritt and a sergeant crawled up to it and popped grenades through the gun slits. His task completed, Merritt went back to headquarters and told Lt Buchanan, 'I've just bombed out a pillbox. Try it some time before breakfast. I recommend it.' As Pte Vaughn Storey put it, 'The colonel was full of inspiring courage.'

Despite the gallantry of their colonel and others, little progress could be made by the lightly-armed Saskatchewans against the well-sited defences. Radio communication on Green Beach was poor and rendered more difficult by the frequency with which snipers picked off signallers. HMS *Albrighton*, standing offshore to bombard the headland east of Pourville, was unable even to lend the support of its 4 in. guns because of the danger of hitting friendly troops.

The Canadians' 3 in. mortars proved ineffective in subduing the opposition for several reasons – the high rate of losses among the crews, the inability to get the cumbersome mortars within range of the enemy positions which were causing the most damage, and the desperate shortage of ammunition. 'Half as many mortars and twice the shells would have been better,' said Lt Buchanan. The small arms with which they had been issued were also less than ideal. Lt Leonard Dickin complained after the raid, 'Sten guns are no damned good. I did not see one, and have not heard of one, that fired more than one magazine before jamming. One spot of sand and they stop.'

Secure in their emplacements, the defenders were able to inflict considerable damage. 'The German soldier seemed a very brave man at 200 yards and would die at his own gun,' said Sgt Basil Smith, 'but at close quarters he would run rather than fight.' And Buchanan noted, 'The Germans definitely hated our in-fighting. The bayonet seemed to paralyse them.'

Desperately though they tried, the soldiers from the prairies were rarely able to get close enough to inflict that sort of damage. One German position was overrun when Pte Oliver Fenner, tiring of being pinned down, leapt to his feet and, firing his Bren gun from the hip, charged it until his legs were shot from beneath him. His comrades took the position, capturing two prisoners, and dragged Fenner downhill on his back before treating his wounds and returning him to the beach, from where he was safely evacuated.

Little effective progress could be made against the fortified headland and the failure to subdue the defences here was critical for the next phase of the Green Beach landing, the arrival of the Cameron Highlanders.

Although the crossing from Newhaven in the small, wooden landing craft had been uneventful, the Camerons had spent nearly nine hours packed into their boats by the time the coast of France was sighted and CSM George Gouk reflected that 'it sure felt good that we would be able to stretch our legs again on land'. At the insistence of their commanding officer, Lt-Col. Alfred Gostling, the Camerons were half an hour late coming ashore, at 0550 hours instead of 0520, because Gostling did not believe the South Saskatchewans would have cleared the beach and moved off it within thirty minutes.

So, in broad daylight and line abreast, the Camerons' landing craft sailed into Green Beach, with a piper, Alec Graham, standing in the bow of one vessel and playing 'A Hundred Pipers'. 'Everyone was feeling in the best of spirits and that made us feel better,' said George Gouk. It was quickly apparent that the earlier landing had not been completely successful as shells began to fall among the incoming boats. In the commanding officer's craft the naval officer Sub-Lt John O'Rourke recalled, 'Gostling was very cool and collected, calling out to his men explanations of the different types of fire under which they found themselves.'

The beaching was, like that of the Saskatchewans, a blunder because many of the landing craft put in to the west of the River Scie, whereas all should have gone in east of the river's mouth. Col. Gostling's boat immediately came within range of machine-guns and he was killed seconds after stepping ashore, the Camerons' first casualty.

The plan to advance against St Aubin aerodrome along the eastern bank of the Scie was thus compromised at the very outset, with the battalion split and temporarily leaderless until Maj. Tony Law, the second-in-command, was able to take over.

The Camerons who landed east of the Scie were delayed while they tried to cut the sea wall wire. Eventually Capt. John Runcie, a Scotsman and formerly a Hudson's Bay Company employee, reconnoitred and found exits cut by the Saskatchewans and not dominated by German guns. As Runcie and his group entered Pourville, they were met by the indefatigable Merritt. When Runcie asked whether he should attempt to join the rest of the Camerons at the western end of the village, he was told he would be better employed helping the hard-pressed Saskatchewans to clear the eastern end of Pourville and reinforcing those who had managed to get over the bridge. Maj. Law was contacted by radio and agreed to this change of plan.

Another party of Camerons, led by Capt. Norman Young, got over the sea wall and pushed up the eastern bank of the Scie 'to do as much damage as possible' according to George Gouk. They were under heavy fire and Pte Clarence Flemington reported, 'I was kind of worried about all those bullets, but Mr Young told us they weren't very good shots during the last war and that he didn't think they had had much practice since, so I took his word for it and kept going.'

Capt. Young was soon a victim of the marksmanship he had scorned. As he stepped through a gate in a stone wall, Young was hit in the stomach by a bullet and as he was falling he was struck and killed by a mortar bomb.

George Gouk estimated that the group penetrated about half a mile inland to attack a cluster of houses. 'Snipers and machine-guns seemed to be in every house, so we got busy on them and were doing a fairly good job cleaning them out with rifles and grenades when all of a sudden they opened up on us with their mortars. It sure was hell. Our casualties started mounting then. Every corner you turned you seemed to run into mortar fire and they sure could place their shots. Well, there was no stopping the boys then. They were seeing their pals for the first time being killed and wounded at their side and the only thought that seemed to be on everyone's mind was to have revenge. It was great to see the boys with blood all over their faces and running from wounds in their arms and legs not worrying about getting first aid but carrying on in a systematic manner, clearing out the Nazis from the houses just as they learned to do on the Isle of Wight.'

Eventually the group was reduced to a dozen men, a mixture of Camerons and Saskatchewans. Pte Clarence Flemington commented, 'We had lost our company commander and our sergeant-major had left with some men to go to work on a few stray Huns he had seen someplace.' The situation was similarly confused all along the eastern heights as the Canadians struggled to hold on against superior fire-power and increasing numbers of enemy reinforcements.

The experience of the special platoon in attempting to capture the radar station was typical. After an earlier Commando raid against another radar post the Germans had cleared the surrounding land of all obstructions and girded the station with barbed wire and gun emplacements. Every approach route was covered. Sgt Basil Smith recalled, 'We were met with very heavy machine-gun fire and were forced to ground. We tried to beat down this fire and advance but this was impossible.... We then moved back about 50 yards and to the right, planning a flanking movement. Here again we came under heavy fire, the enemy always supporting one another.... The Germans then brought mortars to bear on us. We could do nothing, so tried a left flanking movement. Here we met the same results.'

The radar expert, Jack Nissenthal and his closest 'bodyguard', Sgt Roy Hawkins managed to get near to the station but were forced to admit in their official report, 'We were at no time able to reach any of the objectives set for us.'

As the official report of the operation commented, 'When it became apparent that the capture of the objectives east of the village was impossible, the remains of the Saskatchewans and elements of the Camerons took up defensive positions on the ground they had gained and held them until it was time for the withdrawal....The enemy was content to limit himself to holding his positions; admirably disposed in posts chosen long before, he had no desire to initiate counter-attacks which would bring him to closer quarters with the men who had come from the sea.' Or as Cpl Henry Conroy put it, 'Jerry had plenty of reinforcements but he did not have enough guts to attack us.'

Several of the Canadians wounded in the attack on the radar station were treated by a French family, though Sgt Smith warned them not to get involved because of the risk of reprisals and handed them printed notices to this effect which the raiders carried ashore.

'These leaflets were of thin, flimsy paper so that they wouldn't be bulky in our already laden uniforms,' wrote Wallace Reyburn. 'We handed them round and a boy in his teens read his closely and with an obvious interest. He asked if he might have some more. He seemed a keen youngster and we concluded that he wanted to dash off and distribute them. But as he folded the leaflets and put them in his pocket, it dawned on me that his request had been prompted by the more prosaic fact of France's dire shortage of toilet paper.'

Many French people were friendly and helpful. 'They wanted to fight with us, and assisted our wounded with hot coffee and wine,' said Lt Buck Buchanan. 'One pub keeper opened up his bar and gave away all his beer.' Some Canadians sniping from behind mattresses placed at bedroom windows were fed with wine and cakes by French girls.

'Their complete disregard of personal danger was remarkable,' said one Camerons officer. Wallace Reyburn watched a farmer rounding up his cows while the battle raged around him, and marvelled as an elderly man cycled along Pourville's main street with a long loaf sticking out of his basket. 'Then there was this kid, playing cowboys and Indians,' said Reyburn, 'sticking his beret out round a corner. He had obviously seen a few Westerns. If nobody fired at the beret he would run across the street. He was a cute little kid.'

Maurice Mallet's cousins from Rouen had not picked the best of times to visit him and his wife at their home overlooking Pourville. They had arrived on 18 August and were up at 5 am to catch the early train home. As his wife prepared breakfast Mallet noted a lot of air activity. 'But that was a fairly frequent thing,' he said. 'Suddenly soldiers appeared near our house. We knew they were British because they were wearing flat helmets. Since ours was only a little house we didn't have a cellar. One of my cousins was a little scared and suggested we dig a trench in which to shelter. I told him, "Shit, by the time we finish it the war will be over".'

The advance to the south-west of Pourville by Maj. Tony Law and his group of Camerons was the furthest achieved by any forces on Operation 'Jubilee'. Having been landed at the wrong place, Law decided to make his way up the Scie valley and cross the river inland to reach his planned rendezvous with the Calgary Tanks at Vertus Wood. As they struck out along the road towards the village of Petit Appeville they were fired on from Quatre Vents farm so they took to the woods by the side of the road. The group were making for the road and rail bridges spanning the Scie at the hamlet of Bas de Hautot just in front of Petit Appeville but as they approached there were signs of considerable German activity in the valley.

Pourville and the Scie Valley had always been regarded as the greatest point of danger to Dieppe's defences and afterwards the Germans were at a loss to understand why the Canadians did not push inland more rapidly towards St Aubin airfield. German intelligence surmised (wrongly) 'Presumably they were halted by command because the frontal attacks on Dieppe had failed.'

To check the advance from Green Beach a bicycle platoon and some elements of the reserve battalion of the 571st Infantry Regiment were alerted as early as 0530 hours, but it took the cyclists almost an hour to prepare for their departure and even longer to get to the scene because their overloaded machines kept collapsing or puncturing. Even so, they had been preparing their counter-attack for some time before Law's Camerons appeared, though the seriousness with which they treated this part of the Dieppe Raid is evident in the stand-by-order issued to a reserve company of a hundred hospital patients who were considered fit enough for emergency action.

If tanks had been landed at Pourville, as the Operation 'Rutter' plan had proposed, success might have attended the Green Beach landings and the story of Dieppe could have been a very different one. Cecil Merritt considered that, despite the height of the sea wall at Pourville 'tanks or gun carriers could have got over at each end'. Once over, they would have encountered no problems crossing the Scie Bridge, which was not mined as Allied planners had feared. The capture of Quatre Vents farm and the radar station would not have been difficult against an enemy who possessed no tanks and few anti-tank weapons, and the headland dominating the western part of Dieppe's main beach would probably have fallen.

As it was, Law's poorly-equipped group was no match for the light artillery and mortars now being lined up against them, even though the German equipment was horse-drawn.

It was now 0845 hours, no Churchill tanks were in sight and taking the Camerons' objectives was clearly out of the question. The only Canadians to reach Vertus Wood, in fact, were dead ones since it was here that the war cemetery was later sited. Law decided to force the bridge at Hautot and cut across the valley to attack the stubborn Quatre Vents farm. They managed to knock out a horse-drawn mortar detachment but were beaten to the bridge by a section of close-support infantry guns. Since the Cameron's own 3 in. mortar had been destroyed in Pourville they possessed nothing powerful enough to silence these German weapons. They were also coming under increasingly heavy and accurate fire by now so at 0930 hours, abandoning all idea of getting across the Scie, Law ordered a withdrawal to Pourville. Almost immediately, his signallers intercepted a message to the South Saskatchewans from the headquarters ship *Calpe*: 'Vanquish from Green Beach at 1000 hrs.' Vanquish was the codename for withdrawal.

Aboard *Calpe*, Gen. Roberts had been kept slightly better informed about the progress of the battle for Green Beach than he had been at Yellow or Blue Beaches. The ship's intelligence log noted the landing of both the South Saskatchewans and the Camerons, though it also logged a false message that the radar station above Pourville had fallen and that the Saskatchewans were closing in on Dieppe itself.

A request timed at 0846 hours for evacuation ships at Green Beach, intended to take off casualties sheltering beneath the sea wall, was misread aboard *Calpe* as an attempt to initiate a total withdrawal, and permission was given for a general withdrawal to begin at 1030 hours. Within minutes this had been amended to 1100 by Roberts himself, a decision which was to have fearful repercussions for the men ashore.

Roberts explained, 'The original time set by me was 1030. It could have been only a few minutes later that I changed it to 1100. My reasons were two-fold. (i) Fear that there might not be sufficient time to contact the Camerons, who I knew had penetrated some distance inland and who were out of wireless touch and (ii) on last-minute advice from the Air Advisor, Air Commodore Cole, who told me that the extra half hour would ensure adequate air support for the withdrawal.'

So a withdrawal time originally understood by those ashore to be 1000 hours was in fact an hour later. This mistake led to the early evacuation by the Canadians of ground overlooking the beach, with disastrous consequences. The Saskatchewans and Camerons would soon undergo an ordeal by fire in trying to get away from Green Beach worse than anything they had so far experienced.

CHAPTER NINE
Red and White Beaches

'They say war brings out the best and worst in people. Mostly at Dieppe it was the best.'

– John Foote VC, Royal Hamilton Light Infantry

The main assault on Dieppe was delivered against the town's mile-long sea front which, for the purposes of Operation 'Jubilee', had been designated as two beaches, Red and White. The eastern landing area, Red Beach, nearest the port entrance, was attacked by the Essex Scottish Regiment while the western landing area, White Beach, which included the Casino building, was assaulted by the Royal Hamilton Light Infantry.

The task of the two Canadian battalions was to occupy the hotels and other buildings fronting the sea along the Boulevard de Verdun. These early gains were to be exploited by a follow-up landing of the Calgary Tank Regiment, supported by sappers and engineers to help blast a way for the Churchill tanks into and through Dieppe to join up with the Cameron Highlanders south-west of the town.

The Essex Scottish were then to take the eastern end of Dieppe, including the harbour, and link up with the Royal Regiment of Canada in overrunning the East headland which dominated the harbour entrance. After taking the western part of Dieppe, the Royal Hamiltons were to hook to the right and meet the South Saskatchewans on the West Headland, knocking out batteries and strongpoints along the way.

The preliminary bombardment against the town and its cliffs would be delivered as the landing craft went in by the 4 in. guns of the destroyers *Garth, Bleasdale, Berkeley* and *Albrighton* and six squadrons of cannon-firing aircraft. Three other squadrons were to lay a smokescreen across the front at the moment of landing.

This close support was only a part of the Royal Air Force's commitment to its biggest operation since the Battle of Britain in an attempt to draw out and destroy the Luftwaffe in the West. The 63 squadrons thrown into battle by the RAF were also to provide fighter cover and general protection of the ground forces against German air attack, and to fly reconnaissance missions over France to report on any build-up of enemy reserves.

The Channel crossing of the Essex Scottish and Royal Hamilton Light Infantry in the troopships *Glengyle, Prince Charles* and *Prince Leopold* had been free of incident and they transferred to their landing craft at 0320 hours on what the Hamiltons' commanding officer, Lt-Col. Robert Labatt, termed 'a wonderful night – sea calm and a slight breeze from the land, ideal for our purposes'. As he entered his boat for the eight-mile run in to the coast, Labatt joked with the naval officer in charge of the flotilla, 'How about landing us on the right beach for a change?' On their final rehearsal, Labatt's battalion had been put ashore seven miles west of their objective.

As the soldiers huddled low in the boats, wearing their gas capes back to front to protect them from spray, the flotilla slid away from the mother ships and Labatt recalled, 'There was no doubt in which direction France lay. One section of the horizon was a regular fireworks display … it was a little like the opening moments of Ravel's Bolero, with the big noise yet to come.' The 'fireworks display' was No. 3 Commando's collision with the German convoy.

'As it grew gradually lighter the outline of the coast became discernible,' Labatt reported. 'Soon we were able to pick out landmarks. We were headed dead on our beach. We reduced speed and the craft following surged up on either side, changing formation from line astern to line abreast. The sea presented an inspiring picture, hundreds of small craft heading for the land with fast support boats zig-zagging well ahead.… Everything was deathly quiet on the beach.'

*

The approach of the 'Jubilee' fleet was not reported by German radar. When von Rundstedt's GHQ West was informed at 0445 hours of the sea battle, it was dismissed by the Naval Group Command West as 'a customary attack on a convoy', though because of the noise of battle the defences to the east of Dieppe were alerted. Von Runstedt's report of the raid said 'Single targets were briefly registered after 0300 hours by the radar at Tréport ... and taken in connection with engine noises which had been reported were held to be aircraft.'

It was only when the landings began on either side of Dieppe that the central defences were alerted. A German tugboat carrying a pilot was waiting off Dieppe, together with three harbour protection ships, to escort the convoy from Boulogne into port when, at 0445 hours, they spotted 'destroyers and many other vessels' a mile and a half away. Firing an alarm starshell, they made a dash for shelter.

On the headland above Dieppe harbour Capt. Richard Schnösenberg was peering out to sea to spot the German convoy. 'As I looked out beyond the mole I suddenly saw a big shadow in the mist. A marine said "Don't shoot, that's our convoy coming in." Then the mist lifted and I saw the ship was flying the White Ensign. That was the end of the conversation. I shouted "Fire".'

The four British destroyers opened up on the Dieppe waterfront at 0510 hours. Drew Middleton, the Associated Press correspondent, reported watching shells smash into 'seafront hotels once sacred to honeymooning Britons'. Aboard the deputy headquarters ship *Fernie*, which did not take part in the bombardment, the American general Lucian Truscott confessed 'It was not nearly so heavy and impressive as I should have liked to hear.'

As the landing craft got within a mile of the beach the air attack went in, right on time. 'There was a roar overhead and a flight of Hurricanes swept low over the water and attacked the buildings immediately ahead with machine-guns and cannon fire,' said Labatt. 'Flashes of flame ran up and down the esplanade as the bursts exploded. It was all over quickly, too quickly. The men who had been standing up to watch were disappointed. "Is that all?" they asked.'

Lt Herb Prince of the Royal Hamiltons remembered, 'We had been told that saturation bombing of the town front would perhaps obliterate landmarks. But one of the first things that struck me was that everything was exactly as it had been described. Even the windows were still there. Everything looked intact to me.' Saturation bombing, part of the original 'Rutter' scheme, had long been abandoned in the 'Jubilee' plan but nobody had got around to passing on the news to junior officers and other ranks.

Corroboration of the ineffectiveness of the air raid is provided by Richard Schnösenberg, who was on the receiving end. 'The planes came in such close formation that two of them collided and crashed into the sea. We lay down on the ground as they flew over us. Some fields were burning but not even one weapon was destroyed.'

With the headlands wreathed in smoke laid by the RAF, the German guns opened up along fixed lines at the approaches to the beach but as the Dieppe Port Commandant noted, 'As the landing craft could soon be clearly discerned a change was made to observed fire.'

The extreme right flank of the Royal Hamiltons' vessels suffered the heaviest mauling from guns on the West headland and two platoons were virtually wiped out. A mortar bomb fell among a bunch of Bangalore torpedoes on one landing craft carrying Lt Fred Woodcock. 'I only remember the sound, because I was blinded. The boat filled with water and I was soon up to my neck. I couldn't hear at all after that for a long while but later there were faraway noises as if I were listening to something over a very poor connection on a long-distance phone call. It seemed that my limbs wouldn't move. I wanted to brush the blood from my eyes and couldn't. Then, a long time later, I could feel something touching my face and realised that it was my hand.'

Only one other soldier survived that explosion apart from Woodcock who, though permanently blinded, struggled ashore, was captured and subsequently repatriated.

In the centre of the landing wave, although the boats came under fire from the Casino and its pillboxes, there were few casualties in the final few moments before touchdown, while on the left flank the

Essex Scottish passed almost unscathed through the fire coming from the East headland. Capt. Donald MacRae, the only officer in the Essex Scottish to land at Dieppe and get back to England, reported, 'The troops rushed out of the assault craft in perfect drill order and up to the first wire obstacle. So far as I know only one man was lost in this crossing.' Capt. Dennis Guest resolved the problem of the first wire barricade by vaulting over it, while Pte Tom McDermott, an American who had crossed the border at the outbreak of war to volunteer for the Canadian army, unselfishly threw himself on to the wire so that his colleagues could scramble over it using his body as a mattress.

It was when the Essex Scottish got to the second, double apron wire barrier on Red Beach that the full fury of the German fire fell upon them. Mortars operating on fixed lines inflicted considerable casualties, though the fact that the shells usually buried themselves in the beach pebbles before exploding minimised the damage they caused, apart from cuts inflicted by flying shingle.

Pte Eugene Cousineau reported, 'The first blast of heavy fire stunned us for a moment but we soon recovered and when we reached the protection of the sea wall most of our section were present. We couldn't see the Germans, who were hidden in the buildings along the waterfront, but their machine-gun and mortar fire was very intense. Early on, the morale was high despite the casualties and the men were all smoking and laughing.'

'It is amazing that, despite the intensive shelling, the numbers of casualties were not as great as might have been expected,' Capt. MacRae noted.

Enough of the Essex Scottish had now reached the sea wall to try scaling it but as soon as a breaching of the sea-wall wire was attempted almost all the troops were shot down. Despite this, a second assault was launched under cover of smoke but it suffered a similar, bloody fate. 'Every time you showed your head over the wall the snipers went at you,' recalled Cpl R. Carle. 'The men took all Jerry had without a whimper, they died like men.'

On White Beach the Canadians faced an additional hazard, the defences in and around the Casino which fronted on the beach itself, though once this building had been captured, at heavy cost, it provided shelter for the attackers from the guns of the West headland. The Casino itself was not heavily defended, being manned mainly by snipers, but in front of the building was a heavy pillbox and embedded in the north-west corner of the building was a gun emplacement. There were machine-gun positions on each side of the Casino and on the promenade immediately east of the building was a long low shed containing machine-guns and an anti-tank gun.

Since there were no naval vessels in Dieppe harbour at the time of the attack, the 360 German sailors based there helped in the defence of the town. The Port Commandant's headquarters section reinforced the infantrymen in trenches around the Casino, while another 60 occupied positions on the promenade in front of the Hotel Metropole. They were involved in the heaviest fighting on White Beach and suffered 28 killed and 25 wounded.

According to Leo Marziniak, one of the German soldiers brought back to England as a prisoner, the guards near the Casino had been roused by the sounds of firing about 0500 hours but the NCO in charge of their post had received no warning of an impending landing, nor did he ever receive one. It was not until landing craft appeared in front of Dieppe that they realised they were under attack. The defenders opened fire without any specific orders and when they were driven from their pillbox Marziniak and some others took refuge in the Casino, where they were eventually captured.

After passing through the outer belt of fixed line fire, the boats carrying the Hamiltons covered the final 100 yards to White Beach in comparative calm. 'Suddenly the towers of the Casino loomed above us,' said Col. Labatt. 'We could see them firing from the upper windows and from gun emplacements on the ground floor level.' As Labatt's boat grounded and the ramp swung down, the naval officer in charge leapt ashore to hold the bows firm and, as Labatt sprinted past, he yelled, 'Drinks – Newhaven – tonight.'

'There was a momentary lull in the firing as we touched down, then it opened up again with terrific intensity,' said Labatt. 'The Bolero reached its deafening crescendo and maintained it for the next eight hours.'

Most of the Royal Hamilton Light Infantry to the right of the Casino had been wiped out on the run-in or immediately after landing, but Lt Llewellyn Counsell led a small group towards the first wire barrier, where he found two gaps. Since they had clearly not been made by attackers, Counsell feared that they would be mined or booby-trapped and ordered his men not to go through them. Instead, under murderous fire and at heavy cost, they attempted to cut a way through the wire. In fact they could have rushed through the gaps quite safely, since there were no mines on Dieppe beach. One passage had been opened by the Germans to permit the collection of stones for ballast and the other, wide enough for two people to pass through, was used for bathing.

While Lt Counsell and Cpl Percy Haines were cutting the wire Counsell was wounded by a mortar bomb. 'I put a dressing on the wound,' said Haines, 'and while I was doing that he got another in the hip, so I helped him back to the water's edge. On the way back he got hit a third time. I then put dressings on all the wounds and told him to lie quiet while I went for a stretcher. On the way to see about it I received a shrapnel wound in the shoulder and before I could get back to Lt Counsell I was all battered up myself.'

Pte Ernest Merrell described the fearful losses in those early moments on White Beach. 'We could go no further because the mortar and machine-gun fire was so intense and accurate. A mortar bomb dropped and many of the boys were hit. Pte A. Pringle, although badly hit in the face, went on firing. Cpl Comfort went to help him and was wounded in the legs doing so. He still carried on, and was hit again. This man did some wonderful work and looked after the wounded even though he had to drag himself around ... I had the Bren gun blown out of my hands and was hit in the hands and face by shrapnel. We had to keep on moving as the snipers only missed once with any of their weapons.... Pte Cornelius was badly hit in the face when the Bren magazine exploded. We fixed him up and then a sniper got him through the heart.'

'It was really terrible,' said Pte Frank Boucher. 'We were being mowed down like flies.' Pte James Holland remembered, 'I must have made a burrow in the ground where I crawled. I never knew I could get so close to the ground and still be on top of it, but it's surprising what you can do when you have to.'

Gordon Ryall, a naval telegraphist attached to the Hamiltons whose job was to direct the fire of the destroyer *Berkeley*, said, 'As I crawled up the beach the mortar fire was so heavy that stones were being thrown up over my head, legs and back. I remember very distinctly this sailor being blown up into the air and his bell bottom trousers floating, waving in the air, as he cartwheeled down. I think he was blown up about 50 feet.'

One mortar bomb landed in Maj. Tom Heyhurst's lap and blew him to pieces, but the Canadians soon discovered that virtually a direct hit was needed to kill. As Pte H. J. Truman observed, 'They could land ten to 15 feet from you and as long as you were well down they didn't hurt you.' As Col. Labatt and his adjutant, Capt. Herb Poag, lay on the beach a bomb landed between them. 'It touched neither of us but the blast deafened me for several days,' said Labatt, who was in considerably more danger when Poag nearly shot off his head while attempting to fire his Sten gun at the Casino.

The snipers concentrated on officers and key personnel, such as signallers. Maj. Norris Waldron, advancing on the Casino with pistol drawn, cursing at the top of his voice, was shot dead; Lt Reginald Baisley was killed the moment he attempted to cross the sea wall; the mortar platoon officer Lt Ian Wright fell seconds after landing and Capt. George Matchett was cut down by a machine-gun. In the Second World War the Hamiltons lost a total of 37 officers. Ten of them died that morning at Dieppe.

Individual acts of bravery eventually managed to subdue the defences outside the Casino. Cpl Johnnie Williamson watched in astonishment as Pte Leo Lesynski cut through the wire, 'standing right up without any cover, and then holding back the wire while the rest of us galloped through'.

When progress towards the Casino was blocked by a pillbox, smoke canisters were fired at it and Pte Harry Wichtacz worked his way round to the back and pushed a Bangalore torpedo through the firing slit. Returning to cover, Wichtacz was hit by fire from another pill box and badly wounded in both legs, one of which had to be amputated later.

Labatt watched Pte Hugh McCourt worm his way through wire to another gun emplacement, stand up and push a grenade through the slit. 'Seconds later I saw his helmet being jerked up and down on the end of his bayonet as a sign of victory.... Thus the first Casino strongpoint was taken.'

Labatt then ordered Lt John Currie to take all available men with him to exploit the breakthrough against the Casino. 'He started at once but there was momentary hesitation in following. Speed was essential. So I sat upright with my back to the West cliff and directed traffic in language no London bobby ever used. This had the desired result. They left me quickly and did a first-class job.'

The Hamiltons were desperately handicapped in their attack against the Casino by the lack of heavy weapons. The guns which they did possess were far from satisfactory and there were many complaints about the malfunctioning of the Stens with which they had been issued. 'Our Sten guns are no good' was the opinion of Pte Jack Shuart, and Pte Frank Farr concurred: 'They aren't worth a damn.'

Many of the mortars carried in the landing craft had been lost, or their vital baseplates dropped into the water, as the Canadians struggled ashore. 'When we attempted to fire our mortar without its baseplate it slipped about and fell over, breaking the sights,' said L/Cpl Joe Whitehead. 'The shots were very wild.' Pte Al Richards, one of the few men left alive between the Casino and the West headland, tried to fire smoke bombs from his 2 in. mortar, despite a painful wound in his left shin. 'My number one man got clobbered and I was left alone. It was slow work. I managed to get the job done but by this time it was hopeless, the platoon was pretty well wiped out. I was scared as hell. I don't think there was anybody who wasn't scared on that beach. The thing I remember most is the stink of blood around the water's edge. It was just like being in a slaughterhouse.'

Needing fire-power to suppress resistance inside the Casino, Col. Labatt put out an urgent message to the headquarters ship *Calpe* on his one remaining radio set: 'Get Johnny forward.' Johnny was the code name for the Calgary Tanks commanded by Col. Johnny Andrews.

When the German naval units in Dieppe were being trained, as part of their port defence duties, in coping with an attack by tanks, Port Commandant Wahn reported, 'I demanded as a final phase an advance by a tank across an elevation of gravel. Within a short time the tank was stuck so firmly that it could no longer be moved. The tracks had to be removed and cleaned. At the time I made the observation "Now we know that the British cannot land here with tanks".'

Now a battalion of Churchills from the Calgary Tank Regiment were heading for that same beach. They were late, having been given a wrong fix for their position when they were some distance out at sea. Instead of touching down immediately behind the infantry as planned to provide cover for the landing with their 6-pounder guns the first Churchills were 15 minutes behind schedule as the tank landing craft (LCTs) approached Red and White beaches at 0535 hours.

Each of the 195-foot LCTs carried three tanks and a scout jeep which were to disembark first, followed by support infantry, beach signal parties and sappers and working sections carrying rolled-up strips of wood known as chespaling and railway sleepers to assist the tanks up the beach and over the esplanade wall. The first flight of the first wave, consisting of LCTs Nos 1, 2 and 3, came under devastating fire as it lumbered towards touchdown.

LCT 2 was on the extreme left and made a perfect landing near the harbour mole. Its three tanks, Cougar, Cat and Cheetah, disembarked safely but slowly. Each one stalled on the landing ramp because the engines had not been warmed up and almost 15 minutes elapsed before they finally got off.

'I had a clear view of the tanks as they left the craft,' said Sgt J. W. Marsh, a member of a Black Watch of Canada mortar detachment aboard LCT 2. 'The first tank was hit three or four times but kept going. It went through the wire but much to my surprise the wire seemed to spring into place again after the weight of the tank had passed over it. After receiving a couple of shots from the French tank cemented into the mole alongside where where we had landed, our tank opened fire and scored a direct hit.'

In fact the French tank continued to wreak a tremendous amount of damage throughout the action. It was at first unmanned but a sentry on guard nearby, who had been trained in the handling of its 3.7 cm. gun, climbed inside as he saw the invasion fleet approaching, fired all of his 185 rounds during the morning and afterwards emerged to take a dozen prisoners.

Having safely negotiated the pebbles, the leading tank Cougar mounted the sea wall, which had been rendered negotiable at that end of the beach by drifting stones, and turned right along the promenade. It was followed by Cheetah, which made straight for a pillbox as it moved up the beach. The German defenders fled in panic and were shot down by machine-gunners aboard LCT 2.

The third tank Cat, which was towing a scout car ashore, became stuck half on the beach and half on the ramp. In a bid to clear it the LCT's captain, Lt Benjamin McPherson, put his engines into reverse to pull the ramp from beneath the tank but at that moment a shell severed the winch cables and left the ramp hanging vertically into the water. 'The tank, now released, rapidly pulled the scout car through the wire and also tore through the wall,' said Sgt Marsh. 'The last I saw of the scout car it was tearing like hell up Boulevard Foch.'

During the 15 minutes it had taken to clear its cargo of tanks, LCT 2 suffered a pounding from the East headland immediately on its left. Pte Cliff McKenna, one of the Toronto Scottish Regiment's machine-gunners posted on the LCTs to provide anti-aircraft and beach covering fire, was manning a Vickers gun on the port side. McKenna had tested his guns soon after departure the previous evening by shooting at seagulls. Now he found a more dangerous target: 'I opened fire on a German mortar section up against the cliff which was bombing our LCT. It became sort of a little game to see who could get who first. They were firing at us and I was trying to knock them out. I was lying on the exposed deck with my number two, Herb Lyons, feeding the belt in. Our ammunition was piled up in front of us and on the sides. When we beached they landed one mortar in the water that splashed all over us, and the next one landed behind us. I guess about six of them just missed before one landed in front of us and set our ammunition on fire, and it started to explode. The next bomb hit Herb, shrapnel wounds all down the back of his legs. About a minute later one got me and took half of my heel away.'

Pte G. St-Onge, one of a detachment of Fusiliers Mont-Royal aboard the LCT, commented on McKenna's '*bel ésprit de combat*' as he continued to operate his Vickers gun with half his foot blown away. 'Eventually the pain was so bad I stopped firing,' said McKenna. 'We both lay there feeling sorry for each other, and finally I couldn't remember a damn thing about anything.'

Pte A. M. Sinclair, the Toronto Scottish machine-gunner on the other side of LCT 2, counted 17 hits by mortar bombs in 16 minutes. 'My remaining ammunition was so riddled by shrapnel as to be useless,' he said. The naval personnel manning the Bofors guns were all killed or wounded with a few minutes. O/S Thomas Lee crawled away from his post and reported to Lt McPherson, 'I can't do anything more for you skipper'. Afterwards Lee had his left leg amputated.

Major Bert Sucharov, in charge of the beach assault engineers, ordered them under cover until the tanks had been landed and to 'wait on my orders to go'. But as the German fire increased Sucharov decided it would be suicidal to put his men ashore. In any case, the sappers' main task had been done for them, as all three tanks on LCT 2 had reached the esplanade. The mortar men of the Black Watch of Canada also sat tight, and in fact never expended one of the 640 rounds of mortar bombs they had carried across the Channel. 'The fire was so intense that it would have been impossible for anyone to have left the ship,' reported their commanding officer Capt. A. L. MacLaurin. Pte J. Laurie thought so too. 'The way the shells were hitting our tub the whole beach was a pillbox.'

Sucharov ran to the bridge to ask Lt McPherson to put his boat in again further towards the centre of the beach but the smashed ramp dangling beneath the LCT prohibited any attempt to get in close enough for a reasonably dry landing. Soon after, LCT 2 suffered five direct hits on the bridge, which killed or wounded all except Lt

McPherson. Its engines going astern and a foot of water swilling around its hold, the battered ship limped out to sea and took no further part in the raid.

LCT 2 was the only one of the tank landing craft in that first flight to get away from Dieppe. LCT 1, aiming for the centre of Dieppe beach, suffered just as heavily and the Hamiltons' padre, Capt. John Foote, watched from the shore as 'one of its guns was hit and all the Navy fellows just disappeared in one big blob'. Its three tanks, Company, Calgary and Chief, were landed, together with a scout car, in three minutes. Company crossed the sea wall successfully, while the other two moved to support the attack on the Casino. Its engines crippled, LCT 1 drifted away from the beach and eventually sank.

LCT 3, carrying three flame-throwing tanks, was trapped in the even more devastating fire from the West headland as it moved towards the beach. 'About 200 yards out a terrific concentration of fire opened up on our craft,' reported Capt. Dick Eldred of the Calgary Tanks, who had been assigned a beach control role. 'Most of our gunners were quickly knocked out of action and though their places were immediately taken these too became casualties.'

A Toronto Scottish private, Jack Fowler, formerly a dance band drummer, lost his left hand and had a hole gouged in his leg by a piece of shrapnel. 'I stopped firing for a moment, placing my hand on my knee. A shell took off my hand and at the same time ripped out a piece of my leg.'

The engineer lieutenant, Jerry Wood, recalled 'I glanced across the deck at an exceedingly serious-faced young naval lieutenant. A blinding orange flash folded him in a heap. If you could be that close and get away with it I wasn't going to worry. Then they started dropping all sorts of stuff inside the craft. A warmer reception than programmed. This was going to be a tough ball game.'

About a hundred yards from the beach the ramp was lowered halfway in preparation for landing, at which Capt. Bill Purdy inside the leading tank, Boar, immediately drove forward, smashed through the ramp and disappeared over the bows into the sea, the LCT scraping over the top of its submerged turret.

Now the mortars had got the range of LCT 3. One bomb burst on the bridge, killing the captain, Sub-Lt W. H. Cooke, and knocking out the remainder of the personnel there. 'Realising the situation I dashed up to the wheelhouse just as the craft came into the beach,' said Lt P. Ross, a passenger in the vessel as Naval Beach Officer of White Beach. Although Ross managed to stop both engines the ship's momentum carried it hard on to the beach. Its ramp had folded back underneath the craft on impact, leaving a ten-foot drop to the beach, but the remaining two tanks, Bull and Beetle, made safe if extremely heavy landings, though in getting ashore the third tank added to the carnage already wrought inside by German shells and bullets. The tank's left hand chock had not been removed and as it climbed the obstacle it crushed some soldiers against the side of the landing craft. 'We yelled and beat on the sides,' said Jerry Wood. 'Closed down, the crew couldn't hear. The tank stopped and reversed. We cleared the chock. "Look", shrieked a youngster beside me as two bodies slumped forward.'

LCT 3's emergency skipper, Lt Ross, made desperate attempts to get the vessel afloat again. Though the telegraphs had been blown up, Ross passed verbal messages to the engine room but the landing craft had been driven ashore too hard and with the tide ebbing it was stuck fast.

The second flight of the first wave, LCTs Nos 4, 5 and 6, followed five minutes behind the first flight, led in by Lt Arthur Cheyney aboard LCT 4. In broad daylight, the landings had now reached the one-sided stage of a duck shoot. LCT 4 was set on fire about 200 yards from the beach and Cheyney reported, 'Flames swept over the bridge, not only making visibility difficult but threatening hundreds of spare boxes of ammunition stowed on the deck.'

All three tanks were disembarked, Maj. Charles Page going ashore first in Burns, followed by Bolster and Backer. By now, however, the Germans had realised that the fire-power available to them at that time was ineffective against the Churchills' armour, so they switched their attention to the more vulnerable tracks. The tanks from LCT 4 had rumbled ashore at the most difficult part of the beach, where shingle had been cleared so recently from in front of the wall that the mechanical excavator was still in position. 'I gave orders to turn to the right and that's when I was hit,' said Maj. Page. 'I was just on the crest at the top of the trench dug by the excavator and the right track was blown off. The left one went on for a few seconds and kind of pulled me into the trench.' Both Backer and Bolster were similarly halted by direct hits on their tracks before they could get off the beach.

The smoke laid earlier by the RAF had now completely disappeared and the shore batteries turned their full attention to the beached LCTs. 'We received hits on the waterline and in the starboard fuel tanks,' said Cheyney. 'Another shell burst on the bridge. Most of the fragments were deflected down the funnel and all the engine room ratings standing at the controls immediately below the funnel were wounded. By now the last tank was ashore and the engines, which had been put to full astern, took us off with a rush. I was surprised to see about 20 troops in the water and 250 soldiers still in the hold. Thinking these men were vital for clearing the way for the tanks stranded on the beach I went in a second time.'

On this occasion Cheyney, already twice wounded himself, took advantage of the partial shelter offered by the beached LCT 3 on his starboard side. 'But nothing could be done about the port side. We received a direct hit in the engine room and another shell burst on the armour plating of the bridge, the blast from which perforated my eardrums. The troops did not take the second opportunity to disembark, so I came astern again. There was no response from the engine room so I went below to find that it was in darkness and we were making water fast.'

Having arranged to pass orders by word of mouth, Cheyney returned to the deck, where he found a wounded naval rating lying in the open. 'As I endeavoured to move him to shelter a shell exploded against the ship's side and killed him in my arms. By now most of my crew were injured so I ordered the helmsmen to steer due north and we steamed slowly out to sea.'

Cheyney went back to the engine room where he found a wounded stoker, Eric Ellis, trying to plug the shell holes with hammocks and duffle coats. 'There was now four feet of water in the engine room and it was gaining rapidly,' Cheyney reported, 'so closing the watertight doors we reluctantly abandoned the engine room.' The engines stopped about three hundred yards from shore, with the decks awash. A motor launch pulled alongside to evacuate the wounded, the soldiers who had opted not to land were transferred to a passing group of Eureka landing craft, and soon afterwards LCT 4 sank.

LCT 5, which lowered its ramp directly in front of the Casino, landed its cargo of tanks, Buttercup, Blossom and Bluebell but, engines and bridge shattered by shells, it never got off the beach again and was abandoned as it caught fire and ammunition on board began to explode.

LCT 6 also got its tanks, Bert, Bob and Bill ashore but was only able to close the beach on its third attempt after helmsmen had twice been killed during the run-in. As Bert, Bob and Bill moved down the ramp they were followed by one group of engineers, but about 30 troops remained aboard, reluctant to face the storm of fire beyond the protection of the LCT's steep sides. His bridge a shambles of dead and dying, his vessel repeatedly struck by shells and swept by machine-guns, the captain Lt Thomas Cook waited patiently for the men to disembark. They would not move. Finally, the ramp was winched up and LCT 6 pulled away from the beach. In his official report Cook, apportioning no blame, said, 'All the infantry except thirty were landed, and after waiting fifteen minutes for the remainder to go ashore, I withdrew from the beach.'

As LCT 6 began to move away, the ramp still down, several of the rifle section who had followed the tanks ashore crawled back on board 'badly wounded and half drowned' according to Pte Bill Simpson of a Calgary Highlanders mortar platoon. 'A piece of shrapnel struck a chap close by me and made a mess of his head. As the heavy fire hit through the barge it killed several of the gun crew on the pom pom and also set on fire a smoke candle. That smoke gave me more assurance than anything else right then.' Though Simpson thought that 'several times it looked as if we were not going to have enough barge left to keep on floating with', the battered ship pulled safely out to sea.

Those sappers, engineers and infantry who followed the tanks ashore from the LCTs suffered cruelly. Bill Lynch of the Royal Canadian Engineers described the horror of going ashore carrying a 70 lb pack of high explosives: 'The front door is down, the tanks rumble off ... hell is let loose. No unopposed landing here, as we engineers were told. Off at the double, bayonets fixed, staggering on loose beach and cobbles. The tanks are having awful trouble with those cobbles, their tracks are jamming. I stagger forward with heavy pack and cumbersome 1916 rifle.

'The Essex Scottish had blown gaps in the wire right where I was. Big dark-eyed Gagne, one of our boys, always on the beer in England, but what a lion here, rushed at that gap like a bull.... Down he goes. I thought he had had it. He's wriggling out of his pack ... he's hit, an awful groove right around his forehead. He rushes past me, dark eyes flashing, covers my left arm with blood as he tears backwards, saying, 'I'm hit. Got to get to the boat. Good luck.'

'I hesitate as I see the terrific fire on that gap. At the same time there are explosions. My section – a group of them – go up in black smoke. My God, it's their own packs blowing! Too many bunched up to the left so I make my way to the right, flopping down halfway between two tanks, right bang up against the wire at the top of the beach. My God, look at that boy. He's a flaming torch, burnt and blown by his own pack of incendiaries.'

Lynch discarded his own highly-dangerous pack, wriggled through a gap in the wire and took cover behind the promenade wall, which was only about three feet high at that point, with a mixed bunch of engineers and infantry 'dead and alive, all bunched together'.

Sapper Vic Sparrow, also laden with a pack of explosives, recalled, 'The first wave was supposed to have cleared the way and all we had to do was go in and put our explosives on some rolling stock in a tunnel, then blow the whole works. But as soon as we hit the beach we were pinned down right there, though some of the boys did get through the wire. Two of our group got caught up on the wire and were just burned to a crisp when they got hit with their packs on. I saw some of our wounded actually get run over by the tanks. It wasn't the fault of the drivers, they couldn't see.'

One sapper, L/Cpl Milton Sinasac, was luckier than most. He was carrying a demolition charge in his arms when a burst of machine-gun fire struck the dynamite but only wounded him in the hand.

Pte C. J. McDonald of the Royal Canadian Ordnance Corps, went ashore behind the tanks from LCT 4. 'I was one of about six or seven who followed the tanks off, at which the LCT pulled out, leaving us behind. We crouched in the shelter of the tanks and crawled from one to the other trying to get further inland but the firing was so intense that we couldn't do it. One chap from the RCASC supply column was lying alongside a burning armoured car when the petrol tank exploded and his clothes ignited. He rushed to the sea and jumped in.'

The human torch, not badly burned, decided to keep on swimming and headed for another LCT which was just about to pull off the beach. McDonald and several others decided to follow his example. 'By the time we reached the water the LCT was about 25 yards out. I dropped my rifle so I could swim better. The landing ramp was still down so I was able to climb on board without difficulty.'

Aboard the stranded LCT 3, Lt Jerry Wood lay on the deck near the bow. 'Stuff was falling inside and it certainly hadn't cooled off outside. What the hell to do?' Suddenly a young naval sub-lieutenant crawled towards him, Sten gun in hand, saying 'Let's do *something*.' Wood admitted, 'That boy shamed me, he couldn't have been more than eighteen. So I decided to make a shore recce.'

Dropping into the water, Wood made his way to the beach and decided to try to ferry explosives ashore in case they were needed. Back at the LCT he asked for half his platoon to come out and form a human chain to the shore. 'Seven men came, four sappers and three Fusiliers Mont-Royal.... I demanded the rest of the men and was told they were all casualties. I didn't believe it. Meanwhile five of my men outside the LCT had been wounded.' Then Wood himself was hurt. 'My arm felt as if somebody had hit it with a baseball bat just below the left shoulder.... A searching hand found no gaping hole. I could still use it but most of the strength was gone.'

Wood sent back his only unwounded man Sapper Knowles ('He had been useless in England, but now the chips were down he was bloody-well magnificent') with instructions to 'throw every son of a bitch out of the LCT'. Still nobody emerged, so Wood struggled back to the landing craft and, though hampered by his arm wound, managed to get back on board.

'The sight made my head spin,' he wrote. 'Blood ran in the gutters, and that is no figure of speech. It was there, and it was running. What I looked at was quite as fantastic a scene as the Confederate hospital in the movie *Gone With the Wind*. Here were what was left of our men. Two RN medical orderlies, both with shrapnel in their arms, moved unobtrusively about their work in the worst shambles of their experience.'

The casualties among the tank support parties were appalling. Of the engineer groups 169 landed, of whom 152 were killed or captured, ten returned wounded and seven got back unhurt, a loss rate of 90 per cent. Among the sapper and demolition parties 98 landed, of whom 90 were killed or made prisoner, and of the eight who returned to England six were wounded, a casualty rate of 92 per cent. The beach and assault parties disembarked 71, of whom 62 were killed or captured. Four of the nine who returned were wounded, a loss of 87 per cent. Pte L. Fortin was one who returned, and said 'Afterwards you ask yourself how you came through it. I keep asking myself that. It seems impossible.'

Despite the havoc wrought among the first wave, the second wave of LCTs moved in on schedule at 0605 hours. It consisted of LCTs Nos 7, 8, 9 and 10 carrying a further dozen Churchills, including Col. Johnny Andrews and his three-tank battalion headquarters, and the commanders of the 4th and 6th Brigades, Brig. Sherwood Lett and Brig. William Southam. Lett and Southam were supposed to set up their respective brigade headquarters in churches near the Dieppe seafront. Lett's 4th Brigade consisted of the three Ontario regiments, Essex Scottish, Royal Hamiltons and the Royal Regiment, which had been crippled before he got anywhere near the beaches. Southam's 6th Brigade had under its charge the two battalions which had gone ashore at Pourville, Saskatchewans and Camerons, plus the floating reserve, the Fusiliers Mont-Royal.

Southam was aboard LCT 7, and had a narrow escape when fire was opened on it: 'I climbed a ladder to go on deck and had just reached the top when there was a flash which seemed to be almost in my face. My immediate thought was that someone had thrown a thunderflash. However, I was tumbled off the ladder and landed on a man below me.'

Lt Edwin Bennett had been up in the bows of LCT 7 to look at conditions on the beach and was returning to his tank Bellicose when a shell detonated some hydrogen cylinders, burning him severely on his hands and face and wounding him in one eye. 'After picking myself up I managed to get the crew to help put out a fire on the back of the tank caused by a blazing tarpaulin. The tank was slightly damaged and the turret traverse was completely jammed.'

In company with LCT 7's other tanks, Beefy and Bloody, Bennett's Bellicose disembarked safely while its commander applied soothing jelly to his burned face. 'The burns were the least of my troubles when we landed,' he reported. 'They seemed to have everything but the brass band out to greet us.'

With an encouraging shout of 'Here we go, lads', Southam attempted to gather his brigade headquarters group around him and follow the tanks to the beach, but he was promptly knocked flat into the water by a near miss. Southam was unhurt but many of the others were less lucky. Another shell which exploded in the front of LCT 7 decimated the brigade signals section and, since it was rapidly being blown to pieces, the boat pulled away from the beach, leaving Southam stranded ashore with only a handful of his headquarters staff. This landing craft was the only one of the second wave to be lost, and it was sunk subsequently, rather than at the time of landing its tanks, when it attempted to return to the beach to pick up troops on withdrawal.

When Southam went ashore with a copy of the 'Jubilee' military plan tucked under one arm in a waterproof package, he committed the day's most controversial act. By nightfall it was in German hands and one sentence in the plan ordering that all prisoners were to be trussed to prevent destruction of documents provided them with valuable propaganda afterwards. Southam and Lett had been authorised to take ashore two copies of the plan each, and though this authorisation was swiftly recognised by Gen. Roberts to be unwise and was countermanded, Southam apparently never received the new order, or if he did he ignored it.

The third tank to leave LCT 7, Bloody, towed off behind it the scout car containing the battalion's signals officer, Maj. Gordon Rolfe. At the sea wall Rolfe pulled a lever to disconnect the tow line but when Bloody stalled on the edge of the esplanade it rolled backwards, crushing the front of the car. So Rolfe perforce set up his undamaged signals equipment on the spot and for the remainder of the action this was the only effective link between that part of the beach and those at sea, since Southam's communications equipment was destroyed when a tank ran over it.

Aboard LCT 8 Sherwood Lett was attempting to join Southam ashore but without luck. As the landing craft touched down, the Calgary Tanks' adjutant Capt. Austin Stanton gave the instruction to the driver of his tank Ringer, 'Advance'. Stanton recalled, 'As I looked through the periscope there was a naval officer lying on the beach. He was dying, lying on his stomach, facing out to sea. The first thing that flashed through my mind was "Keep your head down boy, they're playing for keeps today".'

Unfortunately Stanton's tank did not advance very far, bogging down just off the ramp and blocking the exit for the tanks' commanding officer, Col. Andrews, and his second-in-command, Maj. John Begg. Stanton maintains to this day that he had been told he was to land on a sandy beach and would have to cross a sea wall no more than a foot high. 'What we hit was heavy shale and the sea wall looked about eight feet. I told my driver not to back up until we could see what was happening, and as I turned the periscope round I saw the landing craft was going like hell back out to sea.'

As LCT 8 withdrew half a mile offshore in preparation for a second landing, LCTs 9 and 10 successfully unloaded their tanks. On LCT 10 Sgt S. L. Hart of the signals section aboard reported, 'The first tank was stopped by a direct hit. The second one followed off, then an officer came out of the first tank with his face streaming blood and one eye shot out, jumped into the second tank, swung the gun turret round and let go two quick shots at the gun on the pier.'

Another signaller, Cpl Tom Gorman witnessed the incident, terming it 'the most conspicuous case of bravery I saw', and then watched in horror as the third tank jammed in the landing craft's watertight doors then freed itself, taking the door with it. 'Everything seemed to be getting very sticky by that time,' said Gorman. 'We received a very bad hit directly on the front of our boat that carried away the front end. At about the same time we got it in the stern, making our rudder useless and rendering our craft unmanageable. I resigned myself to my fate and awaited my turn, which I was quite convinced would come, along with everyone else on board.'

Sgt Hart, intending to follow the third tank ashore, turned back to collect a wireless set. 'When I looked again the ramp had been blown off. Shells had also exploded the smokescreen tank on the upper deck and the whole boat was filled with smoke. When at last it lifted I found we had drifted some distance off shore.' In this fashion those still on board LCT 10 survived.

Soon, at the urging of Brig. Lett and Col. Andrews, anxious to get ashore to take over their commands, LCT 8 prepared to go in again, despite the fact that Lett, who had briefly been in touch with Col. Labatt on White Beach and announced his intention of landing, had been told 'For Christ's sake don't' before the line went dead. As LCT 8 approached Dieppe for the second time the final act in the tragedy of the tank landing craft unfolded.

On LCT 8's first landing there had been no casualties, according to a Royal Marines sergeant, Thomas Badlan. On the second occasion they went in alone and much closer to the guns of the West headland. 'We were really catching it this time,' said Sgt Badlan. 'During the final approach we were repeatedly hit.' Badlan was a member of a Marine beach provost detachment under Lt-Col. Bobby Parks-Smith, the oldest serving officer at Combined Operations Headquarters. Parks-Smith, who had helped Sir Roger Keyes build up the organisation and was described by Lord Mountbatten as 'the one really live wire at the time I joined Combined Ops' should never have left his duties in London but he insisted on going along on the raid, a decision which cost him his life.

Parks-Smith was wounded twice and was looked after by Badlan. 'I gave him a cigarette and assisted him to the starboard side which afforded greater protection from the shellfire. As I did so I saw four or five people in the water. Apparently the order to abandon ship had been given.'

No such instruction was given. The men had been blown there by shells hitting the landing craft. One of those in the water was Capt. Laurence Alexander, a medical officer attached to the Calgary Tanks. While treating the injured on the exposed deck he was knocked overboard by a shell blast, but he climbed back on board and carried on with his work of mercy.

Lett was also hit about this time. Lt H. McMillan was offering the brigadier a cigarette when it happened. 'I was near enough to hand him the pack of cigarettes, yet when the shell exploded in the air he was hit and I wasn't, much to my amazement since he was so much shorter than I was.'

As Sub-Lt John Whitehead gave the order to lower the ramp door in preparation, the chains were blown off, an explosion which wounded Whitehead in the left arm and right eye, and the door fell open, touching down in eight feet of water. Believing that a normal landing had been made, Col. Andrews drove off in his tank Regiment, which was entirely submerged except for the turret and, like Capt. Purdy's tank earlier, was 'drowned' since the rough waterproofing which had been applied to the Churchills only extended to a height of six feet. 'I am baling out' Andrews reported. Though he evacuated his tank successfully, Andrews was killed on the beach. For the rest of the action his commanding officer's pennant on the wireless mast fluttered over his otherwise submerged tank. The third Churchill aboard LCT 8, Maj. John Begg's, never got ashore.

So heavily battered was LCT 8 that Lt-Col. Robert King, assistant quartermaster of the Canadian 2nd Division, who had taken over command of army personnel aboard after Lett's wounding, insisted that the ship was literally blown off the shore by the volume of shell fire directed at it.

All the naval personnel both on the bridge and in the engine room were put out of action and the shattered craft was eventually taken away from the beach by a Canadian major, Paul Garneau, and the Marine sergeant, Tom Badlan, neither of whom possessed the slightest navigational experience. Garneau threw the engines into reverse and managed to get them started by pulling all the switches in sight. Badlan, who had been about to abandon the LCT with his mortally-wounded colonel, Parks-Smith, noticed that the starboard screw was turning and the vessel was slowly going astern. 'So I went to the bridge, where I found everybody dead. Then I went to the wheelhouse, after finding out where it was from Col. Parks-Smith. There I found the helmsman minus a leg. The wheelhouse was shattered, there was a small fire which I put out with a helmet full of water and the compass was broken but the wheel itself was undamaged. I was able to steer clear of the beach with the assistance of another marine sergeant on the port side and a Canadian officer on the starboard side giving me verbal orders trying to keep me in the centre and out of the way of the guns. We went out of the bay zig-zagging.'

Eventually a naval mechanic who had been blown overboard but climbed back aboard, took over the engines from Garneau, while Sub-Lt Whitehead, wounded when the ramp was lowered, made his way to the bridge and – despite a broken arm and severe eye injury – helped Badlan navigate the ship away from the danger zone.

The painful retreat of LCT 8 marked the end of the part played by the tank landing craft at Dieppe. The ten LCTs which managed to touch down landed 29 of their 30 Churchills aboard. Five of those LCTs were sunk and three more were so badly damaged that they were out of commission for a long time afterwards, and half the crews involved were killed or wounded. Capt. C. A. Stanfield, commander of the LCT flotilla, reported to Mountbatten 'These losses, with so little to show for it, have been a blow to the flotillas on the South Coast.'

Of the 29 tanks put 'ashore' at Dieppe, 15 – more than half – got on to the esplanade, two were drowned through disembarking prematurely and the other 12 never got off the beach, either because they bogged down in the shingle or because their tracks were shot off.

Probably the greatest pity of Dieppe is that those 15 tanks, which could have done so much to sway the course of the battle, were forced to cruise impotently up and down the seafront until immobilised because no demolitions men survived the crossing of the promenade to blow up the barricades which ran across the head of the streets leading from the town on to the Boulevard de Verdun. These anti-tank walls were about seven feet high and four feet thick, surmounted by barbed wire and extending right across the streets.

'That is the one thing that irks me and has irked me for all these years,' said Trooper Dick Clark in 1979. 'We had no trouble at all when we got off the landing craft and we went right up on the promenade, although we had no idea we were going to land on a beach with stones the size of baseballs. There were several of us up there on the promenade, waiting for the order to advance into the town itself. We were just going round in bloody circles, using up our ammo, using up our gas, being shelled, rolling over people.'

Clark maintains that there was room for a tank to get past the roadblocks in the Rue de Sygogne, which runs immediately under the Castle. He claimed that Lt Jack Dunlap in Bill was trying to get into Dieppe through this roadblock 'but he threw a track and blocked the street.' Clark added, 'When I was taken prisoner I walked up through there. There was lots of room for tanks to get through, thirty feet on either side.'

Maj. Allan Glenn said, 'We realised it was hopeless after only half an hour or so. Then over the radio they started talking about sending reinforcements. I yelled my bloody head off, "Keep them out, it's no use sending them in here. They can't go any place." We had too many tanks there already. But if they had sent just one tank to Green Beach to help the South Saskatchewans, how different things might have been. Green Beach is where we should have landed.'

Some of the most vigorous tank action was taken by the appropriately-named Bellicose, commanded by the burned and wounded Lt Edwin Bennett, which made for the Casino trying to find a low point in the sea wall. 'It was a pretty grim trip as there were so many wounded lying helpless in our path, but we managed to get around them as the tide was going out,' said Lt Bennett. Not all were so lucky, however. Pte Fred Nickol of the Hamiltons watched as 'a big tank went right over a lad lying on the beach and there was only a red spot left.'

Bennett's tank eventually managed to mount the sea wall near the Casino and was immediately able to lend spectacular assistance to the troops attacking the building. 'We made a dash for the Germans who were pinning down our infantry on the near side of the road,' said Bennett. To our surprise they poured out from everywhere, running like hell. Both gunners opened up and we got plenty of them. Even had the pleasure of running down one who tried to dodge us. Then we tried to get into the town behind the Casino but all the streets were very narrow and were blocked with solid concrete. We were finally hit properly and our steering was buggered.... When I tried to fire through the pistol port at a stray German running for cover I realised that I was unable to see clearly any longer. The burns had closed up my left eye.'

Although under constant fire ('It was like hail on the roof,' said Austin Stanton) the tanks marooned on the beach were able at least to offer some form of retaliation against the headlands. 'But it was disappointing, completely frustrating, to sit there and feel so helpless,' according to Stanton. 'We didn't have a hope in hell. They had allotted us half an hour to reach objectives we couldn't have taken in an hour and a half on exercise.'

When it finally bellied down in the shingle, the tank containing Trooper George Volk was right in front of the Casino. Volk, the hull gunner, climbed out of the tank to see if he could clear the shingle from the tracks, was wounded while doing so and eventually evacuated as a casualty. Trooper Percy Aide, who had swum ashore from Capt. Purdy's drowned tank, was the only other member of the

Calgary Tanks to get off Dieppe's beach. Of the remaining 170, 12 were killed and the rest made prisoner.

Dieppe's three-storey Casino, a stucco building stretching some 250 feet from the edge of the beach to within a few yards of the town front, provided not only the lone means of protection from the incessant threat of bullets and shells but was the obvious means by which the Canadians could best funnel men into Dieppe with the least exposure. Well aware of this threat, the Germans had started to demolish the building shortly before the raid. A rambling structure, with hallways and gambling rooms extending on each side of a large lobby and many smaller rooms on all floors, it was ideally suited to the delaying battle fought by the comparatively few men manning it, and its honeycomb of rooms and passageways was never properly cleared.

With the arrival of tanks, the remaining outer defences of the Casino were soon silenced. As Pte Tom Graham threw smoke canisters at the entrance steps, Lt Tony Hill stood up, shouted 'We'd better get out of here,' and charged at the head of his party through the doors and into the building. Next to get inside the Casino was Graham's group, under the command of Capt. Denny Whitaker, formerly a star quarterback for the Canadian Hamilton Tigers football team. Whitaker went first at a suitably athletic pace and was shot at from a long hall by a sniper who missed. Graham was next to chance his life against the sniper's accuracy and get away with it, but the man who attempted to follow him was killed as he sprinted across the hallway. Graham threw a grenade down the hall and five Germans emerged with their hands in the air.

So began the slow, grim task of winkling out the snipers, who in some cases had protected themselves by destroying the communicating stairs to their posts. L/Cpl George McDermott, regimental policeman, met a group of Hamiltons who were trying to track down a group of three snipers and joined in the hunt with relish. 'I spotted the three enemy and worked my way close enough to throw a grenade but they didn't seem afraid, for they threw one back which hit me on the right foot. I ran about 40 feet before it went off, knocking the rifle from my hand. I threw another grenade, then went ahead but they had gone, leaving a pool of blood, a rifle, three grenades, two bayonets and a large amount of ammunition.'

Other sniper hunters were more obviously successful. Pte Frank Jenner reported, 'I looked around upstairs on my own. The only two men I ran into, I shot, as they would not come out when I wanted them to.' Mounting an impressive, sweeping staircase with three other soldiers, Pte Al Oldfield ran into four Germans cautiously descending. The enemy turned tail and were pursued into 'a little cubby-hole' where they were killed. 'We also found one sniper and I threw a grenade and put him out of action,' said Oldfield. 'Then I went after him with my bayonet and killed him.'

The risky business of flushing out Germans was entrusted to Sgt George Hickson, a Royal Canadian Engineer in command of 'Hicks Party', a group of seven whose task was to blow up Dieppe's telephone exchange. 'Hicks Party' was accompanied by a covering group of 35 infantrymen but by the time they gained the shelter of the Casino only four sappers and a handful of the protection group were left. Hickson took command of the survivors and began to blow his way through the Casino by the simple expedient of moving from room to room, dynamiting the walls.

The heavy gun emplacement on the seaward side of the Casino was still firing on the tank landing craft at point-blank range, so Hickson and his party decided to silence it. The two machine-gun posts flanking it were put out of action with grenades the crews surrendering comparatively easily, but the emplacement itself was a different matter – a two-storey concrete structure which had defied the shells directed against it. The lower storey, barred by a steel door, contained the sleeping quarters of the crew and the gun itself was in the upper level. Hickson demolished the steel door with a 3 lb limpet charge, killing or stunning the gunners in the confined space of the upper chamber. While the survivors were dragged outside, Hickson destroyed the gun with a charge up the breech.

Soon, prisoners were being taken at a rapid rate. Altogether 23 were captured inside the Casino, though only three were brought back to

England on the evacuation. Sgt Barney Lowe commented, 'The prisoners I saw did not appear to be in very good physical shape and were young – about 16 to 22,' while Pte Jack Taylor noted 'They all looked terrified, especially when they saw the tanks.' Pte Tom Graham, firing his anti-tank rifle from the Casino at snipers in buildings on the Boulevard de Verdun, was startled when a German sergeant suddenly appeared in the room behind him and announced that he wished to surrender.

In accordance with the instructions contained in the 'Jubilee' battle plan, but in contravention of the Geneva Convention, the prisoners had their thumbs bound behind their backs with fish twine. Once on the beach, however, they were untied to help with the evacuation of the wounded.

Eventually, at 0712, Gen. Roberts on *Calpe* was informed that the Casino had fallen, but in capturing it the Canadians had exhausted themselves. 'The operation had been costly and had used up the centre and most of the reserve companies,' reported Col. Labatt. What the Germans themselves considered a fine opportunity to roll up the beach along the flanks from the wedge driven into the defences by the occupation of the building was lost because the Allied forces simply did not have enough men left to exploit it.

The effort poured into the attack on Dieppe provoked alarm and nervousness among the German defence planners. Von Rundstedt's GHQ West issued regular 'Appreciations of the Situation' through the day and the first of these, put out soon after the main beach landings, said 'Because there have been simultaneous landing attempts in several localities on a front of 20–25 km. and in daylight it is possible that the landing is a major effort.... Situation still unclear.'

The Germans were deeply suspicious that the Dieppe Raid was a diversionary attack as a preliminary to the launching of a Second Front elsewhere on the northern coast of France, and it was some hours before this doubt was removed. After all, the generals at GHQ West did not possess the grandstand view afforded to Capt. Richard Schnösenberg on the East headland, who said, 'The main thing people don't realise is that the outcome was decided after half an hour. It was a stupid thing to do, to land in daylight on an open beach.'

At 0625 hours, an hour after the First Appreciation, GHQ West ordered an Alarm Scale Two for the 10th Panzer Division, 60 miles away at Amiens, and three minutes later the same alarm was transmitted to the S.S. Adolf Hitler Division, which had been based in Vernon, midway between Rouen and Paris, for only a month since its return from the Russian front. The S.S. division, under its fervent Nazi commander Sepp Dietrich, was quickly prepared for the 80-mile haul to Dieppe but the 10th Panzers, for such a vaunted organisation, were pathetically unprepared. The alarm call was delayed for several minutes because the division's General Staff Officer could not be contacted, and when the commanding officer, Gen. Wolfgang Fischer, attempted to contact the 81st Corps for further instructions the telephone line was dead. Next the commander demanded maps of the Dieppe area so that he could brief his officers, only to suffer the embarrassment of being told that the division did not possess any. A dispatch rider had to be hurried 80 miles north to Lille to obtain maps detailed enough for the Panzers to work out where they were supposed to go into action.

The lack of maps was not the only area in which the Panzers were caught unprepared. Several groups of the division's soldiers had to be called back hurriedly from harvesting and other duties from as far away as eight miles and, after its mauling in Russia, the 10th Panzer Division was short of spares, operating worn-out equipment, running on bald tyres and so deprived of petrol supplies that the new drivers drafted into the division had been unable to obtain the convoy experience needed for such an emergency.

When Fischer was ordered to move out his vanguard at 0900 hours and his main force an hour later, he set off without any detailed maps. The journey to the coast was marred by overheating engines, punctures and breakdowns of tanks and trucks, and afterwards the Panzers' speed of advance was criticised by the Fifteenth Army HQ as being no better than the approximate rate of movement of a bicycle formation.

Elaborate arrangements had been made in Dieppe for the destruction of port installations and secret documents in case of attack. Explosive charges had been laid at the pumping stations, swing bridges and floodgates to the docks. Though none of these charges was set off, there were examples of nervous reaction to the raid. When the naval harbour protection group attempted to destroy their secret papers by sinking them, one of the boxes had not been properly perforated and continued to float. A hand grenade was tossed at it, and though the box was blown up and sunk, documents were left floating all over the harbour waters by the explosion and had to be fished out after the battle.

Destruction of the papers belonging to the 38th Minesweeper Flotilla was similarly bungled. When the flotilla's billet, the Grand Hotel, came under fire the naval men believed they were about to be overrun and a 54-year-old engineer named Breier, who had won an Iron Cross in U-boats in the First World War, was detailed to burn the records. So thoroughly did Brier soak the documents in petrol that when he applied a match to them he also burned down the hotel.

Von Rundstedt was highly critical about the amount of ammunition expended by his inexperienced troops: 'One troop fired 1,300 rounds of shells in half a day's fighting. There was also a shortage of ammunition for quick-firing machine-guns and one company used up all its ammunition by the end of the morning.' The most dangerous period for the defenders came between 0800 hours and 0930 when the artillery firing on to the main beach ran out of shells and fighting was carried on solely with infantry weapons. 'The enemy did not take advantage of this very unfavourable situation for us,' the Germans reported. By then, though the Germans did not know it, the Allies were preparing to abandon the Dieppe Raid.

In his Second Appreciation, issued at 0700 hours, von Rundstedt ordered a state of the 'highest alertness' for all forces in the West. Alarm about a possible Second Front continued: 'The operation has greater extent and seems aimed at taking possession of Dieppe as a bridgehead,' the Field Marshal announced, and he asked for a U-boat attack against the fleet lying off Dieppe, only to be briskly turned down by the commander of German naval forces in the West 'because of the danger from mines and enemy air superiority'. Next von Rundstedt turned to the Luftwaffe, requesting an air effort 'against everything that floats'.

The Luftwaffe was entirely unprepared for the Dieppe Raid. The earliest Allied air attacks encountered opposition only from the ground, and the first German fighter squadrons were not alerted until 0600 hours. Luftwaffe personnel in France had been allowed out on late night passes in the usual way and slept in their billets away from the airfields. Nor had any precautions been taken to have the aircraft fuelled and bombed up ready for instant take-off. The captured crew of a JU 88 bomber confirmed the surprise element. They were asleep in their quarters away from the aerodrome at Creil when the warning was first given about 0630 hours, and when transport arrived an hour and a half later to collect the airmen, the pilot was found still asleep. He had failed to hear the alarm.

The capture of the Casino and the covering fire which Bren gunners were able to give from windows on the town side of the building enabled small groups of Canadians to achieve their first penetration into Dieppe itself. Lt Tony Hill led a dozen Hamiltons along the colonnaded portico that stretched between the Casino and the Boulevard de Verdun and a final, breathless sprint took them safely into the cover of buildings bordering the boulevard. Apart from their rifles and grenades, Hill's party possessed only one Bren gun and one Sten.

After trying without success to climb over a tank barricade blocking one of the streets into the town, they broke the glass windows of a large building and found themselves in the storeroom of a cinema. Moving into the amphitheatre, Hill's group removed the steel bars sealing a side entrance and swung the door open. Cautiously they edged into Dieppe. 'The sniping was bad,' said Pte Archie Liss, the Bren gunner. 'We couldn't see the flash of the rifles and couldn't locate them.' It was a sniper who claimed the only victim among Hill's party, shooting L/Cpl Sam Harris in the back. A wireless set which was not working but which Harris had not bothered to discard cost his life, as the snipers concentrated on officers and signalling personnel. 'Before we could get the set off his back he was dead,' said Pte Donald Gayler.

As they attempted to penetrate deeper into Dieppe, the little group exchanged shots with German patrols and were saved from disaster several times, according to CSM Jack Stewart, by civilians tipping them off about the proximity of the enemy, though Pte Gayler thought 'it would have been better if they had stayed out of our way, as they were giving our own position away'. Just after one brush with a patrol, Stewart watched in astonishment as a woman carrying a basket emerged from her house, walked to a bread shop a little way down the street and made the return journey carrying a loaf.

As at Pourville, the French people's cool reaction to the battle raging around them was amazing. While Georges Guibon, his First World War helmet on his head, watched the fighting, a milk cart rolled past him with its driver grumbling that he hadn't been able to make his delivery to the public nursery because there was shooting nearby. One of the strongest German post-raid recommendations was that in future emergencies all civilian traffic in the area should be halted. 'French motor vehicles were actually going into and out of Dieppe during the battle', said a report.

Since they were being encircled by German patrols, Hill ordered his own group back to the shelter of the cinema, where they were joined by half a dozen men led by Maj. Harold Lazier, who had safely crossed the promenade. While Hill and Lazier planned to blow up the tank barrier near the cinema with the explosives Lazier's group had brought with them, Archie Liss was posted at the cinema door with his Bren gun to hold off the German advance. As the officers talked, the cinema's elderly caretaker was at work near them, sweeping under the seats and emptying ashtrays. Plans to blast a way through for the tanks had to be abandoned after Lazier's men found that their explosives packs contained no detonator charges.

Eventually, under cover of smoke grenades, the Germans rushed the cinema. Jack Stewart and Liss held them off long enough for the rest of Hill's and Lazier's parties to scramble across the promenade and back into the Casino.

One other group of about 18, led by the Casino's demolitions expert, Sgt George Hickson, managed to cross the Boulevard de Verdun under the covering fire of a Churchill tank, suffering no casualties. Once in the narrow streets of the town, however, they quickly ran into the harassing fire of snipers. Hickson, still trying to reach his main target, the telephone exchange, was a good deal more suspicious of the presence of locals in the streets than Hill's soldiers had been. 'I was very much surprised to find civilians, or at any rate people in civilian clothes, moving freely about the streets. After watching them for some time we became convinced they were giving away our position to the snipers, so we cleared the streets with Bren gun fire.'

Soon Hickson's party began to run short of ammunition so, cutting telephone cables and inflicting as much other incidental damage as they could along the way, they withdrew across the sea front to the Casino.

Lacking the shelter of the Casino, the attempts of the Essex Scottish to get off Red Beach were almost totally repulsed by the fire sweeping the front from the East headland. In the smoke and confusion, however, small groups of Canadians survived the crossing. After blowing a gap in the wall wire with a Bangalore torpedo CSM Cornelius Stapleton led a group of 15 across the promenade, and the handful who got all the way over forced an entrance into houses on the Boulevard de Verdun.

In another group Pte J. T. Fleming crossed the wall with eight others but by the time he reached the town front only one man was still on his feet with him. Gradually the assorted individuals who had got across the esplanade gathered together under Stapleton and, exchanging shots with snipers, they managed to reach the Quai du Hable, overlooking the harbour. Here Fleming was wounded in the right arm by a sniper on the East headland, and the rest of the small group were driven back by the volume of fire.

Ordered back to the beach, Fleming came across an hotel which appeared to be a German billet and contained ammunition, which he blew up with a grenade. Recrossing the promenade Fleming was again wounded, this time in the left arm.

Reception of messages by Gen. Roberts on board *Calpe* had been sporadic in the extreme because of casualties and the destruction and malfunctioning of wireless equipment. Following the brief excursion across the promenade by Stapleton and others from Red Beach, a message was received by Roberts telling him 'Essex Scottish across the beach and in houses'. This, combined with the news of the fall of the Casino, persuaded Roberts to perpetrate what the official records called 'one of the most unfortunate errors of the whole operation' and commit his floating reserve, the Fusiliers Mont-Royal, to the battle.

CHAPTER TEN
Disaster

'People felt they had been abandoned. Later on they realised they were sacrificed. We felt it in retrospect and we feel it today'.
— Al Richards, Royal Hamilton Light Infantry

The journey over from Shoreham in their small wooden landing craft had been cramped and uncomfortable for the Fusiliers Mont-Royal and, after arriving off the French coast, they had been condemned to a further spell of inactivity in the boat pool awaiting orders while the thunder of battle floated out to them from behind the pall of smoke which cloaked Dieppe.

Eventually orders were received that the Fusiliers were to land at Red Beach to exploit the breach opened by the Essex Scottish, and their commanding officer, Lt-Col. Dollard Menard, popularly known as Joe in his regiment, swept through the bobbing boats aboard a motor launch, steel helmet tilted at a rakish angle over one eye and a machine-gun dangling under his arm, to tell his troops through a loud hailer that they were about to get the action for which they had been thirsting. 'We'll show 'em what we're made of', he shouted. 'Good luck, boys.'

Menard then transferred to his landing craft and led the twenty-six frail boats towards the smoke blanketing their destination. 'It was a grand sight, this deployment of little white skiffs', according to Sgt Lucien Dumais as the Fusiliers Mont-Royal (Regimental motto: Never Turn Back) moved towards their doom.

As the landing craft broke through the offshore smokescreen and emerged into the bright sunshine for the final couple of hundred yards to touchdown, they were enveloped in the curtain of shells and bullets which had shrouded the tank landing craft earlier. Those ships had at least possessed steel plating; the Fusiliers' tiny wooden boats suffered terribly. Aboard one, the naval officer in command later counted fifty bullet holes in the White Ensign alone. Lucien Dumais described the reception they received as 'one continuous roar, unbroken even for a fraction of a second'.

Two of the small boats were wrecked by direct hits. Pte Marc Pilote was thrown into the sea from one of these crippled craft: 'I had no rifle, no nothing. I took off my boots, my tunic, the lot, and when I crawled ashore I was wearing only my trousers. All I could do was throw stones, so I just lay there and acted dead.'

'I was in charge of five boats; the other four were hit and men wounded but mine wasn't touched, how I don't know,' said Major Guy Vandelac, a company commander who is now Gentleman Usher of the Black Rod in Canada's Parliament. Lucien Dumais confessed to a feeling of self-pity mixed with vulnerability on those last few yards into the beach. 'I began to think the enemy was definitely unreasonable to be doing this to me. It was very dangerous and he might kill me.'

It was not until they emerged from the offshore smoke that the Fusiliers realised they had been carried well off course by the strong westerly set of the tide. Instead of putting in at Red Beach, they were headed for White Beach and, in the most extreme cases, straight for a narrow strip of shingle at the foot of the West headland.

As he watched the boats come ashore Lt P. Ross, the Naval Beach Officer at White Beach, thought they were the ones he had requested to evacuate the wounded, and he prepared to move the injured to the water's edge. Instead the boats disgorged more armed men and immediately pulled away. 'They did not touch down but dropped the troops off knee deep in water and made off as quickly as possible out to sea,' said Ross. 'As the craft never came within hailing distance it was not possible to detain them.'

Lt Jerry Wood also witnessed the Fusiliers' arrival: 'It burned me up to see the men jumping out with their 50 lb packs of ammunition into water up to their necks, almost as if the engines were reversed.' Pte Ray Geoffrion, a Bren gunner, was laden with a pack full of magazines for the weapon and when the naval officer aboard his landing craft yelled 'Prepare to land' Geoffrion jumped overboard. 'I sank like a stone in about 15 feet of water, but as I bobbed to the surface the boat was still going past me so I grabbed hold of it and was towed into the beach.'

Geoffrion was dragged ashore right under the guns of the West headland where he joined the unfortunate group of French Canadians who, in the words of the official report, 'were unable to accomplish anything at all, except add to the losses being suffered'. Geoffrion recalls how he staggered up the beach. 'All around I could see men falling ... I ran under the cliff and tried to fire off a few rounds but couldn't see anything to aim at. The Germans were dropping grenades down on us but they were exploding halfway down the cliff. Water was also dripping on to us and the rumour spread that it was oil and that the Germans were going to set fire to it and burn us out of our hiding place.'

Col. Menard's second-in-command, Maj. René Painchaud, disembarked from his boat just as a machine-gun neatly cut off the leg of the coxswain. 'On my right hand side, close to the cliff, I saw what looked like a company of men lying down,' said Painchaud. 'My first reaction was, why did they stay there? They should have tried to take cover at the bottom of the cliff. Then I realised they were all dead or wounded. Then I was hit by a bomb and I didn't see much of what went on after that.'

On the boat carrying Lucien Dumais's mortar section only Dumais and half a dozen others had managed to get ashore before it began to back away carrying their mortars with it, and the remainder of the soldiers aboard hurriedly began jumping into the water. In the belief that the naval officer in charge was over-anxious to get out of danger, Dumais pulled his pistol and threatened to shoot. The man appeared to duck out of sight, but in fact he had been killed by a bullet.

Maj. Guy Vandelac encountered a different problem on landing. 'All my soldiers were so shocked they couldn't move, they stayed there like they were set in jelly. We couldn't give any orders, there was too much noise, so I just waved and started running up the beach, and they followed me like sheep to the sea wall.' As he made for the wall Vandelac came across an officer from what he politically termed 'another formation' who pleaded with him, 'Don't open fire, otherwise we will all be killed.'

'We realised it was pretty hopeless the minute we saw the tanks knocked out on the beach,' said Vandelac. 'The minute you saw that you knew damn well the whole thing was *kaput*. Everything was so detailed, we couldn't *believe* it would go wrong. We were never told there was a big sea wall, we thought it was just a plain beach we were landing on.'

As the Fusiliers struggled up the beach trying to find any sort of shelter from the holocaust, the familiar horrors that had befallen the Essex Scottish and Hamiltons were re-enacted. Col. Joe Menard recalled, 'I think I had taken three steps when the first one hit me. You say a bullet or a piece of shrapnel but the word isn't right. They slam you the way a sledgehammer slams you. There's no sharp pain at first. It jars you so much you're not sure exactly where you've been hit – or what with.'

The first wound had been sustained in the right shoulder, knocking Menard over, and he confessed to 'the sort of feeling you get on the football field after being tackled from behind; stunned, surprise, frustrated. I got to my feet and brought my left hand around and felt my right shoulder. It was damp and sticky. I looked at my hand and it was covered with blood.'

He was quickly struck a second time. 'There was pain with this one because the shrapnel burned through the cheek and tore away quite a bit of flesh. I brought my left hand around again and felt my cheek. It's funny the way you instinctively try to feel where you've been hit. The cheek felt raw, as though someone had ripped a fish hook through it.'

Still trying to advance on a pillbox ahead of him, Menard was wounded a third time, on this occasion by a bullet. 'It knocked me backward on to a steel picket, seriously injuring my spine. The bullet went clean through my right arm above the wrist and smashed two bones. I barely felt it, yet under ordinary circumstances I'll bet a man would pass out if a heavy-calibre bullet smacked into his arm like that.

'My rage pulled me along to the pillbox, and I found that our men had cleaned it out.... Then shrapnel got me again, this time in my right leg above the knee. I could feel myself slipping, getting weak. I fell, tried to get up again but couldn't. My whole right side felt warm and soggy. Then the pain began to come and I started praying, harder and harder. And then I passed out.'

A signaller Pte Jean Napoleon Maurice, said 'What we went through was unbelievable. I saw a corporal trying to set up his mortar directly under the Jerries' machine-gun fire. He didn't have a chance. He got hit fast but even as he went to his knees he kept trying to get that mortar in place and open up on the cliffs. He just wasn't able.'

As he lay there, wearing only his trousers and pretending to be dead, Marc Pilote remembered, 'I wasn't frightened because I had done the training for the job, just like a boxer training for a fight. But some of the men were frightened, they were screaming. I just kept my mouth shut. If you moved you were dead. A nervy bloke would get shot.

'Oh, there were some terrible sights on that beach. One man named Marcotte was sitting up trying to drink from his water bottle. He had been shot through the jaw and it was hanging off. He was pouring the water into his mouth but it was running straight out again. Another man a short way away from me must have had one single bullet cut through his belly and all his guts came out. I did move away that time, because it would have made me sick.'

Within minutes of landing the Fusiliers had been reduced from a fighting unit to dazed groups seeking to survive. Seeing his platoon commander, Lt Pierre Loranger, lying with both legs smashed Lucien Dumais took command of what was left of Loranger's force and led them into the Casino. Few of the French-Canadians were able to achieve any positive action, but Pte Leo Filiault, the only survivor of his section, joined forces with two sappers to attack a pillbox. Lacking any tools, Filiault dug a hole for the explosives with his bare hands before the charge was detonated, wrecking the emplacement.

*

Still Roberts aboard *Calpe* was receiving piecemeal and misleading information from Red and White beaches and soon after 0800 hours the Military Force Commander believed the situation on White Beach was so satisfactory that additional forces landed there might be able to get into Dieppe, fight through to the back of the town, swing left and silence the guns of the East headland. At 0817 hours *Calpe*'s intelligence log contained the entry 'Have control of White Beach', so Roberts decided to commit his other floating reserve, the Royal Marine Commando.

The Marines, a group of 17 officers and 352 other ranks of No. 40 Commando (RM) under the command of Lt-Col. Joseph 'Tiger' Phillips, had made an early bid to carry out their original assignment of sailing into Dieppe harbour in their Chasseurs, led by the gunboat *Locust*, but were driven back. Cdr Robert 'Red' Ryder, who had won the Victoria Cross at St Nazaire five months earlier, was in charge of the attempt to get *Locust* and her accompanying vessels into the harbour and when this failed he went aboard *Calpe* to obtain further orders, returning with the news that Red and White beaches were clear of opposition.

By now the story of the Royal Regiment's failure at Puys had reached Roberts, so he ordered the Royal Marine Commando to make good this setback by 'landing on White Beach and skirting the town to the west and the south so as to attack from the south the batteries placed on the East cliff above the town'. As one French author has pointed out, 'This meant a mere walk of two and a half miles along the Rue de Sygogne, where no one had yet advanced more than 20 yards;' even the official historian of the Canadian Army termed it 'an over-optimistic plan'.

At first it was intended that the Marines landing should be supported by sending in another 18 Churchill tanks still lying offshore, and though an order to this effect was sent out, it was countermanded. For the landing, the Marines transferred from the Chasseurs which had carried them from Portsmouth into five landing craft and two larger motor launches. They formed up off Green Beach and then sailed east parallel to the coast, with the Chasseurs on either side to screen them from the shells of the shore batteries, before turning hard to starboard and heading into White Beach.

Lt Malcolm Buist, the senior naval officer in the Chasseurs, said 'It was not long before I realised that this landing was to be a sea version of the Charge of the Light Brigade. There was a barrage coming from the cliffs which showed only too well that White Beach was under a very heavy fire.... Shells started to burst all around the group of landing craft, which we endeavoured to screen by smoke. I shouted to Col. Phillips to ask what he thought about going on, but I doubt whether he heard me. Anyway, he merely waved his arms and grinned to show that he meant to land at all costs.'

What happened next was witnessed by Capt. Peter Hellings. 'Immediately the fire became intense Col. Phillips took up a prominent position sitting on top of the motor launch in order to direct the remainder of the party from this position. Thus, leading the boats and under the most intense machine-gun and mortar fire, he led his commando into the beach. As the range shortened and the smoke cleared there was no doubt in any man's mind that an attempt to reach town over that beach would mean certain death to the majority.

'In spite of all these facts my commanding officer refused to turn back until he had proved the uselessness of the adventure by his personal action. Realising now the futility of further action he stood in the stern in full view of all, placing his white string gloves on his hands and waving to the boats astern to return to the cover of the smoke. His final order undoubtedly saved the lives of a further 200 men. He went cheerfully and happily to a death which he had said the night before could not be better.'

As Phillips fell to the deck of his motor launch mortally wounded, the following vessels were able to veer away and head for the smoke curtain, though the two small landing craft which had been on either flank of the launch continued into the beach. Lt Ken Smale raced ashore from one of them: 'The scene on the beach was one of absolute horror and carnage. The whole air was full of the smell of blood and all the people who had been blown to pieces. We charged up the beach towards this tank. It was very heavy going but we were spurred on by the bullets coming towards us. I never realised I would be so keen to press my nose against a lump of steel. When some mortars fell just behind the tank we took our first casualties. I thought I had been hit in the thigh. I put my hand down and it felt sticky and wet, but the shrapnel had only broken my hip flask of rum.

'There was one unfortunate who I saw three or four times actually going along the beach. He had been shot through the temple but he was still going up and down the beach cursing the Germans in a good accent, but his eyeballs were hanging down by his nostrils. And for some unknown reason he walked through that hail of fire three or four times.'

Most of the 66 Marine Commandos killed or captured were in the two landing craft which got to White Beach, though the others did not get clear without casualties. The bravery shown by Col. Phillips, at the cost of his own life, in diverting most of his force from catastrophe marked the end of attempts to reinforce the unfortunates already stranded on Dieppe's main beach. Apart from the tanks and the limited incursions across the promenade, those ashore were incapable by that time of doing much apart from trying to stay alive, as Friedrich Wilhelm Schlie, in command of a 75 mm. gun battery on the West headland near the Castle, recalled: 'We fired 946 rounds of shell at the tanks and men. They were easy targets because there was nowhere they could go. We felt very sorry for the enemy because he had no chance. He was as a mouse going into a trap.'

Many of the men who survived on Red and White beaches stressed the accuracy of the German gunners. Maj. Guy Vandelac, huddled against the sea wall and trying to get in touch with *Calpe*, found his signalling equipment was a particular target. 'The minute you showed your finger it would get hit. They killed my radio man, his wireless set was split and I was wounded in the shoulder by shrapnel. They mortared all the antennae. They were very sharp.' As he hugged the beach Pte Alf Collingdon watched the pebbles moving: 'I thought at first that land crabs or some other creatures were moving the stones. Then I realised it was shell fragments or bullets from the cliffs.'

Maj. Brian McCool who, as Principal Military Landing Officer, was Roberts's representative on the beach came under particullarly severe fire because his group took ashore a dozen signalling sets. 'We had most of our small party blown up within three minutes of landing and whenever we collected another half-dozen the same thing happened. All the sets were knocked out and the men operating them killed. The first time I hooked up and tried to get headquarter a voice said in English, "I heard, I heard. Heil the Führer." They had our frequencies.'

Eventually McCool discovered an undamaged two-way radio in a wrecked scout car on the esplanade and in order to keep in touch with Roberts he made several highly risky trips from the beach on to the promenade: 'I would go there every 15 minutes or so, and sometimes send others. The technique was to run a few yards, fall down to give the impression you had been hit, roll around, then get up again and go.' As he pointed out in a letter to his wife in Toronto from prison camp he was frequently hit on these excursions: 'They drew claret out of me five times but nothing more than skin deep.'

As McCool's communications group huddled behind a beach groyne they were harried by a sniper operating from the harbour mole overlooking their position. 'A naval officer was on one knee by my side – he was so close we could have kissed – and trying to yell a message at me. Suddenly a hole appeared in his head. So I went up to the scout car and said, "For God's sake knock out this target on the pier." A bored voice said, "Have you ascertained there are no friendly troops in the area?" I replied "For Christ's sake, they are knocking us off." The voice said, "The matter will be treated as urgent," and in a couple of seconds they blew the whole thing up.'

Huddled under the sea wall with an undamaged radio set and what was left of his battalion headquarters, Col. Robert Labatt of the Hamiltons was the only one of the group not hit at some stage of the morning. A message from the wounded Lett aboard the battered LCT 8 had ordered Labatt to take over command of the 4th Brigade on the beach, though there was little to command. Labatt later wrote, 'It was a grim feeling to be in command of the finest brigade in the Canadian Army only to find it in a position to which there was no tactical solution. The Royal Regiment could not be reached, the Royal Hamilton Light Infantry was practically wiped out and any movement on the part of the Essex Scottish meant its destruction and the end of organised resistance ... the greatest bravery in the world (and much was cheerfully shown all day) could achieve nothing unsupported.'

Labatt paid tribute to the Germans' efficiency ('their fire plan was well laid out and beautifully co-ordinated') and noted that, in comparison to the volume of fire they produced, very few Germans were actually seen. All this changed with dramatic suddenness when CSM Lloyd Harris, who had been ordered to keep field glasses trained on the West headland for any sign of the South Saskatchewans arriving, suddenly shouted to Labatt, 'By God sir, take a look at that.'

'I focussed on a shoulder of cliff jutting out beyond the West headland', said Labatt. 'At first I thought they were civilians because of their light and multi-coloured clothing, but on closer inspection they turned out to be a large group of German officers, some in white summer tunics. From the glitter I judged that it included pretty high-priced help. These people were standing right in the open, obviously out to see the fun. Some were smoking cigars. I switched two Brens on to them. Both guns opened fire at the same time and the target was cleared in split seconds. We must have hit some of them, anyway they never came back. Their carefree holiday attitude, however, confirmed my fear that the South Saskatchewans had not been able to approach from the West.'

The gaudily-dressed group were the German war correspondents, who had been rushed to Dieppe still wearing the white jackets in which they attended the late-night dance for the *Helferinnen*, accompanied by officers and some of the air women. Before ducking for cover one of the correspondents, Ulrich Haussmann, had time to note that 'the castastrophe was approaching its end'. It appeared that way too to Lt-Col. Fred Jasperson and his hard-pressed Essex Scottish, who had by now suffered more than seventy-five per cent. casualties and were running out of ammunition: 'Mortar and shell splinters were whistling all around me, some as close as eight feet, but none got me,' said Jasperson. 'The most I suffered was periodic showers of stone on my tin hat and body which did me no harm. The experience was quite harrowing and how I was missed God only knows. The scene of it all will be imprinted on my mind for ever.'

Among those scenes at Red Beach imprinted on Jasperson's mind were Lt Douglas Green, his left foot blown off, continuing to hobble around with the stump bound up until a mortar bomb finished him off, and another Essex Scottish officer, Maj. John Willis, already badly wounded in the chest, both arms and head, being killed as he tried to pull an injured man from his company to safety.

Though few of the men pinned on the beach were able to do much in the way of offensive action, the Essex Scottish managed to set on fire a large seafront building believed by intelligence to be an ammunition depot. In fact it was a tobacco factory and 140 tons of tobacco literally went up in smoke, to the dismay of the Dieppe population.

One of those who *was* able to test his qualities of marksmanship was Lucien Dumais of the Fusiliers. Following a solarium wall on the outside of the Casino he suddenly spotted a German helmet: 'It was a soldier coming along on all fours. He saw me and tried to raise his sub machine-gun in his right hand. My Sten gun was in my right hand but automatically I drew my pistol and fired first. He collapsed and his feet beat the ground in a rapid tattoo. I kept my gun in my hand, ready to fire again, but it was not necessary; there was a small hole in his helmet and blood was running down his forehead.... It was only constant pistol practice, that single movement firing as you drew, that saved me.'

The Churchill tanks on the beach provided dubious cover, since the main fury of German fire was concentrated on them. As Dumais watched, a soldier lying behind one was crushed when the tank suddenly lurched backwards and another man in front of it was decapitated when he stood up just as its machine-gun opened fire.

The fact that one tank appeared to be doing nothing at all surprised Brig. Southam, who made his way to its side and contacted the commander. 'He informed me they were nearly blind as the waterproofing cover had not been completely blown off the front,' said Southam. 'I was able to cut away sufficient material to enable them to see and suggested they get on to the promenade.' It was not until six months later, as he sat in his POW camp writing a report of the action, that Southam confessed it had not occurred to him at the time that he might have boarded the tank, got on to the promenade and reviewed the scene for himself in comparative safety.

None of those who stayed inside their crippled tanks on the beach was wounded, though Capt. Austin Stanton remembered, 'I was looking through my periscope, which was a piece of prismatic glass about four inches wide, six inches long and an inch thick, when bingo, it was shattered. Since we had spares I put in another. This happened about three times. I didn't think too much about it at the time but about six months later I was sitting on my bed in POW camp and I broke out in a sweat because I realised I should have got it right between the eyes three times. It was only that glass that saved me.'

When he ran out of ammunition in mid-morning Stanton sensibly kept his crew in the tank. 'Nobody was getting hurt and I wouldn't let them make a run for it because people were dying like flies on the beach. We fired up the Primus stove and had some pork and beans and bread while we waited for them to come and take us prisoner.'

Though the Germans showed no mercy to those still trying to wage war against them, they immediately respected the makeshift Red Cross flag which Alf Collingdon fashioned by ripping the Cross of St George from a Royal Navy ensign and fixing it in a prominent position aboard the stranded LCT 3. No more shells were directed at the landing craft, though the occasional sniper's bullet ricocheting off the open ramp served as a warning to those inside that they should stay there.

The other beached tank landing craft, LCT 5, was also used to house the wounded. Capt. Wesley Clare, the Hamiltons' medical officer, although hit in the head himself, treated those being brought to him through the organisation and brave efforts of the chaplain John Foote, who scorned all danger to seek out injured men and carry them to safety.

LCT 5 had been set on fire earlier and eventually the blaze began to explode the ammunition lockers. 'It was very uncomfortable,' said John Foote, 'so when the the tide went out we put the wounded in the lee of the landing craft. There was a little chap from the Royal Navy helping. He didn't look to me to be over 16 or 17. He was a really wonderful lad. He looked like a little schoolboy.'

The Royal Hamilton corporal, Al Comfort, continued to treat the wounded in the open even after a mortar bomb blew him into the air, badly damaging both legs. Comfort painfully pulled off his bloodstained trousers, dressed his own wounds and then carried on helping the injured who crawled towards him, though he was again hit in the shoulder and his battledress was torn by near misses. Pte Al Oldfield reported, 'He refused to be looked after himself but insisted on having as many wounded as possible brought somewhere near so that he could attend to them.' Eventually, his first aid equipment used up, Comfort dragged himself painfully down to LCT 5, where he continued treating those in pain.

As the tide receded more and more soldiers, not all of them wounded, sought the shelter of the two beached LCTs. Lt Jerry Wood described the lee side of LCT 3 as 'a mass of men; we ran out of stretchers, bodies had to be piled to make room for the living'. Among those sheltering from German bullets were several Luftwaffe personnel, who had been brought down in the fierce air battle now going on and had parachuted into the water and swum ashore. They were wet, shaken and understandably unhappy at being shot at by their own side.

Those Canadians remaining in the open and still unhurt made the best of their plight. Cpl Robert Derube recalled, 'I just lay on the beach playing dead until it was time to re-embark, but I managed a smoke'. Pte Raymond Bellaire, pressed up against the sea wall with a group which included his brother Leo, said 'We didn't even know if we would come out alive, but one of the boys kept telling jokes and we couldn't help laughing.'

Some, however, were shattered by the experience and Lucien Dumais saw a young private from his battalion 'crying his heart out, just about uncontrollable with fear; I could hardly blame him.' By now some were thinking about surrender, but when a wounded man suggested to Lt Jack Prince of the Essex Scottish that they should give up, Pte Stan Carley recalled, 'Mr Prince said no, he was not surrendering for nobody'.

Out at sea the remaining tanks and their crews, who would never be landed now, listened grimly as comrades ashore radioed their plight. The Reuter correspondent, Alan Humphreys, aboard LCT 13, wrote, 'The Calgary men in our vessel are getting quiet and not a little dispirited. Their pals are fighting and dying within their sight and they are just waiting.... Some of them are even sprawled out on the canvas covers, quite oblivious to the constant explosions of guns on shore, guns at sea, guns in the air. As I write I can hear the ping and whistle of bullets which, from a mysterious somewhere, go close to my head. I slip my tin hat a little more forward over my right eye, hunch my shoulders and strive to keep both my notebook and pen from shaking. The doctor comes to the rescue. "Three Star Martell," he says as he hands me his flask.

'Then the tank radio gives the word everybody has been expecting for some time. Evacuate, says the radio.'

In the operations room of HMS *Fernie* the American observer, Gen. Lucian Truscott, asked the Deputy Military Force Commander, Brig. Churchill Mann, how things were going and was told, 'General, I am afraid that this operation will go down as one of the greatest failures of history.'

Aboard HMS *Calpe* the unmistakable stink of disaster was in the air. The Naval Force Commander, Capt. Hughes-Hallett, reported 'By nine o'clock it was obvious that the military situation was serious and it was becoming steadily more difficult for ships and craft to close the beaches.' Roberts was urged to order a withdrawal 'but was loath to abandon hope and reconcile himself to the failure of the operation', according to Hughes-Hallett. Then, in the words of the American correspondent Quentin Reynolds, 'Suddenly Roberts, who had gotten older during the past two hours, looked at the plans of the time schedule and said softly, "Bring them home".'

The formal order to withdraw was issued, under the codename 'Vanquish'. In order to provide enough time for the RAF to mount an effective air umbrella and to lay smoke, the time set for evacuation of the beaches was 1030 hours. At 0950 a message to this effect was coded and prepared for dispatch but, in the words of Hughes-Hallet, 'Roberts then informed me that he would prefer to wait until eleven. This was amended and dispatched.'

In the *Daily Sketch* of 20 August, Gordon Webb reported, 'I have seen the greatest daylight Allied air activity of the war. There has scarcely been a minute of the day when the sky has not been filled with British aircraft crossing the coast.... The thud of explosions from France rocked houses in British seaside towns 65 or 70 miles away. Some people reported that the din was equal to that of Dunkirk.'

Under a date-line 'South-East Coast' Reginald Foster wrote in the *Daily Herald*, 'Almost continuously since I was awakened at dawn today by a roar of aircraft so loud and long that dogs barked in alarm, squadrons of British aircraft have been crossing and recrossing the Channel in endless formation.... People on this coast have found it the most exciting day in the air since the summer of 1940.'

Massive organisation was needed to mount the biggest Allied air effort since the Battle of Britian. On that occasion the RAF pilots had been fighting over their own territory. At Dieppe they were working more than 60 miles from the English coast and in some cases over a hundred miles from their bases. One of the major handicaps was that in 1942 British fighter production was still wedded to the Spitfire, a fine defensive aircraft but one which suffered the serious defect in offensive operations of possessing a very short range; and 48 of the 67 RAF squadrons thrown into the Dieppe battle were composed of Spitfires. In some cases these aircraft were able to spend only five minutes over the landing area before being forced to head back to England to refuel.

Much of the bravery shown by the pilots in the early stages of Dieppe was wasted. From his landing craft off Blue Beach Ross Munro watched Hurricanes, acting as fighter-bombers, attacking the headlands lower their undercarriage to slow them down and afford better aim at the target. Their light bombs and cannon shells inflicted negligible damage, and easily the most effective support was provided by three squadrons of smoke-laying Boston and Blenheim planes. The Germans commented on the 'rapidly laid and efficient coverage' which had handicapped their defences, and the RAF's resources were severely strained by repeated requests for additional smoke-laying missions. 'I could quite easily have done with treble the number of smoke aircraft,' said the Air Force Commander, Air Vice-Marshal Trafford Leigh-Mallory.

Almost 500 bombs were dropped on the five heavy coastal batteries around Dieppe, without doing the slightest damage. The German guns were sited in deep, sandbagged pits against which a near miss was ineffective and too often the RAF came nowhere close to achieving even this. When a dozen Bostons bombed the Hitler Battery from a height of 8,000 feet they missed by more than a mile, and an Air Ministry report officially condemned such efforts as 'a waste of resources'.

The RAF's heaviest losses in a pointless cause were suffered by the four tactical reconnaissance squadrons flying Mustangs out of Gatwick. Their task was to patrol inland from Dieppe, well beyond the area of fighter cover, checking on possible reinforcements moving towards the port. The information obtained was scanty; the Mustangs failed to throw any light on what had happened to the Royal Regiment at Blue Beach or to spot the German troops assembling for a counter-attack on Pourville.

The four squadrons flew 72 sorties and lost ten planes, not all of them to enemy fire. The fact that the Mustangs, new American aircraft, with square wing tips, were similar to the Messerschmitt 109 caused them to be fired on by Allied warships as they flew low over *Calpe* to radio their reports, despite the fact that they were carrying a yellow band on each wing to assist recognition.

Quentin Reynolds witnessed the demise of one Mustang from HMS *Fernie*: 'An aircraft that was neither a Spitfire nor a Dornier came wobbling towards us. It looked like an Me 109. The ack-ack started to bark angrily and the approaching plane was framed now by ugly black bursts of smoke. But fortunately not one bullet found its mark, fortunately because as it wobbled closer we saw that it had RAF markings; it was an American Mustang.

'It seemed out of control and then it glided down to land on the water 20 yards from us. It hit with a great splash and the pilot, as though shot from a cannon, catapulted out of his seat into the water. A motor launch picked him up and brought him to us. He was a tall, good-looking Canadian. His motor had been put out of commission over Dieppe and instead of baling out he had decided to glide into the water as close to our destroyer as he could. "Only one thing worried me," he said as he stripped off his wet clothes. "Our own ack-ack".'

Mustangs were not the only friendly planes to suffer at the hands of jumpy naval gunners. Five RAF aircraft were shot down by their own guns and Capt. G. C. Wallach of the Royal Canadian Artillery aboard LCT 17, recalled, 'I was standing beneath the bridge when two Bostons escorted by Spitfires flew very low over us. The naval gunner opened up, followed by several machine-guns mounted on the deck, followed by five of our Oerlikon guns. I dashed up to the bridge and asked the officer why the goddam gunner was firing on our own aircraft. His answer was non-commital so I then dashed over to the gunner and asked him what he was firing at. He replied 'A Focke Wulf torpedo bomber". We were recompensed for our mistake by having the escort of Spitfires spray us liberally with machine-gun fire.'

One destroyer continued to shoot at a damaged Spitfire even after it had fired its two-star recognition signal, and when Sqn-Ldr Johnny Johnson, commanding 610 Squadron, dived to sea level to escape the persistent attentions of an FW 190 he was fired at by the British warship for which he was heading.

In view of the magnificent cover provided to the troops and shipping by the RAF, Gen. Roberts insisted after the raid, 'We *must* drive this lesson home. Not only were our own aircraft shot down but there was a tremendous waste of ammunition when everything opened fire at targets far out of range.' Capt. Hughes-Hallett also recommended that in future the noses of friendly single-engined planes should be painted a distinctive colour and that gun crews and control personnel should undergo special recognition courses.

Though they were opposed by heavy anti-aircraft fire, the early sweeps over Dieppe encountered no enemy air opposition, partly because German fighters in the Dieppe zone were prevented from taking off by early morning mist. Enemy fighter strength in the West was less than 300, half that available to the Allies, though the Germans had two clear advantages at Dieppe: shorter distances and quicker refuelling turn-round, and the superiority over the Spitfire of the FW 190, probably the best fighter flying at that stage of the war.

By 0700 hours FW 190s and Me 109s were appearing over Dieppe. One Mustang, piloted by a Canadian P/O Charlie Stover, was jumped by a bunch of FWs but made a spectacular escape by diving to ground level, despite ramming a cement pole which tore off four feet of one wing.

Another Canadian, Flt-Lt Jack Godfrey, who is now a Senator, kept a diary of what he called 'the most hectic and exciting day of my life,' flying a Spitfire over Dieppe and escorting Hurricanes in a strike against Dieppe's West headland:

'Of all the jobs that could have been assigned to us this undoubtedly was the worst.... We took off at ten o'clock and met the Hurri-bombers over the southern coast of England, and away we went with one other squadron of Spitfires with us. We flew about five feet above the waves, cruising quite slowly. About five miles off the French coast we gradually opened up so that we hit the coast going flat out to the right of the town.

'Up over the headland we went and flew inland about three miles, weaving amongst trees. Then we swung to the left. I was following Flying Officer Johnny Brookhouse, slightly to the right and about 75 yards behind. After making our turn we were in a bit of a gully with trees on either side and no trees ahead. The ground started to rise and there at the top was a big flak position. We were on it before we realised it. All hell was breaking loose. There were heavy ack-ack guns and I don't know how many machine-guns blazing away at us from point-blank range. We had come up a funnel completely exposed. The next thing I saw was the tail of Johnny's kite just blow, and the fuselage broke in two right behind the cockpit. His kite seemed to go slowly over on its nose. I didn't see it hit the ground as I was past but one of the other lads saw it and it really spread itself all over the ground. I don't suppose poor Johnny even knew he was hit before it was all over.

'As we crossed the coast on the way home we fully appreciated the reception we were getting. There was literally a shower of splashes all around us from ack-ack which followed us about three miles out to sea. Why I wasn't hit I don't know.'

German bombers were slower than the fighters to arrive on the scene because of the need to arm and fuel the unprepared squadrons, but eventually all available resources in the West were thrown against the Allied armada off Dieppe, including black-painted night bombers and a number of reserve planes used for crew training purposes. Though they suffered heavy losses these bombers (Junkers 88s, Heinkel 111s and Dornier 217s) pressed home their attacks with great determination and bravery and Capt. Hughes-Hallett commented that at one period 'the air attacks were serious and certainly far exceeded in intensity anything I saw in the Norwegian campaign'.

One Dornier squadron based at Eindhoven in Holland had only seven serviceable aircraft and four of these took off at 0900 hours to attack the Allied shipping. Three were shot down and the fourth crash-landed at Amiens and blew up just after its crew had escaped. The remaining three Dorniers did not take off until the afternoon, with orders to bomb British troops on Dieppe's beach, but on arrival they could find nothing to attack.

Another Dornier squadron based at Deelen was promised fighter protection during its bombing run and took off in pairs at 0930 hours. One captured pilot told how, on approaching Dieppe, he saw what he took to be the promised escort as he came down to 5,000 feet to single out a target. Unfortunately the planes were Spitfires and after he had managed to release only two of the four 500 kg. bombs on board his Dornier was shot down.

The wildlife expert, Peter Scott, spent the early part of the morning aboard his gunboat SGB 9 'steaming slowly along the enemy coast as bold as brass; at this moment in the bright morning sunshine we were lulled into a most curious and entirely false sense of security'. The peace was rudely shattered by the appearance of a pair of FW 190s carrying bombs. As the first one dived into the attack, Scott ordered hard a' starboard and rang up the revs to 28 knots. The bomb fell in the ship's wake close astern.

The bomb from the second FW 190 was only 20 yards short. 'There was a pause, then a heavy shock and a huge waterspout, but the ship was still afloat and still steaming.' said Scott. 'I remember thinking it must have been a very small bomb not to have damaged us more.' The second Focke Wulf, damaged by the SGB's fire, crashed into the foot of the cliffs.

Drew Middleton of Associated Press wrote vividly about an attack by Dorniers on the small vessel from which he was reporting the Dieppe Raid. 'They were flying about 6,000 feet in echelon. They looked big and very black as they whirled closer. Our little ship jumped under the recoil of her Oerlikon and machine-guns. The leading bomber swerved slightly and out of its belly tumbled four bombs. You could see them dropping ahead and to port. They landed with explosions that nearly lifted us out of the water.

'The second and third bombers dropped their loads but anti-aircraft fire drove off the fourth. The bombs missed the target but now everyone was watching the Dorniers, the first blazing from hits by anti-aircraft shells and the other two hotly pursued by three Spitfires. The first fell flaming into the sea near the shore. The other two tried desperately to avoid the fighters which hung like black crosses above them. There was a furious burst of machine-gun fire and one after another the two Dorniers turned lazily over, burst into flames and fell into the sea.'

While Middleton's craft was fixing a line to tow a disabled LCT which was three times as large as their own vessel, it was again attacked. Two bombs fell to starboard and fragments went through a tiny cabin shared by the ship's two officers. 'They gravely estimated the damage at half a pint of gin, a picture of HMS *Suffolk* and a teacup,' Middleton wrote.

There were vastly exaggerated accounts about the numbers of German aircraft shot down as several ships cheerfully claimed the same plane. Aboard the flak landing craft LCF 6 a Marine lieutenant, W. K. Rogers, told how 'three JU 88s attacked us in quick succession.

We opened up with everything. We blew the first one up – it seemed to disintegrate completely in mid-air – the second never came out of its dive and went into the sea with a roar about 50 yards from us and the third could not face it and sheered off. The crew went quite mad, dancing around, giving thumbs up and shaking each other by the hand!'

A similar story was reported from LCF 3 to Lt John Hargreaves Heap of the Royal Marines, whose craft was attacked by a pair of Me 109s. 'When the leading plane was about a thousand yards astern the starboard gun opened fire. The effect was electrical. The very first burst scored a direct hit and the plane just evaporated. One minute a plane, the next minute hundreds of small bits. The second plane was also hit but disappeared into the thick smoke before we saw it crash.... It was the first time we had ever fired against enemy planes and we had *one* certainty and *one* probable.'

As the Luftwaffe offensive grew in ferocity, requests for air cover and assistance mounted. The number of squadrons patrolling the skies over Dieppe at any one time was doubled from three to six, then increased again to nine to ward off the bomber attacks and the continual presence of up to 30 German fighters. There were desperate pleas for rocket and smoke-laying missions to subdue the fire from Dieppe's headlands, and planes were turned round at top speed at their English airfields. Under the headline WAAFS RAN A DIEPPE BUFFET the *Daily Mail* reported, 'Returning fighter pilots ate meals and drank coffee sitting in the cockpits while their planes were refuelled. The food was cooked and carried by relays of WAAFs who had been up since dawn. One girl said 'We had almost to thrust the food into the hands of the aircrews, they were so anxious to be off again.'

The American Air Force also struck against the German air effort when 24 Flying Fortresses, escorted by four squadrons of Spitfires, dropped high explosive and incendiaries on the airfield at Abbéville, the nearest operational station to Dieppe. The attack was highly successful. Wg-Cdr Kingcombe, leading one of the fighter escort wings, said 'The Americans did not waste a single bomb on the middle of the aerodrome, but buildings around the edge went up in clouds of smoke and débris.' Abbéville was put out of action for two hours and the Germans admitted three FW 190s destroyed, another one damaged and many buildings shattered.

None of the Fortresses was lost but the fighter escorts ran into opposition on the homeward run. P/O Don Morrison's Spitfire was crippled when the FW 190 he was firing at exploded no more than 25 yards in front of him. The débris from the Focke Wulf, the Candadian pilot's fourth 'kill' of the war, smothered his windscreen and hood with oil and damaged his plane.

'Suddenly my engine started to cough and the aircraft shuddered violently. I realised that I was going to have to bale out, so I started to climb. My engine then cut out completely but I had reached 2,000 feet.' Morrison then prepared to make his first parachute jump, which was not without its alarms. As he attempted to throw himself clear of his stricken plane his parachute became entangled and he was not able to free himself until he was some 250 feet above the Channel. 'My Spitfire plunged into the water below me just as my parachute opened, and somehow I got a nasty clip over my eye.' Morrison fell into the water and two Spitfires circling overhead directed an Air Sea Rescue launch to collect him after only 15 minutes. He was 17 miles off Dieppe.

Morrison's next few hours aboard the rescue boat were, in his opinion, 'more frightening than participating in the dog fight,' as the ASR launch dashed around off Dieppe collecting downed fliers. At one stage it was attacked by a pack of FW 190s. 'I have been in a few tight spots but this beat them all,' said Morrison. 'I have never felt so helpless in my life. Their bullets were spitting all around us and our radio was put out of action.... Only when they had run out of ammunition did they fly off.'

Two Air Sea Rescue launches nearby were attacked and set on fire by enemy fighters and when Morrison's boat went to collect the survivors he dived overboard to save a wounded man. 'We picked up 14 survivors, most of them very badly wounded, so we returned to port at full throttle.'

During the day the Air Sea Rescue boats answered 47 'May Day' calls, mostly close to the French coast, and though they rescued 14 pilots it was a costly effort. Three launches were lost and they suffered 15 killed and 14 missing.

Not all the Allied airmen were so fortunate as Morrison. Aboard HMS *Garth* Goronwy Rees watched an RAF fighter crash nearby, and the destroyer altered course to search for the pilot. 'The wreckage floated on the water in an inextricable tangle of wires and broken struts, the tip of a wing showing above the waves like a shark's fin. Not far away a dark round object bobbed on the waves like a football and coming up to it we saw, with a sudden feeling of sickness, that it was the pilot's head, its black hair sleek and wet as a seal's, neatly severed at the neck.'

Several Luftwaffe personnel were plucked from the water by British ships. One, collected by *Calpe* and taken before Hughes-Hallett, complained bitterly that he should not have been in such a predicament as his leave was not due to end until noon that day. Another, rescued by SGB 8, obviously had the Second Front very much on his mind and enquired, 'Are they all coming over today?' Peter Scott's SGB 9 fished out two more. One was almost drowned and was transferred to a medical launch while the other asked politely, 'Where shall we be landed, England or France?'

Scott also rescued two Allied airmen, one a Norwegian 'grinning, perfectly well and happy', and the other an American 'sitting quite comfortably in his rubber dinghy in spite of a badly broken leg and an injured arm'. On the way back to England Scott went below to talk to his German prisoner. 'He was a likeable youth who could speak no English and I found him sitting between the Norwegian pilot and his guard, who was fast asleep with his head on the German's shoulder with our black kitten on his lap. We had a short philosophical discussion on the senslessness of war to the limits of my German. He had apparently much impressed the ship's company by the way he helped with the wounded.'

The onshore winds were kinder to another Luftwaffe man, who parachuted safely on to Dieppe's East headland only 150 yards away from Capt. Richard Schnösenberg's command post. 'He walked up to me, stated his name and rank and requested to be allowed to join in the battle until he was picked up,' said Schnösenberg. 'I told him I considered it a stupid question; there was no chance of my not granting permission because there were several thousand of the enemy coming against us. He was collected two hours later and went off to fly a new machine.'

On 21 August the *Toronto Globe and Mail*'s headline trumpeted ALLIED FLIERS BAG 280 NAZI PLANES IN DIEPPE and Winston Churchill told an admiring Commons in September that 'Dieppe was an extremely satisfactory air battle which Fighter Command wish they could repeat every week.' Both statements were nonsense.

Months after Operation 'Jubilee' the Allies were still claiming German air losses of between 150 and 200 and the official Combined Operations report on Dieppe considered the air side of the action 'highly successful'. Even the RAF's official claim of 91 victories and 44 probables was wildly out. German records showed that they lost 48 planes, including those destroyed on the ground at Abbéville, and 24 damaged. Losses in personnel, taking into account men at flak batteries and radar stations, were 104 dead and 58 wounded.

In contrast German claims, as in the ground battle, were highly accurate. They announced that 112 Allied aircraft had been shot down and the RAF admitted 106 losses due to enemy action in 2,614 sorties – 88 fighters, ten reconnaissance aircraft and eight bombers or smoke-laying planes. The international nature of the Allied air effort could be gauged from the casualties. Of the 67 pilots killed, 44 were from the Royal Air Force, 11 Canadians, four Free French, two New Zealanders, two Americans, one Australian, one Pole, one Norwegian and a South African.

Fourteen other RAF planes were written off because of miscellaneous causes such as engine failure, faulty undercarriages, heavy landings and crash on take-off. One pilot ran out of fuel through misreading his gauge, another could not find his base because of a deterioration in the weather and crashed, while a third forgot the emergency apparatus for lowering his under-carriage.

The losses were the heaviest suffered by the RAF in a single day in the whole war and brought a swift end to Fighter Command's plan to draw away German strength from the Russian Front by 'trailing its coat' over northern France. The gesture in the summer of 1942 cost nearly a thousand aircraft and almost as many pilots.

The Navy's attempts to provide effective support for the troops ashore was hampered by the lack of heavy guns and smoke which obscured the target. Without this smoke the naval units would have had to retire four miles offshore to avoid being constantly shelled, instead of lying less than a mile from the beaches. But if it screened the ships from German batteries the smoke also blanketed the progress of the battle. Since radio communications were poor and most of the observation officers landed to direct the warships' fire became early casualties, there was little scope for effective naval bombardment.

Attempting to cover the withdrawal from Green Beach HMS *Brocklesby* bombarded the cliffs 'with a feeling of considerable ineffectiveness,' as her captain later recalled, 'since no point of aim was discernible'. At the same time the destroyer was shelled by a shore battery which scored several shrapnel hits.

HMS *Garth* fought a gallant but hopeless battle with the guns of the East headland. Her captain, Lt-Cdr John Scatchard, reported 'Their fire was extremely accurate and it was impossible to go in and carry out a steady bombardment. It was a matter of going in through the smoke till close, squaring off and then retiring, then circling round and repeating the manoeuvre. On each occasion we were straddled and it seems extraordinary that more ships were not hit.'

Scratchard's terse description revealed none of the drama of a destroyer sailing right in under the towering headland to take on impossible odds. Goronwy Rees, on *Garth*'s bridge as an observer, recalled 'Each time it became harder on the nerves, especially after we had been hit, but the commander imperturbably repeated the same orders; once again we emerged from our smokescreen. The petty officer on the bridge looked at me, shrugged his shoulders, raised his eyebrows and muttered under his breath, "The old bastard's going in again." It was spoken in a tone in which wonder, tolerance and admiration were all equally combined.'

By 0845 hours *Garth* had fired more than 600 shells and was forced to halt the bombardment to conserve ammunition. When Cdr Scatchard reported this to *Calpe* he was ordered to escort the LCTs which had not landed their tanks back to England. So *Garth* withdrew from the action, having suffered one shell hole in her charthouse, another in the engine room above the waterline and two splinter holes in the funnel. The shell which entered the charthouse did not explode and while it lay spinning on the deck A/S James Dobson picked it up and threw it over the side. There was a similar instance of bravery aboard HMS *Albrighton* when Stoker James Norris collected an unexploded shell in the boiler room, carried it on deck and dropped it overboard.

The smoke almost brought disaster to *Brocklesby* when the destroyer moved into White Beach during the evacuation. 'I approached as close as I considered navigationally safe in thick smoke and then turned parallel to the beach,' said her captain, Lt-Cdr Nigel Pumphrey. 'Since I could give no assistance commensurate with the risk to my ship from staying so close inshore I altered to port to open from the shore but as the ship turned her stern grounded. I continued to go ahead and she came off but hits from shells emptied the lubricating oil reserve tank and shot away the lubricating pipes, putting both engines out of action.' As *Brocklesby* drifted helplessly Lt Albert Lee saved the ship by repairing the system while under fire, and within three minutes the destroyer was under way again.

As ships of all sizes clustered round *Calpe* seeking advice and orders and offering assistance, Hughes-Hallett thought the headquarters ship resembled a fleet flagship on regatta day: 'There were seldom fewer than six to ten craft alongside; their presence was rather an embarrassment to the commanding officer when he wished to manoeuvre to avoid fire.'

One of the ships which was near *Calpe* was Peter Scott's SGB 9. 'We have plenty of 3 in. ammunition, can we help?' he signalled, and received the reply, 'Closer support is required, offer of help appreciated.' With smoke blanketing the shoreline Scott sent a further message. 'Can you give us a bearing on to which to lob shells?' but got no answer. So Scott moved alongside HMS *Berkeley* and shouted, 'What's happening?' to her captain, Lt James Yorke. 'But he shrugged his shoulders,' said Scott. 'No one knew.'

As the instruction was passed to commence the withdrawal at 1100 hours, there were two tragic misinterpretations of the order. Aboard the armoured flak landing craft LCF 1, Lt F. M. Foggitt thought the signal referred to his ship alone and at the appointed hour turned to seaward and returned to Newhaven, accompanied by a group of vessels which could have done invaluable work in taking off troops.

The more serious misunderstanding, however, involved the officer in charge of the boat pool, Cdr H. V. McClintock. After putting their troops ashore, all landing craft returned to the central pool off the main beach, where they lay protected by a smokescreen in readiness to go in again for the evacuation. When told that the withdrawal would start at 1100 and that all landing craft were to move in at that time without further orders, Cdr McClintock asked his assistant Lt-Cdr J. H. Dathan to pass this news to the western half of the landing craft while he dealt with the eastern half.

'I got about as far as abreast of the end of Dieppe breakwater when I was attacked from the air, and I rather think that we were also under fire from the shore,' McClintock reported. 'At any rate, I retired very hurriedly to seaward, followed by quite a few landing craft. The end of this attack found us rather disorganised as we had three or four serious casualties…. I had come to the conclusion myself that it was not possible to evacuate from Blue, White or Red beaches. I told such landing craft as had followed me to form up on a course for home. I then went in search of HMS *Calpe* to report what I knew to the Force Commander and to exchange information, but could not find her, so made a signal in plain language. He replied "If no further evacuation possible withdraw to four miles from shore." This message was received by me as "No further evacuation possible, withdraw." Foolishly I made no reply to this signal, so left the Force Commander in the dark as to what I was doing.

'I must admit I had some difficulty making up my mind at this time as to the exact action to take. The difficulty was caused by the fact that I could see nothing to shoreward of me owing to the smoke and did not know really where all the landing craft were. There was a group consisting largely of LCPs in company with me. These I had difficulty in communicating with, as my loud hailer was out of action, but no difficulty in keeping together because wherever I went they followed. After a certain amount of hesitation I decided the best thing was to withdraw with this group.'

Lt Jack Koyl of the Royal Canadian Navy, the senior boat officer of the troopship *Duke of Wellington*, was moving inshore with his group of empty landing craft when he came across McClintock's small fleet. 'I was ordered by the Boat Pool Officer to follow him. We turned about and proceeded seaward at full speed under cover of smokescreen.'

McClintock got back to Newhaven at 1930 hours 'very glad to be home but with a somewhat guilty feeling that the Boat Pool Officer, who had expected to be one of the last arrivals, was in fact one of the first'.

While the Allied planning and activity was being directed towards the impending withdrawal, the German High Command was still deeply suspicious that it was faced with the Second Front. Reconnaissance aircraft had spotted various concentrations of shipping in the Channel: six transports 25 miles west of Dieppe, another group of three 37 miles from the French coast (both of which were ships making their way back to England from Dieppe) and, more seriously from the German point of view, a convoy of some 26 ships, 'decks crowded with troops' according to the Luftwaffe and escorted by three destroyers near Selsey Bill. Though this was merely a routine convoy of coasters on its way from the mouth of the Thames to the Isle of Wight, von Rundstedt issued his Fourth Appreciation of the battle at 1010 hours and warned, 'The enemy undertaking may be the beginning of an attempt to establish the Second Front.' Accordingly, a full alert was issued to defences as far away as Brittany and Holland.

Even when the British convoy was later reported to be heading in the direction of Portsmouth, von Rundstedt's doubts persisted. 'To move the convoy of transports nearer the strongly-defended naval port of Portsmouth did not necessarily mean the enemy had given up his intentions.'

Second Front or not, the German C.-in-C. West ordered his troops: 'It remains our task to batter and wipe out the enemy at Dieppe with all our means in the shortest possible time.'

CHAPTER ELEVEN
Withdrawal

'We were sent into the raid, in my opinion, largely to prove to our people, the Americans and the Russians that a Second Front just wasn't on. And we proved it.'
– Forbes West, Royal Regiment of Canada.

The shape of the troubles to come in getting away from Green Beach at Pourville was apparent long before the official order to withdraw was issued. When the Naval Beachmaster, Lt-Cdr Redvers Prior, radioed a request for landing craft to evacuate those wounded in the early fighting he failed to raise a reply so this brave officer, who would be wounded four times during the morning, stood on top of a captured pillbox on the promenade at Pourville and, while being shot at, waved semaphore flags in a bid to attract the attention of ships lying offshore. At 0930 hours one landing craft moved in towards Green Beach but was driven off by machine-gun fire. Half an hour later another boat went in and spotted Prior's beach party huddled under the sea wall. One man who tried to run towards the boat was cut down instantly.

The withdrawal of the Camerons and South Saskatchewans towards Green Beach was accomplished with few casualties. The Camerons arrived back in Pourville with 80 per cent. of their force still intact and the German counter-attacking forces were content to follow the retreating Canadians warily, inflicting casualties when the opportunity arose.

The fact that Col. Merritt was away from his battalion headquarters attempting to oversee the retreat into Pourville contributed to the confusion about the timing of evacuation of Green Beach. 'I was running around trying to find out what was going on and when the order came to withdraw it was passed direct to my various companies without reference to me,' said Merritt. 'On the headland east of

Pourville my company commander, Major Claude Orme, a very determined fellow, got the message and quite properly he thought it had come from me, so he, came down. When I got back to my headquarters and realised what had happened we tried to reoccupy the high ground and cover the withdrawal, but it was too late.'

The war correspondent Wallace Reyburn wrote later of Merritt's disciplinary influence as the Saskatchewans withdrew. 'As we set off along the road to the promenade I heard Merritt's voice, "Don't run, men. Slope arms and march to the beach." I saw the man in front of me shoulder his rifle and start marching. I'd been dashing forward in a crouching position, hoping that I'd be less of a target for the snipers but automatically I raised myself erect and marched with the other men around me.'

As the Germans cautiously began to reocuppy the Canadians' abandoned positions, the retreating forces settled down to await the arrival of the boats. Because of the mix-up over timing, they would have to wait an hour, the longest hour of the day and, for many, the last hour of their lives. Reyburn found himself sheltering in 'some sort of casino' on the promenade: 'It was a classic scene for a movie. We were waiting for the boats and a Panzer division was coming the other way. Who would get there first?'

At 1104 hours four landing craft appeared through the offshore smokescreen laid by the Navy. The Saskatchewans' medical officer, Capt. Frank Hayter, who was preparing the wounded for withdrawal, watched them come in: 'As they neared the beach it almost seemed as though the water was boiling around them from the number of mortar shells which were exploding.'

All four beached safely, but because the tide was low they were separated from the sea wall by some 200 yards of stony beach and wet sand, and by now the Germans had had time to set up machine-guns and mortars firing down on to the evacuation area. It had been agreed that the wounded and the Camerons would be taken off first, with the more seriously hurt being carried by stretcher bearers and prisoners, of whom about 50 had now been taken.

'I knew it was going to be hell getting to the boats as we could see the bullets knocking up the sand and shells bursting along the beach,' said CSM George Gouk. 'Well, nothing for it but to make the attempt, and off we go. The Nazi gunners sure took a heavy toll. It was pretty hard to see the boys being knocked out after all they had done. Those left crawled and dragged a pal along with them until they got near a boat.... Our troubles weren't nearly over yet. The Germans kept sniping at men on deck and got their mark time and again.'

Lt Buck Buchanan paid tribute to the stretcher bearers who made the long and murderous journey to the boats and then came back for more: 'Many of the lads owe their lives today to the stretcher bearers' coolness and guts.' An indication of the dangers faced was the fact that only one of the German prisoners pressed into service to help with the wounded was brought back to England.

Of the four landing craft which had come in, one was so badly damaged that it never got off the beach, a second was so overloaded that it sank under fire 200 yards out and though the remaining two managed to reach destroyers offshore they were so severely battered that they were useless for further evacuation and had to be abandoned and sunk.

By now more landing craft were heading in through the smoke towards Green Beach, among them a group which had been ordered into Red Beach but had been carried to the westward by the strong set of the tide. Lt David Flory RNVR in LCA 197 reported, 'Going in through the smoke I found men swimming out to get away from the machine-gun fire. There were some corpses in the water and those that were alive had little strength left. I picked about 20 men out of the water and, amid their protestations, proceeded towards the beach. By this time one engine was not working and the steering appeared to be defective.

'I stopped the boat before a group of men who had waded some hundred yards out, four carrying a severely wounded man on a stretcher. We were now bow on to a machine-gun position and it was impossible to manoeuvre the craft owing both to the mechanical defect and the weight of men clambering over the bow and stern; many were shot in the back as we pulled them over the bow. When every man in the vicinity was on board we had great difficulty dragging the injured men away from the lowered door. I gave orders to go astern on one engine, which was a slow progress, but by this time the steering had improved and we were able to put out to sea.'

LCA 198, commanded by Lt Denis Woodward RNVR, collected survivors from the overloaded landing craft which had gone down off Green Beach. 'Steerage was difficult as there were nine stretcher cases and everyone arrived exhausted. Craft down by the bow, ramp piled with bodies, taking water forward,' Woodward reported. 'Astern movement inadvisable due to many men hanging on to propeller guards.' The skipper of LCA 187, Sub-Lt Kenneth Tew, also collected swimmers and survivors of other sunken craft: 'My boat was packed out, unable to close the ramp door, about 40 men I should think, only six fit ones among them.' One of those picked out of the water was Jack Nissenthal, the radar expert who faced death or suicide rather than capture. As he lay in the bottom of his rescue boat moving slowly towards safety he wondered whether the sea water had spoiled the cyanide pill he was carrying.

As destroyers offshore attempted to douse the fire from the cliffs overlooking Pourville, without ever knowing what they were shooting at, more landing craft gallantly went in to Green Beach to collect the South Saskatchewans. The medical officer, Capt. Frank Hayter, helped to carry a wounded man to one of them:

'As it touched the beach and let down the ramp it was very quickly filled with men. The water was quite shallow and it seemed to take about ten minutes before the boat had been pushed out far enough to clear the beach. All this was done under very heavy fire. Some men were still coming towards the craft, carrying wounded. I climbed on board, lifted one man by the shoulders as he was being passed in, stepped back a few paces with him and tripped over a steel rail on the bottom of the boat. Then another man was thrown half over the first one I had helped and I was pinned down to the bottom of the boat. I managed to get partly up when a chap standing beside me was shot through the head and also fell over me. Water was coming in the front of the boat in a fairly steady stream about two inches deep and I was rather wondering if these fellows would float before I lost my wind under water or not. However, I eventually managed to get up on my feet.

'The front of the boat was finally successfully raised, and then everything which counted as any weight at all was thrown overboard so as to lighten the boat, such as steel helmets, rifles and so on, including the man who had fallen across me, who was now dead. I had brought my pack with what remained in it with me and later on, trying to find it, discovered that it had also been thrown overboard. It contained, as well as other medical equipment, the better part of a bottle of brandy, which loss was regretted.'

Wallace Reyburn, who had three landing craft sink under him before he was taken aboard *Calpe*, said, 'It's amazing how difficult it is to kill people, really. When we were coming down to the beach there was only one exit on to it and naturally the Germans aimed everything at that. When I jumped down I landed on a pile of bodies and then ran across the beach. I remember ziz-zagging, thinking I was dodging the bullets, bloody ridiculous. I had picked up a German helmet while I was ashore and was bringing it back as a souvenir. Running down the beach I had my own tin hat on my head and the German one round my bottom, but I dropped it on the way.

'I got a wonderful feeling of relief when I reached a boat but the ramp was up, which meant she was heading out to sea. I was preparing to clamber up over the side when I heard a voice say, "She's stuck. We've got to push her off." I waded into the water and joined the men heaving and pushing. We'd get it out a few yards only to have a wave buffet it back in again.... At last we got the craft out into deeper water and could feel her gathering momentum. We grabbed hold of the rope dangling in long loops from the side and were dragged along through the water.

'As we went I noticed the young lad next to me lose his grip. He grabbed frantically at the rope again but the boat slipped away from him. He was too exhausted to swim after us and stood waist deep in the water, watching us go. I shall never forget the look on that boy's face. It was a look of utter hopelessness. He'd come so far, almost got into the boat, and now we were going off without him.

'The steel was wet and slippery and I hauled myself up on the rope, only to slither back as I found nothing to grasp on the smooth, wet deck. As I prepared to try again I heard a bullet whistle past my ear. It went right through the brain of the man next to me. He fell like a log and his tin hat clinked against mine as he went down.... He floated away, face downward in the water.'

Reyburn was eventually hauled aboard, only to find the boat was sinking, so he leapt back into the water, among dozens of wounded floating among the debris wrapped in their buoyant stretchers 'rolled up like Venetian blinds, helpless'. Reyburn swam to an empty landing craft and again went through the exhausting business of trying to climb up its sheer side. 'That was another example of how difficult it is to get killed. When I climbed over the side it was an eight or ten foot drop from the top into the bottom of the hold. I just dived and landed flat on my back on this ribbed metal and wasn't the least bit hurt.'

Soon this boat went down too, so Reyburn transferred to a third 'which got blown up by something'. Eventually he swam alongside *Calpe*: 'I climbed up a single rope, a hell of a job when you're exhausted.'

As the dazed soldiers on Green Beach swarmed into the water, the indefatigable Beachmaster, Redvers Prior, who had by then been wounded in both hands, the jaw and the left arm, noted 'Some of the troops were completely bewildered and demoralised when they came under machine-gun fire in the sea whilst embarking, holding up their hands in token of surrender. I waded out to them and ordered them to embark.' Having done that, Prior returned ashore again rather than attempt to get away himself.

Every boat which touched down was swamped by numbers and had to be pushed off by those still trying to get aboard, wounded or not. CSM Ed Dunkerley, who had been hit three times during the fighting inland, had crawled back to the beach on one leg and then dragged himself to the water's edge for the evacuation: 'The vessel was badly overloaded and we got stuck in the sand. There were about 40 or 50 of us pushing at the time, but I was only going through the act. You can't do much when you're standing on one leg. Finally a mortar shell exploding nearby freed us. It literally blew us out into the water.'

Cpl Bill Salmond, wounded in the chest, had been taken back to the beach as a stretcher case, but when a landing craft got stuck some naval officers called for volunteers 'and told us if we could move it they would do the rest for us.' So Salmond abandoned his stretcher. 'About fifty of us made a beeline for the shore to get that craft off. We managed it, well some of us managed it, some didn't get that far. We put to sea but unfortunately the boat was sunk and the next thing I remember really was climbing up the side of another boat. The bullet in my chest had been giving me a bit of trouble and I had to look to see if I could find it. Gradually I worked it out of my chest myself. I managed to get hold of it and pull it out.'

After surviving the sprint across the beach, Pte Ross Finlay leapt inside a landing craft only to find it was holed and full of water and dead men. 'I jumped back in the water and waded out to the stern. I felt I was trapped and as an act of defiance I fired three rounds at a building below the cliff and soon got returning fire. About four bullets ricocheted off the deck too close for comfort. I realised that, although I hadn't a clue where these Jerry snipers were, they sure had me taped and any more acts of defiance were just plain bloody foolish, so I crouched down behind the stern wondering what to do next when I was joined by an American Rangers sergeant.

'As far as I can recollect we just looked at each other without a word, then he said, "Let's try to get this scow afloat, it's our only chance." So we started pushing the stern to the left and then to the right to try to ease the bow off the sand but it would not budge. Whilst we were doing this, the sergeant had both his hands up near the top of the stern with his fingers above the deck and when I was looking up at them I saw the middle finger of his left hand disappear. I remember looking at his hand and wondering why it wasn't gushing blood, then I looked at him wondering why he wasn't screaming bloody murder. But he didn't seem to know what had happened. I said, "Hey Sarge, you just lost a finger." He pulled both hands down and held the left one up in front of his face and said, "Well I'll be damned. There goes another ten cents worth of hamburger." I thought, what an incredible thing to say under the circumstances.

'Then he said, "I'm going to try to make that boat out there." He stripped his rifle and threw the parts all about him and then waded in deeper and started to swim and that was the last I saw of him. I considered following him but held back as I never was a Johnny Weissmuller at the best of times. There was a hell of an explosion and I was blown off my feet and I found myself struggling underneath the water to regain my feet, which was quite an effort as I still had a bandolier of .303 ammunition in one pouch and two grenades in the other. I managed to get back on my feet to discover that the landing craft was no more.

'My shield was gone and bullets began to plop in the water about me. I lost no time in shedding my webbing and started swimming out to sea. I can still remember the tracks underwater of the bullets. I expected to get one in the back or head at any second but after five or six shots Jerry must have given up as a waste of ammunition.

'I remember nothing more until I felt something pushing me in the ribs and shouts of '*Raus, raus*'. I opened my eyes and was staring at a pair of boots, with the water lapping over my legs. I was on my stomach and as I rolled over and looked up I saw a Jerry with a rifle and fixed bayonet with the point about two inches from my chest. I was still groggy and apparently didn't respond to the command *Raus* quickly enough, so I felt the point of the bayonet just pricking my skin. I got the message and "Raussed". How I got back to the beach I'll never know. The only thing I can think of is I must have passed out and, as I still had my Mae West on it turned me over on my back and I floated about until the tide washed me up.'

Others, like Lt-Cdr Prior, made their way to shore of their own choice. As Col. Merritt said, 'I didn't think it was my place to leave until all the others had got away, and all my compamy commanders felt the same way about it.' As if Merritt had not done enough to earn the Victoria Cross, Capt. John Runcie reported another act of gallantry by the Saskatchewans' commanding officer: 'He crossed the beach under heavy fire and carried to shelter under the wall a wounded soldier lying at the water's edge. It wasn't human, what he did.' Of this act, Merritt recalled, 'I saw a poor fellow shot in the water. I didn't want to leave cover but I couldn't stand watching so I went out to try and bring him in, and then I got hit in the left shoulder by a sniper. I went everywhere during the battle but never got a scratch until that last half-hour.'

There was no greater example of bravery on Green Beach, however, than that performed by a German sergeant, Friedrich Waltenheimer, one of the reserves brought up by truck for the counter-attack on Pourville. Shooting had ceased when Waltenheimer saw three Canadians clinging to the keel of an overturned landing craft about 500 yards offshore and shouting for help. 'I don't speak English, but I understood that much,' he said.

Stripping off his uniform and helmet Waltenheimer, who held several life saving certificates and in 1936 had saved a regimental comrade who fell into the Danube, sprinted down to the beach, picking up two red lifebelts from a French fishing boat along the way, and swam out to the stranded Canadians. 'The shooting on shore was over but there was still a lot of air activity, so I kept my head down as I swam because it is better to be shot in the behind than in the head.'

When he reached the upturned boat he saw that two of the soldiers were not wounded, so he passed them the lifebelts, told them to make for shore and pushed them overboard. 'But the third man was badly wounded and in need of assistance, so I swam back to the beach and with the help of two of my group, Prögel and Christensen, picked up a badly-holed rowing boat which we plugged with field dressings and articles of clothing. I found one paddle, got Prögel to help me carry the boat to the water and paddled out to the landing craft. When I got there the boat had filled with water, so I tipped it over to clear it, lifted the wounded man inside and swam back, pushing the boat ahead of me. We were strafed by a Spitfire and I was slightly wounded when shrapnel hit the boat and a splinter struck me in the backside. By the time I got back to the beach I was completely exhausted, and Prögel had to pull the boat ashore.'

Thirty-seven years after the incident Waltenheimer was still insisting that what he did was not bravery but 'a normal act of humanity', adding 'I don't want a halo, I only did my duty'. And 37 years afterwards, he was still trying to trace those three Canadians whose lives he saved.

Though many of the rearguard on Green Beach were still expecting to be evacuated, Capt. John Runcie held out no such hopes: 'It would have been suicidal for the boats to have attempted to come in again.'

The Saskatchewans' adjutant, Lt Buck Buchanan, was one of the last to get away. 'No words of mine can describe the sheer display of courage that dominated that half hour of hell.... But at last the ordeal was over and as the last craft left the shore we saw the fellows who had to stay behind waving us on and still keeping the Jerries away from the sea wall.'

So ended the evacuation of Green Beach. Though, as the official report pointed out, 'In spite of the extremely difficult conditions a very considerable number of men were successfully withdrawn,' the casualty figures were still high.

The Camerons embarked a total of 503 officers and other ranks, of whom 268 got back to England, 103 of them suffering from wounds. Sixty Camerons were killed and a further 16 died in captivity or in English hospitals, while 167 became prisoners of war. Only eight of the 32 Cameron officers who set out for France returned unwounded.

The South Saskatchewans took to Dieppe 523 officers and men, of whom 84 were killed or died subsequently; 89 were captured and of the 353 who got back to England 167 were wounded. Only six of the 25 officers who set out got back unhurt.

Of the two battalions' combined embarkation strength of 1,026, the killed, captured and wounded totalled 685, or more than 65 per cent.

The official plan of withdrawal for Operation 'Jubilee' called for the tanks and most of the troops to be re-embarked directly from the beaches in front of Dieppe. When he read the plan the tank adjutant, Austin Stanton felt 'the only thing they had forgotten to mention was that tea and cakes would be served on the beach'.

The orders stressed 'large deviations from this plan must be expected'. So it proved.

At 1045 hours as the first of the rescue craft began the run-in to the main beach, covered by warships churning out smoke with the benefit of an onshore breeze, HMS *Fernie* received the gloomy message from the shore 'Enemy along headlands waiting for Vanquish'. Precisely at 1100 hours, as requested, three smoke-carrying Boston aircraft roared low over Dieppe. 'They were flying at 200 feet along the water's edge,' said Col. Robert Labatt. 'They laid the most perfect smokescreen I have ever seen, from one end of the beach to the other.... Under cover of the smoke which drifted slowly inland small groups began to climb through the wire and move towards the water. The first and largest was a crowd of German prisoners, carrying our wounded from the Casino, some using doors as makeshift stretchers.'

As four landing craft approached White Beach, Bren gunners still holding the Casino were able to provide some measure of covering fire, but the intention first to evacuate the wounded sheltering in the lee of the stranded LCTs was forgotten as the small boats were overwhelmed by hundreds of troops desperate to get away. Lt Jerry Wood was appalled by what he saw, terming it 'worse than moving pictures of mob flight; in my rage I yelled, "Come back, you bastards," but I should have saved my breath'.

The RNVR lieutenant Peter Ross, who had worked so diligently to prepare for the evacuation of the wounded, had managed to load some injured men before the landing craft were deluged by the rush. As Ross plunged into the water and urged the boats to back away, the officer in charge of one of the vessels, Lt Alasdair Forbes, was forced to beat away would-be boarders with a boathook. 'Trying to make any of the men disembark was a waste of time, said Lucien Dumais. 'The one thing they wanted was to escape from the hellish fire.'

Under cover of the smoke three of the boats managed to get clear, each laden to the point of sinking with about 70 men, double the normal complement, but the fourth capsized after being struck by a shell. The bravery of the sailors manning these evacuation vessels was praised by Sapper Bill Lynch: 'Great guys, these naval fellows. All that was left of one of them, as he was steering his boat out, was the stumps of his legs standing up in his boots. A shell had cut him clean in two.'

Eight landing craft were in the first wave which attempted to take off the Essex Scottish from Red Beach. Lacking even the meagre protection afforded by the guns inside the Casino, six of these were destroyed as the smoke thinned. Other vessels ordered into Red Beach went in by mistake two miles west at Green Beach where, as already noted, they did useful work, though this was of dubious consolation to the Essex Scottish, who brought back to England fewer men than any other major unit engaged because of the shortage of available boats. So fierce was the demand for space that, after being dragged aboard a boat pulling off Red Beach, the badly-injured and unconscious Pte James Maier was thrown overboard by someone who thought he was dead. The immersion helped to revive Maier, however, and he was pulled to safety on another craft.

Col. Joe Menard of the Fusiliers Mont-Royal, the only commanding officer who landed and got back to England, was also carried aboard a rescue boat unconscious: 'When I came round planes were trying to machine-gun us.... I was lying on a case of explosives. One bullet would blow the works sky high but by then I didn't give a damn. I thought, what the hell, if they haven't got me by this time they're never going to get me.

'I lay there and watched our Spitfires drive the Nazis away as though I were watching a movie. We got into the clear and a Royal Navy man came along and gave me a swig of rum. Then he came running back. "Pardon me sir, but have you got a stomach wound?" I shook my head. "That's good, sir," he said, "because if you had I shouldn't have given you that rum." That struck me as the funniest thing I'd ever heard. I began laughing and the only thing that stopped me was the pain burning my side.'

Capt. Donald MacRae contrived his own means of escape from Red Beach when he came across a small abandoned rowing boat by the water's edge. Loading it with wounded, MacRae swam out to sea pushing the boat ahead of him for two miles until he and the men he had saved were picked up. Another miraculous escape from Red Beach was that of Pte Roy Jardine. With eight other men he pushed off in a small boat with one oar. Hardly had they got under way before a sniper hit him in the shoulder, then the boat was upset by shellfire and the survivors had to swim for it. Picked up, Jardine was hit again, knocked overboard, rescued once more and managed to get back to England. He had been wounded eleven times.

As the smoke cover thinned, subsequent waves of landing craft suffered more heavily. 'Machine-guns on the cliffs wrought fearful execution,' said Jerry Wood. 'Some of the boats pushed off, all hopelessly overloaded. Then the mortars and field guns got to work, first bracketing the boats, then dropping stuff right inside. It was frightful murder. Murder on our part, not the Germans,' for getting ourselves into such a situation. The sea was full of men and bodies.'

Gordon Ryall, the nineteen-year-old naval telegraphist attached to the Hamiltons, had two landing craft sunk beneath him before coming to the conclusion 'the Germans were determined we weren't going to get away', and swimming back to shore, while Lt Ken Smale of the Marine Commando decided to take his chance in the sea from the start rather than join the hundreds scrambling to get into the rescue boats. 'I tied my footwear around my neck, blew up my lifejacket and paddled into the sea trying hard to look like a corpse. It took me about an hour to get into the smokescreen, then I shouted "help" as hard as I could, and this boat loomed out of the smoke. To my utter surprise it was German and they hauled me out of the water rather unceremoniously on the end of a boathook.'

The boat carrying Pte A. Hutchings of the Royal Canadian Army Service Corps had only gone a hundred yards before it sank. 'Well, it was pretty cold in the water,' Hutchings reported on his return to England. 'I swam around a bit until a British warship picked me up.... It was hell on earth while it lasted. Boy, I couldn't hear a thing, I was deaf for three hours. I can't believe I am here yet. I know what it is like now to see dead men all around me. But I would go again.'

Lucien Dumais was on his way from the Casino to the water's edge when he came across a badly wounded corporal from his battalion who could not walk. 'He begged me not to leave him there. As he was a heavy man I couldn't carry him and got two prisoners to take him down to the beach. When we got to the water's edge I got a third prisoner to help and we put him on a piece of rubber dinghy and started pushing him towards a landing craft about fifty yards away. As the prisoners were about to get him on board through the ramp door I went around it to try and climb in by a rope. As I got hold of the rope the boat started backing away.

'Having my full pack on my back and it being full of water I could not pull myself aboard and had to let go. The water was about eight feet deep, my Mae West was only half-inflated and I sank to the bottom. The only equipment I could take off was my steel helmet. I kicked to the top and got a breath of fresh air, went down to the bottom again and thought I was going to drown there, as I couldn't release my equipment, or float, or swim. I was unconscious and swallowed a lot of sea water before I revived a bit and paddled under water, trying to make for shore. The current from landing craft on both sides pushed me towards the shore and I finally got my head out of the water. I was exhausted. As I slowly came out of the water a machine-gun started firing at me. I was too exhausted to care.'

Probably the most dramatic account of a frustrated bid to get away from Dieppe was provided by Col. Labatt. After supervising the destruction of his radio set, Labatt set off down the beach with his adjutant Herb Poag and Maj. Dick McLaren. 'After the smoke had come down and while it was thick, enemy firing faded to almost nothing. As the air cleared, however, fire became very much brisker and so did the movement of McLaren Poag and myself.

'All the boats within our limited range of visibility were loaded and starting to turn, so we moved to the east to see how things were going there. Here the groups who had run across the beach were wading out to the LCAs waiting offshore. We did likewise and clambered into the last and most easterly boat. We were no sooner aboard than the smoke cleared completely, leaving us exposed right under the German guns. The clearing smoke caught most of the LCAs either backing away or in the act of turning. Every German weapon turned on them and all hell let loose. What we had experienced before was nothing to the furious hurricane of fire. In no time the sea was littered with the wreckage of shattered boats and dotted with heads and waving arms. A shell burst inside the crowded boat next to us with ghastly results.

'I could feel our craft being hit but was not conscious of anything amiss until I saw the naval crew jump overboard and found I was standing in water up to my knees. I told the men to inflate their Mae Wests and either to swim out to meet incoming boats or to get ashore and wait for them there. I decided to swim out to an LCT half a mile offshore. I asked Poag if he would care to try for it with me. "No sir, I still don't like water and I'm going ashore if it's OK by you," and off he went.

'By the time I had stripped down to my shirt the boat was practically empty and was floating half-submerged with no indication of sinking further. The engines, of course, had been drowned in the first few minutes and the tide had borne it inshore towards the east. It was in about six feet of water. Just before jumping overboard a voice called out, "Well goodbye, Bob". It was Dick McLaren holding out his left hand. He told me he had just been hit in the right arm and figured his number was up. I examined the wound and found it was nasty but not serious. I assured him that the boat would not sink and that his best chance was to sit tight right where he was. Several others also remained in the boat.

'I went overboard and struck out for the LCT. Hundreds of men were swimming around, some out, others towards shore. I tried to keep clear of groups as they presented tempting targets and the sea about them was lashed into foam by machine-guns, mortars and artillery. As I neared the LCT I realised that it was being shelled and when about 200 yards from it, it received two direct hits in the engine room and began to settle by the stern. I couldn't believe my eyes. I was sure it was an optical illusion and kept on swimming. However, when there was nothing left to be seen but the bows sticking vertically out of the water, I realised that she wasn't in very good shape. Neither was I. I had no idea how long I had been in the water, but I knew that I was tired and very cold.

'As the only other craft in sight was miles away on the horizon I turned reluctantly back towards the shore. The return trip was very trying. The tide had taken me over a bit and I landed behind an LCT stranded broadside. The fire had increased if anything and I was horrified by the number of dead washing up on the beach. Sheltering behind and lying around the LCT were 150–200 men of all units, nearly all wounded. They were in shocking condition and were being constantly sniped, machine-gunned and mortared.

'The beach was hell on bare feet so I clothed myself in some poor dead chap's socks, boots and overalls and an ex-naval rating's duffle coat.'

Brig. Southam met Labatt by the stranded LCT and thought he looked 'pooped'. 'A few minutes later Labatt's adjutant, Capt. Poag, swam into the beach,' Southam said. 'I gave him a hand up from the water and as he stepped away he received several bullets in the stomach from a burst of machine-gun fire.' Poag was given morphine but died soon afterwards.

Lt Tony Hill, who had led the small party of Hamiltons into Dieppe itself, also stumbled ashore, in his case safely. After helping to push off a landing craft that had become stuck he clung to the side for some time but could not manage to clamber aboard and had to let go. By dint of desperate methods others were able to get away. When water poured through the open ramp of his rescue boat, Capt. Denny Whitaker organised a chain of men baling, using steel helmets as scoops, and kept the boat afloat long enough to reach a motor vessel cruising offshore. Pte Frank Farr recalled that in his boat, 'we had to throw out German prisoners, blankets, rifles, and other stuff: the doors couldn't be closed properly and there were only about two inches to go before sinking when we reached an LCT'.

On another LCT which was so crowded the ramp could not be raised properly, Sgt George Hickson, the demolitions hero of the Casino, set those aboard to baling with their helmets and tried to raise their spirits by getting them to sing. 'But this proved difficult,' he admitted, and when he found himself singing alone and decided that this sounded 'rather foolish' he desisted.

A record for endurance and one to match the long-distance swim of the Commando captain, John Smale, was the experience of Pte Al Richards, an English-born Canadian who was a mortar man with the Hamiltons. Richards had been hit in the left shin on landing, and he was wounded three more times, twice in the left thigh and once in the right calf, as he made for a landing craft. 'I stumbled but kept on running. That's the worst feeling anybody can have, to turn your back on all that and run. It was worse than going in. The smokescreen was down but they were just firing blindly into it and I got about halfway to the water before I got hit. I ran right up off the beach, up the ramp and into a landing craft that was beached. I didn't feel any pain from my wounds, I guess I was too keyed up to feel anything.

'We pulled out to sea, happy that we were going home, but the bloody thing had been riddled with shrapnel and it sank about a mile out. Before I swam away I took off everything but my undervest, trousers, tin hat and one sock. It was just a matter of minutes before I made my way to another landing craft. I hung on to the back for a while until I got hauled in. What a feeling of relief to get off that bloody beach. I was looking forward to a good bath, a good day's sleep and a shot in the backside to take the pain away, because by this time pain was starting to creep in. But it wasn't long before we could see this one was going down, too. I was watching the water come up to my knees and I turned round and looked down the boat, it was like a big bathtub full of bodies, floating around.

'I remember making sure some of the wounded had their life jackets on but in a sense it was every man for himself. I was always a good swimmer, never afraid of the water, and my instinct for survival came naturally, so I struck out for the French coast about 14 miles away. In a narrower part of the Channel I could have swum the other way towards England, but I couldn't see the English shore. All I could see was the smudge line of France and that's where I headed, towards the smoke.

'My legs being what they were, I just used my arms. I looked around for a while there and it was rather funny, it made me smile despite everything. All I could see were steel helmets, like turtles on the water, with little eyes peeping out. Once I left the second boat I had my objective in mind and in order to reach it I probably did every stroke in the book. Once a destroyer passed by me a couple of hundred yards away, but there was no way I could get to it, I didn't have the speed.

'It was late evening, getting dark, when I got back to the beach. I don't remember much about it, just that there were people around me, talking. They got my arms around their shoulders and dragged me up the beach. I didn't care whether I was in France or England, all I wanted to do was sleep.'

As a result of the inability to move his legs during the seven hours he was in the water, gangrene set in and Richards eventually had to have both limbs amputated, the first thirteen years after Dieppe and the second in 1962.

As the morning wore on the tone of the messages being passed back to *Calpe* by Major Gordon Rolfe's lone signalling set grew more and more desperate. At 1132 hours: 'Want lots of support … much smoke and air support.' At 1135: 'Can we rush things? Things are getting heavy.' At 1140: 'Small boats have been hit and sinking. Do not consider it possible to evacuate unless you get everything available in here.' At 1154: 'High ground to east and west of beaches *must* be bombed or shelled.' And at noon: 'Support now arriving must be continuous or boats will not get away.'

As morning moved into afternoon those who had somehow survived up to seven hours on the beach at Dieppe huddled in the lee of stranded ships, tanks and anything that would provide shelter from the incessant gunfire. Sapper Bill Lynch, behind an LCT, recalled, 'We were six or eight deep there, hunched against its side. The sea was full of bodies drifting in with the tide. They jammed around my legs. I remember one big fellow; he was face down, the seat of his pants blown off, bobbing up and down there.

'Right behind us many boys were still swimming, the survivors from that awful slaughter in the water. One big fellow made the shallows, started to run as best he could through them, stopped in his tracks, dropped dead as a doornail. I just saw a faint movement of his lips. I've been shooting rabbits and game since I was a small boy. I knew death, and he'd got it very quick.'

Col. Labatt began to supervise the moving of the wounded away from the advancing tide. 'The injuries were appalling and many could neither be shifted nor properly tended, yet I never heard any complaining, and if one cried out or groaned he tried to apologise for it afterwards.' Labatt saw Edwin Bennett, the tank officer temporarily blinded by the facial burns he had suffered, being led by his crew to the shelter of the beached LCT. 'He must have been in agony but his spirit was magnificent,' Labatt said. 'I heard him say, "Remember boys, if it comes, give only your name, rank and number." Despite the pain he must have been suffering, Bennett was able to write later, 'I was fortunate because I could stand but before I was taken prisoner I was in water over my knees and there was a body washing at the back of my legs.'

Southam warned that priority aboard any further rescue boats must be given to the wounded. 'I added that disobedience would be settled if necessary by pistols in the hands of officers.' Southam felt there was no sign of fear or panic among the unwounded 'but they seemed to be stunned and almost incapable of action, and in some cases, conversation'. The same apathy was noted by Jerry Wood when he called for volunteers to go out and bring in some wounded. 'Nobody moved. I was shaken by this lack of response.'

Survivors of the shattered landing craft were still making their way ashore and Wood watched two men drag a limp figure out of the water. 'One of the rescuers was a Jerry. That showed how ridiculous it all is. Wars are a peoples' muddle. "This is just a needless slaughter," said someone sitting by the boat. It didn't make much sense.'

As the inevitable end approached, the work of tending the wounded went on. Capt. George Skerrett of the Hamiltons, who had taken off his trousers and battledress tunic to use as emergency tourniquets, worked ceaselessly in and out of the water in his underwear and socks directing the loading of wounded into evacuation boats, ordering those trying to get away, 'Every man carry a man.'

The citation for chaplain John Foote's Victoria Cross in the *London Gazette* said, 'The calmness of this heroic officer as he walked about collecting the wounded on the fire-swept beach will never be forgotten', and Cpl 'Buff' McNab said of Foote, 'He was a wonderful and brave man, never letting up for a minute to do things that would help others.'

Foote disdained several opportunities to get away. 'By the time I got one wounded soldier slung aboard a boat I was on the deck myself, so the fellow said to me, "Come on," but I said, "No, there are lots of chaplains back in England." I didn't intend to go home because the action wasn't over, my work wasn't done.'

As far as the German C.-in-C. West, von Rundstedt, was concerned, the action was as good as over. At 1215 hours he announced, 'The enemy is withdrawing. It is up to us now – and I am pressing this point – to wipe out as many of the enemy as possible. Drive forward at once! Every available gun barrel must now contribute to the complete destruction of the enemy and the entire front on which he has landed must be cleared in the shortest time.'

One attempt at surrender, when a soldier ran from behind one of the beached LCTs waving a white flag, was brought to a summary halt. 'He was shot, whether by our own people or the enemy I do not know, probably by both for he had no orders to do it,' said Labatt.

By then, however, one group of Canadians on the main beach had already given up. The Fusiliers Mont-Royal trapped under the West headland were gradually enfiladed by Germans who reached the beach by a track down the cliffside. Lt Auguste Masson was still attempting to organise an attack across the sea wall when Capt. Sarto Marchand and a group of French Canadians appeared behind him, followed by a German officer and soldiers carrying sub machine-guns. Marchand told Masson that futher resistance was impossible, so he also surrendered.

*

As those plucked from the Dieppe beach were transferred to the larger ships waiting offshore, these quickly became overcrowded with wounded, dying and exhausted men. More than 300 were taken aboard *Calpe* alone. 'We put them on the mess deck until it was full,' said a crew man, Arthur Brough. 'Then we had no choice but to put them on the upper deck completely exposed. The point came where we had to put bodies on top of others in order to make room to take still more wounded on board.'

Goronwy Rees watched the soldiers being brought aboard *Garth*: 'They looked as if they had learned some terrible lesson.... Many were badly wounded, all were suffering from shock and exhaustion. They had the grey, lifeless faces of men whose vitality had been drained out of them; each of them could have modelled a death mask.'

The ships waiting offshore for the last evacuees to be brought off were by now under constant air attack. 'I wasn't scared in the least when I was ashore because there was something to do all the time,' Wallace Reyburn maintained, 'but when I was on *Calpe* hanging around in front of the beach then I was scared. There we were, jammed in the innards of the ship and any minute she might be blown up.

'I was sitting in the middle of the wardroom and could hear her anti-aircraft guns opening up on the port side, say, and then hear the swoop of the plane followed by the starboard guns opening fire at it. I knew it was stupid, but each time I involuntarily turned my back towards the side of the ship at which they were coming and then quickly reversed my position when they passed over to the other side.

'The stewards were doing the rounds of everyone, giving them brandy, whisky or anything else they wanted to drink. I reached for a sodden roll of notes in my uniform to pay for my drink but with a grin the steward said, 'I don't think the Navy will expect you to pay for this one chum'.

'All of a sudden water started cascading into the wardroom and I thought "Oh shit, we're for it," but it was only the sprinkler system that had been damaged by a near miss.'

It was in these final moments of the evacuation that the Navy suffered its only serious loss of the operation when the destroyer *Berkeley* was sunk. Three Dornier 217s moved in to attack *Berkeley* and though they were quickly engaged by RAF fighters one of them pressed home its run and dropped four bombs. The first two were near misses but the other two struck the ship just forward of the bridge on the starboard side, breaking her back.

'She reared like a bucking horse', recalled Peter Scott, who was watching from his steam gunboat. 'The bridge went up and the fo'csle went down as if there were a hinge. Then for a few moments, as the ship subsided again into the water, the half-detached fo'csle waggled up and down.'

Berkeley had been going hard to port at full speed when she was hit and with the steering smashed she continued to sail at high speed in a circle, heeling over so steeply that some of the crew were thrown off her decks. 'At first it appeared the ship would capsize but when the engines stopped she settled a little,' said her captain, Lt James Yorke. Lt Leslie England of the South Saskatchewans, one of the casualties aboard *Berkeley*, had been unconscious at the time of the attack and came round to see water pouring through a gaping hole at the waterline near him. Abandoning his stretcher, England climbed out through the hole and was quickly picked up.

The prompt action of nearby naval craft in collecting men from the deck of the destroyer and salvaging others from the water meant that only 15 of the crew were lost. Lt Yorke and most of his men were transferred to SGB No. 8 without even getting their feet wet.

Lt-Col. Loren B. Hillsinger, the American Air Force observer aboard *Berkeley*, was one of the more seriously wounded, losing a foot. At the time he was wearing a pair of a new hand-made boots of which he was very proud and after applying a rough tourniquet to the stump with his tie and handkerchief, he took off his other boot and threw it after the first, which he could see floating on the water with his severed foot inside it. After being taken aboard the SGB, Hillsinger refused treatment until other wounded had been cared for, and remained on deck to act as aircraft lookout. Hillsinger was awarded the Distinguished Service Cross for 'extraordinary heroism' and also won his own country's Purple Heart.

After being abandoned *Berkeley* continued to float, although down by the bow and listing to starboard, until HMS *Albrighton* was ordered to sink her sister ship with torpedoes. The first one struck under the bridge and blew off the bows, which sank immediately, but the rest of the destroyer continued to float until a second torpedo struck the magazine. 'A huge reddish-purple burst of smoke and flame belched out of the wreck and went up into the calm sky in a tall column with a mushroom of dense blackness at its top – an extraordinary and unforgettable sight,' according to Peter Scott. 'For a few seconds part of the ship floated so that we imagined she was resting on the bottom, then she disappeared altogether.'

On Red and White beaches the end was rapidly approaching. Maj. Rolfe's radio pleaded at 1301 hours: 'Bombard buildings and pillboxes along promenade. Enemy closing in.' And at 1304: Give us quick support. Enemy closing in on beach. Hurry it up please.'

Orders were passed among the tank crews to destroy their Churchills with bombs brought with them for the purpose. Each tank carried a pair of these bombs, glass balls filled with nitroglycerine and covered by a tin sheath. 'They'd blow a hole through anything,' said Maj. Allan Glenn. Trooper Dick Clark's tank was destroyed as instructed: 'We all baled out and blew it up, but when we went to the water's edge the dead were just lying everywhere and there were no boats so we just lay on the beach, right in the open. We were all captured.'

Destruction of the tanks was hampered in some cases by the fact that soldiers were using them for shelter. There were other reasons. The adjutant Austin Stanton said, 'I left my bombs behind in England, I was afraid they would kill my crew on the way over.' Allan Glenn considered the bombs 'a real stupid idea, one for the birds'. He disposed of his on the Channel crossing. 'I got a sandbag and three lumps of metal and some wire, went down into the tank and brought up these sticky bombs. Then I wrapped them up with our operational orders and lowered them all over the side, very carefully, until they touched the water and let go.'

Just before 1300 hours, although they were unaware of it because of the smoke, HMS *Calpe* and two accompanying landing craft were the only ships remaining close inshore. Roberts, determined not to leave while any hope remained of getting more men away, persuaded Hughes-Hallett to go in for a final reconnaissance. 'Keeping a landing craft on either bow I steered for the eastern end of Red Beach, at the same time opening fire from the foremost guns,' said Hughes-Hallett. Although in severe danger of going aground *Calpe* closed right in on the beach and came in for the exclusive attention of German gunners. 'No sign of troops or landing craft other than derelicts could be seen,' reported the Naval Force Commander, though as *Calpe* turned away Cpl Tom Gorman, aboard an LCT at sea, picked up a message from Rolfe's set 'saying they were making a dash for it'. Soon after a further message came over 'in a voice that was practically hysterical' according to Gorman, shouting, 'We are surrendering to the enemy, a mass surrender on Red Beach.'

Bitterly disappointed, Roberts dispatched a message to England, 'Very heavy casualties in men and ships. Did everything possible to get men off but in order to get any home had to come to sad decision to abandon remainder. This was joint decision by Force Commanders. Obviously operation completely lacked surprise.'

The surrender on the main beach came at 1308 hours just as the 10th Panzer Division lumbered into position on the outskirts of Dieppe. Twenty minutes later the Germans officially conceded that danger had passed: the town garrison's butcher company was given permission to stand down from its defence positions and go back to making sausages for supper.

The Royal Hamilton Light Infantry sent 582 officers and men to White Beach, of whom 197 were killed or died subsequently. Another 175 became prisoners and of those who managed to get back to England 108, almost exactly half, were wounded. Capt. Denny Whitaker, the football star from Hamilton Tigers, was the only officer to return unhurt. When he went home on leave to Canada that winter, Whitaker slipped in the snow and broke his ankle.

The hopelessness of the Essex Scottish position on Red Beach was graphically illustrated by the battalion's casualty figures. Of the 553 who embarked, only 52, fewer than ten per cent., returned and two of these subsequently died in hospital. The Essex Scottish lost 121 killed or died of wounds, while 382 were captured on the beach at Dieppe.

The Fusiliers Mont-Royal were not far behind the Essex Scottish in the total of men made prisoner, losing 354 of their embarkation strength of 584 to the prison camps. Ten of these soldiers died in captivity and a further 105 were killed at Dieppe. Col. Joe Menard brought home to England with him 120 soldiers (four of whom later died of wounds) and four of the 31 officers with whom he had set out.

The brief, doomed foray by the Royal Marine Commando cost them 66 killed or captured and 31 wounded, and the grim count at Red and White beaches was pushed even higher by the severe losses among engineers, sappers, signallers and naval personnel.

CHAPTER TWELVE
Surrender

'Like the German nightmare is Stalingrad, the Canadian nightmare is Dieppe. They should try to come to terms with it.'
— Richard Schnösenberg,
302nd German Division

Although resistance had long ended at Puys before the evacuation order was issued for the main beaches, the grim business of lifting the Royal Regiment's casualties off Blue Beach went on through the morning. After the surrender Ron Beal stopped some of the other Royals setting booby traps for the Germans by priming grenades and hiding them under stones. 'I told them that if we had to clear the beach of our own wounded our stretcher bearers would be the ones to be blown to hell.'

Jack Poolton was sent back to the beach to help lift the wounded from the water's edge before they drowned in the rising tide, and what he saw horrified him more than anything that had gone before: 'There were two German officers down there actually shooting the worst of the wounded, putting them out of their misery. I actually saw this one German officer shoot at least three. He was putting bullets through their foreheads. Even though I realised they were doing it as an act of mercy, I didn't want to see any more because it made me sick. I thought, my God, we're licked, isn't that enough?'

Al McDonald witnessed a different humane side of his captors. With a group of other wounded, he was under guard in a large house overlooking Blue Beach: 'A German soldier came in, all grimy and dirty, and he looked around and saw one of our fellers lying there pretty badly wounded. He had some soup. He squatted down beside him and said in English, "This is my food but you need it more than I do," and he sat there and fed this soup to the wounded man.'

When Ron Beal was marched up the hill away from Blue Beach he was convinced he was being taken away to be executed: 'I don't think anybody had any idea they would be prisoners of war. I expected I was going to be shot.'

But Capt. George Browne, the artillery observation officer, noted that prisoners were treated 'if not with any great solicitude, at least not inhumanely; the German troops were correct in their behaviour and I saw no instance of what might be called the Nazi mind'.

The only exception seems to have been in the case of captured Commandos. 'They are made up from murderers, gangsters and the like,' said an order issued to the 302nd Division just before Dieppe. 'Cold steel is the only way to deal with them.' Trooper John Lerigo of No. 3 Commando and the medical orderly of No. 4 Commando, James Pasquale, both insist that they were lined up to be shot before being reprieved. Lerigo and two others were captured about three miles inland at Berneval while trying to take shelter in a church whose doors were locked. One of Lerigo's captors told him in broken English, 'All Commandos should be shot.' Lerigo said, 'The other two *were* taken away and shot, but I walked on. I was one of the lucky ones. The next thing I knew six of us were lined up against a wall and five Germans levelled their rifles at us. I just didn't have any feeling in me, I was numb. But some officer told them to stop. These stories I have seen about them treating us well just aren't true. I saw them bayoneting the wounded.'

Pasquale, who was captured because he insisted on remaining at Orange Beach with the wounded, said 'I must admit the Germans were very good then. They sent stretchers down, but after a while six of us were lined up against a ditch. They never said anything but it was obvious what was going to happen. Just then a marvellously dressed officer who spoke perfect English came over and stopped them. They were very good after that, gave us a meal later on, but I think the intention had been to shoot us because, after all, our lads hadn't left one bloke alive on that gunsite.'

The Germans were swift to make propaganda capital from the captured Commandos. Wally Dungate remembered, 'A German officer offered one of us a cig. He refused, but the German made him take it so he could take a picture of him. They had all that off to a fine art'. Albert Moore agreed: 'It was a scorching day and we had had nothing to drink. When they marched us back up from Yellow Beach they took us to a football field. They planted buckets of water at strategic places and had photographers there, and when everybody dived for the water they took photos of these animals. But they only got one chance. Immediately we realised what was going on everybody stopped drinking. Now, we said, we'll do it nice and orderly in good old British fashion. That was the first real taste of the German method that I had. They never liked the Commandos, you know. Used to call us "Churchill's rats who kill in the night".'

At Pourville, the rearguard crouched behind the sea wall continued to offer resistance for some time after the last rescue craft had pulled away from Green Beach. 'The process of realising that they weren't coming back was slow to dawn,' said Col. Merritt, but he insists that it was a decision of which he approved. 'The Navy lost quite a number of landing craft and it was a proper order from the Force Commander.'

The wounded naval officer Redvers Prior discussed with Merritt the possibility of getting off the beach and trying to hold out in woods nearby. 'But as we had no ammunition Col. Merritt considered this impracticable. He told me his men were completely exhausted and he could not call on them for any further major effort.'

So Merritt called a conference of officers and it was decided that further resistance was useless. Weapons were destroyed and papers buried, then Merritt asked if anyone had a white flag with which to surrender. Maj. Elmer 'Lefty' White complained that it was very much against his grain to do this. Instead, he suggested that one of their German prisoners be sent out to negotiate the surrender, and this was done.

As the column of more than 250 Canadians captured at Pourville was marched towards Dieppe over the headland they had not been able to subdue, sympathetic French offered them food and drink. 'Women approached us with apples and pails of buttermilk,' said Lt

Felix Walter. 'The German guards made no attempt to interfere, and indeed seemed anxious to get some refreshments for themselves.'

As the firing died away on Dieppe's main beach, Col. Labatt was forced to make what he later termed, 'the most unpleasant decision of my life', and organise a surrender. 'There was nothing further we could do and we were losing lots of our wounded chaps through the rising tide drowning them. We had with us some German airmen whom we had taken prisoner, and I sent one of them out into the open with a white towel. Never before have I seen such a pleased expression come over a man's face. He waved to his pals, and thirty or forty of them leapt up on the sea wall and covered us with sub machine-guns and rifles. Everybody stood up, and that was that.' As he moved forward to surrender, Labatt was wearing only a shirt and underpants.

Lt Jerry Wood confessed to a feeling of 'shame and humiliation' as he gave up. 'I hadn't shot a single German. I hadn't even seen one fighting. I had done no more in the battle than a medical orderly.' Marc Pilote suffered the same despair: 'I heard somebody shout at me *Raus*. I lifted my head and it was a German soldier. That's the first one I had seen all morning.'

Maj. Brian McCool was captured just as he got off a last message. 'There was a crunch on the gravel and I looked under my arm and saw a pair of jackboots. "*Aufstehen*", said a voice, so I stood up. When a German officer appeared I broke my revolver and handed it to him and then asked if he would like a drink from the bottle of Scotch I had brought ashore with me. He saluted, took the revolver but refused the drink.'

Southam, the senior Canadian officer ashore, told those around him, 'Sorry lads, we might as well pack up too,' when he saw white towels and shirts being waved further down the beach, and he later wrote that he and the signals officer, Maj. Gordon Rolfe 'were destroying and burning our papers'.

Rolfe's recollection was different. He noticed with alarm that Southam was still carrying his copy of the top secret military plan. 'I raced to the Brigadier, pointed to the bonfire on the beach and urged that the package be burned immediately. Southam hesitated, saying he might still have further use for it.' Eventually, according to Rolfe, 'he attempted to bury his precious package under the pebbles', but his action was spotted and the plan fell intact into enemy hands.

At his end of the beach, where he was giving aid to the wounded in the stranded LCT, Lucien Dumais prepared sadly for the inevitable: 'I picked up a rifle with my bayonet on it and tied my handkerchief to the end. It was an old khaki handkerchief that had turned yellow with age, so I did not even capitulate under a white flag, but under a yellow rag, the colour of cowardice.' As he stood up Dumais was shot at, so he ducked behind cover until Germans appeared on the beach and moved towards the LCT.

As he lay inside the tank landing craft, Alf Collingdon heard the Germans talking and the noise of their boots on the pebbles as they approached. 'I stood up, pointed to the men and said, "All wounded." The German looked in and smiled. "Well, well," he said in perfect English, "if it is isn't Captain Plunkett and his boys on the road to Berchtesgaden." He had worked in northern Ontario before the war.'

'Two six-foot skinny youths each holding a rifle in one hand motioned us soberly to the front of the boat,' recalled Jerry Wood. 'We dropped our arms in a pile as we filed out.... As I reached shore a young sniper helped himself to my Zeiss field glasses. Fair game, but it burned me up that I hadn't had the presence of mind to destroy them, a legacy from my Dad.'

The German officer, who had collected Wood's copy of *Last Train From Berlin* from the LCT, sauntered off along the beach with the book under his arm, with the farewell, 'So long, gentlemen. Perhaps we'll meet in a bar sometime in London or New York.'

Though Wood insisted that the Germans' behaviour towards the prisoners and wounded was 'correct and mild', the victors were naturally suspicious of what they considered truculent attitudes. When Lucien Dumais insisted on going back to the shore to assist with the moving of the wounded, a rifle was pointed at him and he was told that if he did not do as he was told he would be shot.

As Austin Stanton's crew climbed out of their tank they left the air-conditioning motor running. 'One little fellow was very concerned because he thought there was a bomb set to go off inside the tank, so he poked me with his bayonet and made me go back in and switch it off.'

The chaplain, John Foote, was also urged along in similar brusque fashion when it appeared that he was hanging back on the beach. 'Before going in the water I had taken off my boots. They were a brand new pair of Veldtschoen and I was so proud of them. At the end of the action they were only a few feet from me on the beach but as I went to get them I got this bayonet jabbed into my backside. The Germans wouldn't let me go near them, so I looked at the boots and I looked at the bayonet and I thought, to hell with the boots.'

As he walked off the beach the naval telegraphist Gordon Ryall recalled, 'I was tired, I was hungry and I was thirsty. I thought, maybe they are going to give us tea, surely they will give us something. And I had visions of bread and butter being supplied, and doughnuts and maybe cream cakes. Then I thought, no they won't give us cream cakes. But I did imagine we might get something, just like we did after sports day at school.'

'We were all very thirsty and bellies empty,' Sapper Bill Lynch wrote of the surrender. 'They let a little Frenchwoman give us water from a jug. We filled her pockets with souvenirs and English silver coins. I still had my little Westclox. I was very glad of it. The young Jerry officer had been decent about that. As we filed off the beach the fellows ahead of me said to him, "May we keep our watches, sir?" He replied in good Oxford English, "Certainly you may keep your watches." But what piles of Ronson lighters, they didn't half have a pile of them!'

Austin Stanton requested permission of a group of Germans drinking bottles of beer to return to the water's edge and help remove one of the wounded. 'When we were coming back with the man through a hole in the wire one of them moved the wire over with his rifle so that it was wide enough for us to drag this wounded guy through. With that, the German took the bayonet off his rifle and I wondered what was going to happen. What happened was that he flipped the tops off three bottles of beer with the end of his rifle and he handed one to George Valentine, one to myself and one to the fellow on the ground, who said he didn't want it. This German spoke a little English and turned to me and said, "You look big enough for two," so there I was, standing with a bottle of beer in each hand. After a sip or two it occurred to me just how ridiculous war was. Fifteen minutes ago we were shooting at one another, and now there we were, just a couple of soldiers having a beer.'

Stanton's brief period of relaxation was soon disturbed. He had just given a wounded Hamiltons officer a morphine injection. 'The man suddenly hollered at me, "Duck". We were against the sea wall, he was facing out to sea and I had my back to it. Some Spitfires came over and cut a trench between the two of us. We were maybe a foot apart. He got hit twice more, yet I didn't get touched.'

Survivors of Green and Blue beaches also suffered the further indignity of being shot at by friendly aircraft after having been taken prisoner. At Pourville John Runcie reported that Spitfires machine-gunning the beach 'caused some casualties'. At Puys Leonard Keto recalled, 'We had just given up when, jeez, our own planes started bombing us. My pal Jack Newman hadn't been scratched on the beach but our own planes hit him so close to the heart that they couldn't take the bullet out.' As he lay wounded on the floor of a house above Puys beach, opposite a window with a dump of captured ammunition outside, Al McDonald heard the Allied aircraft attacking. 'I had my boots under my head and I put my steel helmet over my face and I thought, OK, go ahead.'

'Those who could march away from Blue Beach were taken to a schoolyard,' said Reg Hall. 'The RAF were still machine-gunning and bombing. I remember a tall chap standing next to me while it was all going on saying, "Come on boys, give it to 'em." Then they shot us up in the schoolyard and wounded a lot of us. It couldn't be helped, they didn't know.'

As the officers and other ranks were being separated on the Dieppe esplanade, cannon-firing fighters again roared in from the sea. 'Whatever its effect on the target, I confess its effect on us was a bit shattering,' said Brig. Southam. Then he limped to the front rank of the officers, one leg bandaged, his trousers torn and flapping but his Glengarry cap neatly in place on his head and told them, 'I've led you this far, gentlemen, so I might as well lead you the rest of the way.'

Southam confessed, 'I was amazed at the numbers, particularly officers, who were present, and I wondered how in God's name so many had come through.' Southam led the column towards the grounds of Dieppe Hospital, where all the captured were being gathered. Jerry Wood took his last look at the beach 'which was a shambles of devastation ... guts and limbs strewn about, bodies floating in the water and lapped by waves.' The German correspondent Ulrich Haussmann was allowed on to the beach soon after the fighting was over: 'It presented a picture of horror. Hundreds of corpses and moaning wounded covered the hard gravel. Drowned men and dying men, borne up by life jackets, are washed up by the waves and swing, packed closely together, in horrible rhythm.'

One of the seriously wounded left lying on the beach was Cpl John Gilchrist of the Essex Scottish, who had been hit in the face. After being given a morphine injection he lost consciousness and was left for dead until he was finally located at dusk on 20 August, almost thirty-six hours after being hit. When he came round in hospital, Gilchrist's watch was missing but it was returned to him six months later.

At the Hôtel Dieu, the town hospital identified by huge red crosses painted on the roof and marked out in flower beds on the lawn, nuns and medical personnel of both sides treated the wounded. Early in the evening the first hospital train pulled out of Dieppe for Rouen carrying 174 German and 347 Allied injured. Among them was Bill Stevens, wounded twenty-three times at Blue Beach. 'When they finally picked me up they put me on a stretcher and gently carried me up a ladder off the beach. I was put in a horse-drawn ambulance with three other guys and they gave each of us a pack of cigarettes. I was taken straight to a hospital train, lifted in gently and then, from about three feet in the air, tipped over and dumped on the floor of the truck.'

A second hospital train left Dieppe in the early hours of the following morning with another 240 Allied casualties, who had to be looked after by unwounded comrades because of the shortage of trained German personnel.

Six hours after the surrender all those who had come through the raid unscathed or only slightly wounded were assembled and marched in a huge column to Envermeu, nine miles inland. 'All the way down the street Jerry photographers were taking pictures,' said Bill Lynch. 'Many of the boys who had tried to swim away were minus their pants, shoes or socks. They had to march, just the same, a fine sight for the French ladies, who were now out to see us and taking a good look. Some of the boys had on only an undervest.'

'As they marched past they came very close to me,' said Georges Guibon. 'I whispered, "Thank you, thank you." A number of them were protecting their feet with bags secured with string. It was a sad spectacle indeed.'

Col. Labatt recalled, 'As we passed through the streets the townsfolk stood about in tears and passed out little things to eat, wine and water mostly.' When one old woman, in mock anger, pelted the column with tomatoes they were cheerfully and gratefully accepted, though another who leaned out and yelled, 'English pigs', at a passing group of Fusiliers Mont-Royal, 'must have been surprised to receive a lot of French swear words in reply', said Ray Geoffrion. 'We marched out of Dieppe singing the *Marseillaise*,' said Jack Poolton. 'We were as defiant as hell.' And Harold Price remembered, 'The lace curtains in the windows were drawn in the V sign and people kept giving the V sign as we marched past.'

'It was astonishing,' said Geoffrion. 'Morale was so high. On the way to Envermeu we passed a wedding procession coming from the other direction. The men waved and cheered, threw money to the couple and shouted, "Long live the bride".' Stan Darch of the Hamiltons, barefoot and limping badly, was gravely and ceremoniously presented with the shiny patent leather shoes he was wearing by one of the wedding party, a gesture which caused his arrest.

At Envermeu the officers were separated and locked into the village church, while the remainder were marched another two miles to spend the night in a disused brick factory. 'In the church the white-haired old priest walked among us, shaking his head,' said John Foote. 'I remember lying on the stone floor of the church, worn out, rolling around. The church was full of gladioli. I can never see gladioli now without thinking of that night.' Maj. Brian McCool, who had surrendered his revolver on the beach but still had some bullets in his pocket, seized the opportunity to get rid of them inside the church: 'I took out the plug in the baptysmal font and dropped them down there.'

Next day, officers and men were moved by train to Verneuil, about 40 miles west of Paris, where they were temporarily interned in a hitherto-unused prisoner-of-war camp built by the French at the beginning of the war.

The Germans were quick to begin their interrogations after the raid. The wounded Commando captain, Geoffrey Osmond, was collected by car from Yellow Beach and taken for interview. 'I was asked in perfect English where we had come from and how we had got there. I am afraid I was very rude to them because I wasn't feeling at all well. I told them I had imitated Jesus Christ. When they asked me to explain I said I had walked on the water. I was told curtly that that was no way to talk to a German officer and that was the end of the interview.'

Padre John Foote and the Hamiltons' medical officer, Wesley Clare, were helping with the wounded in Dieppe hospital when they were taken away for interrogation because they were wearing uniforms with captains' insignia. 'They put us in a Volkswagen,' said Foote. 'Clare and I sat in the back seat and alongside the driver was a soldier, leaning over the front seat and pointing a sub machine-gun at us. The damn Volkswagen was bouncing all over the road and I said to Wes, "We got away with it on the beach but there's a good chance of us getting killed now if that thing goes off."

'At German headquarters I faced an officer looking very cool and comfortable compared to me. He spoke very good English, perfect.

When he started to interview me I told him I was a chaplain and didn't know anything about the technical part of the war. He quizzed me for a long time without any success but eventually he said, "Well, if you *are* a chaplain I suppose all I can ask you about is the state of morale in England." I told him morale was just fine.'

Jack Poolton recalled, 'Mostly they pumped you about what things were like in England. I was glad I was a buck private, I didn't know anything. Most of us wrote down on the form they gave us that we were farmers, so they would think we were dumb ploughmen. If a guy was an engineer he wasn't going to say. I remember one German saying, "You've got a lot of farmers over there". '

At Verneuil Brian McCool, his identity as Principal Military Landing Officer uncovered, was interrogated over two days. 'They tried to bully me occasionally but on the whole they were pretty correct,' said McCool. 'At the end of it a bird whose English was better than mine said, "Look McCool, it was too big for a raid and too small for invasion. What was it?" I said to him, "If you can tell *me* the answer I would be very grateful".'

A report on the interrogations noted, 'The officers all showed a smiling, superior expression. Many were arrogant, bordering on impertinence. Only scanty information could be obtained from them. The NCOs and men behaved in a similar manner. The Commando officers and men were completely secure. The French Canadians were the ones most willing to talk.'

Noting this, and in an attempt to cause dissension between the French Canadians and English-speaking Canadians, the Vichy government issued parcels of food and cigarettes to the men of the Fusiliers Mont-Royal. The parcels were gratefully accepted, and promptly shared out among all.

Strangely, one of the rare reported cases of violence happened to a French Canadian, Ray Geoffrion: 'An officer who spoke better French and English than I did talked to me about Montreal, named a few streets and said what a good time he had had there. He asked if I would like a cigarette. I reached across the table and was just about to light it when one of the guards standing alongside me slapped me across the face, knocked the cigarette flying and said, "It is not permitted to smoke in the presence of an officer".'

A German war correspondent, Johannes Jørgensen, was allowed to mix with the Canadians and wrote, 'I was struck by the contrast between these men and the captured Bolsheviks, of whom we had seen more than enough on the Eastern front. There, brutalised, sub-human creatures, ragged, shapeless. Here, tall well-built men, good-looking in a way, often fair-haired. When we spoke to them they absolutely refused to talk about any military subject.' Jørgensen confessed to one problem, however. 'Conversation was a little difficult on account of the marked dialect of English the Canadians speak.'

After the surrender ashore, *Calpe*'s continued presence off Dieppe earned the headquarters ship the close attention of shore batteries and aircraft. Quentin Reynolds was standing near the press officer, Lt Robert Boyle, and Air Cdre Cole, the Air Force Commander's representaive on the destroyer, when they were attacked by an FW 190. 'The concussion was frightful,' Reynolds wrote in the American magazine *Collier*'s. 'I bit on something hard and spat out a gold filling. That seemed to be the extent of my injuries. Air Cdre Cole staggered past me holding a hand to his blood-covered face. Boyle was bleeding from the neck and scalp. As I helped him down to the first-aid room he said, "This is one hell of a way to celebrate a birthday. I'm 21 today".'

Still the ordeal of *Calpe*'s crew and the 300 Dieppe survivors on board was not over. The destroyer turned away from the main convoy to seek a pilot reported in the sea nearby and was attacked by a Ju 88, one of whose bombs exploded right alongside a starboard gun mounting, blowing five members of the gun crew overboard and killing and wounding the rest. When *Calpe* turned to attempt to collect the five men in the water she was attacked by another German bomber, so Peter Scott's steam gunboat was ordered to do the job instead. Scott returned to within a mile of Dieppe before sighting *Calpe*'s missing gunners and hauling them to safety.

Just as he was about to leave the area he spotted a derelict landing craft. 'As we approached the boat we saw that it contained three soldiers, two of whom were completely naked except for their Mae Wests. One of them was semaphoring SOS. We passed them a rope, took them in tow and, still miraculously unshot at although we were no more than a mile offshore, we set off again to rejoin the convoy.'

On the return voyage to England the fleet came under sporadic attack from German planes taking advantage of the thickening cloud over the Channel, but there were no more losses to enemy air action.

Even when they were safely in harbour the sufferings of the wounded were still far from over. Although elaborate arrangements had been made for their reception, the sheer volume of injured overstrained the facilities. At the last minute the fleet of ambulances waiting in Portsmouth had to switch to another dockyard, 15 miles away, and arrived to find utter confusion. For a mile, the narrow road to the dockside was blocked by hundreds of vehicles and when the warships arrived they had to berth side by side and manhandle the stretcher cases across the cluttered decks of other vessels.

At Newhaven the tide was low at the peak return time and stretcher cases had to be hauled out of the ships by dockside cranes. Jetties were crowded with returning soldiers, would-be helpers and journalists, making it difficult to clear the later boats of the injured and eventually the harbour had to be closed to further arrivals for a 75-minute period to disentangle the jam. One tank landing craft carrying several seriously wounded had to wait hours for a berth and the last craft with casualties aboard did not dock until 0215 hours the next morning.

Although Mountbatten was able to tell the War Cabinet, truthfully enough, the next day that two-thirds of the Dieppe raiding force had returned safely, the fact that many had never even landed distorted the fearful extent of the carnage among those who had gone ashore. The Canadians alone suffered 906 killed (56 officers and 851 other ranks) and of the 5,000 men who sailed into battle 3,367 were killed, captured or wounded. In nine hours at Dieppe the Canadian army lost more prisoners than in the 20 months of the Italian campaign. The 2nd Division was practically wiped out and its battle worthiness reduced drastically for many months. Not since the Somme in 1916 had a Canadian formation suffered such losses. On top of the Canadian casualties, the Commandos counted 270 killed, wounded and captured and the Royal Navy 550.

The terrible truth was slow to dawn at the various regimental headquarters in southern England. At Littlehampton, the Royal Regiment received word at 1700 hours that survivors were on their way. A hot meal was prepared for 500 men. It remained untouched in the kitchens. At 2100 hours the first two Royals reported back 'in an exhausted condition', and as the regimental history has pointed out, 'Before midnight it had become obvious that the Royal Regiment of Canada had virtually ceased to exist as a unit.'

At Middleton-on-Sea the Essex Scottish cooks worked overtime to feed their returning colleagues but only a few stragglers put in an appearance and the regiment's war diary noted the following morning, 'The sun is bright but the day is a sombre one.'

Pte John King of the Royal Hamilton Light Infantry got up to go on parade on 20 August. 'Instead of hundreds of men there were ten of us. We had to go round and collect our mates' personal gear and put it in envelopes to send back home.'

On his return to England Ray Scott of the Royal Regiment was interrogated at a naval station near Portsmouth. 'When I came out I asked a marine where my regiment was. He said, "First hut on the left." I went down to the hut and looked in. There were two guys. I thought there had been a mistake so I went back to the marine and said, "I think you misdirected me, I'm looking for the whole regiment".

' "That's it buddy," he said, "that *is* your regiment."

'There were only about 13 Royals on muster the next morning. It was really pitiful because if you put all those regiments together who were at Dieppe there wasn't enough to make a battalion out of the whole shooting match of us.'

CHAPTER THIRTEEN
Aftermath

'The Duke of Wellington said the battle of Waterloo was won on the playing fields of Eton. I say that the battle of Normandy was won on the beaches of Dieppe.'

– Earl Mountbatten of Burma

Though the German NCO who exulted to Georges Guibon in Rue Chanzy after the raid, 'We have captured five thousand prisoners,' was exaggerating, the true total of 2,195 was impressive enough. Equipment which fell into German hands included 29 Churchill tanks, seven scout cars, a personnel truck, 1,300 rifles, 170 machine-guns, 42 anti-tank rifles, 70 light mortars, 60 heavy mortars and a vast quantity of ammunition, explosives and clothing. The collecting of the booty proved a hazardous business. One German NCO was killed and eight men wounded clearing the beach.

After visiting the main beach the journalist Johannes Jørgensen wrote, 'It is a scene of death, destruction and horror. Dead soldiers lie in heaps. The corpses are being carried away, salvage squads collect weapons and other material. You have to put your foot down carefully so as not to set off one of the dangerous explosive charges. Helmets, discarded rifles and ammunition belts are too many to be counted. We step on blankets, haversacks, water bottles; uncountable are the personal belongings that the Tommies threw away before capture … everything from comb to safety razor, toothbrushes to salt boxes, field dressing pack to biscuit tin, helter-skelter.'

At 1915 hours on 19 August, in his Sixth, and final, Situation Appreciation, von Rundstedt announced, 'The enemy has been battered to destruction. He has suffered heavy, gruesome losses.' When the news was passed to Hitler, he immediately requested von Rundstedt to convey his 'thanks and appreciation' to all those who had taken part in such a memorable day for German arms, and all soldiers wounded in the action were granted additional rations which included a half-bottle of Sekt, ten cigarettes and two tins of biscuits.

The casualties suffered by all three German services were given after the action as 591 and later revision only took the total to just over 600. The Army lost 132 killed and missing, including eight prisoners taken back to England, and 201 wounded. The Navy suffered 78 dead and missing, which included the whole crew of 46 aboard the blown-up submarine chaser 1404, and 35 wounded, while the Luftwaffe's losses, including ground personnel and anti-aircraft gunners as well as aircrews, were 104 dead and missing and 58 wounded. The Germans lost 37 prisoners, 25 sailors, eight soldiers and four airmen. In addition 15 horses of the transport section were killed. Apart from 813 Battery at Varengeville, their equipment losses were negligible: two French field pieces, four anti-tank guns, three machine-guns, two trucks and a field kitchen.

On the evening of 19 August a telegram was sent in secret cypher to Churchill in the Middle East reporting on the raid: 'It is certain that casualties have been heavy and that generally speaking objectives were not attained.' The Prime Minister's reaction was swift: 'Consider it would be wise to describe 'Jubilee' as quote reconnaissance in force unquote.' So before the day was out the attempt to play down Dieppe had already begun.

For the public in Britain, Canada and the United States, however, the initial news was of a smashing blow delivered against Hitler. Next morning the *Daily Mail*'s eight column headline read 'Dieppe Victors Come Back Singing'. The *Mail* told its readers that Commandos had seized Dieppe racecourse and held it as an emergency airfield for Allied pilots, adding, 'Scarred Canadian tanks were rolling home safely to their headquarters last night, cheered by crowds which saw them pass. With the return of the tanks the raid has proved that armoured vehicles can be both landed and withdrawn under fire.'

The *Daily Sketch*, too, was exuberantly incorrect in this matter: 'Did we bring back any of the tanks we landed? The answer is WE DID!' *The Times* described Dieppe as 'heartening news' and although the

News Chronicle also reported the raid as a triumph, the description by its correspondent W. B. Robson of the return to Newhaven should have provided the British public with an inkling of the desperate fighting involved: 'Even hard-boiled staff officers saluted these fellows as they wandered down the gangway clad in filthy rags, blankets strapped round the middle, bandages round their heads and wearing every variety of garment the Royal Navy could lend them.'

American newspapers awarded Dieppe the biggest headlines since Pearl Harbor, heavily overstressing the involvement of the US Rangers: 'US and British Invade France' (*New York Journal-American*); 'Yanks in 9-hr Raid on Nazis' (*Daily News*) and 'We Land in France' (*New York Post*). The *Post* trumpeted, 'Not all the eloquence of Goebbels is going to be able to gloss over for the German people one nightmare fact – the Americans are landing in France again.'

In New York a cat with a black mark under its nose, giving it a resemblance to Hitler, was kicked in the face by its owner after news of Dieppe was announced. When a picture of the cat, its face bandaged, appeared in a paper, readers sent in 8,000 dollars to pay for the animal's broken jaw to be mended.

The early reaction of the Canadian press was similarly enthusiastic. 'The battle of Dieppe will go on Canada's roll of honour with Ypres, Vimy, the Somme and Passchendaele' (*Toronto Star*); 'The knowledge of inevitable losses will be forgotten in the sheer joy of getting to grips with Jerry' (*Winnipeg Free Press*). It was only slowly that the cost in Canadian lives came to be realised. In Hamilton, the *Spectator* published the names of 17 casualties among the Royal Hamilton Light Infantry on 21 August. The next day a further 26 were named and on Monday 24 August another 122.

The same day the *Toronto Globe and Mail* filled a whole page with the names of casualties and in its leader column reported, 'Dieppe, the name that thrilled the nation with high hopes scant days ago, has brought deep gloom to hundreds of Canadian homes. Already the names of 418 Canadians are on the list of dead, wounded and missing. That gloom will be slow to lift. No brilliance or valour in the field, no tale of sacrificial courage is quite enough to speed its passing.'

There was spirited reaction to the news. The Royal Hamilton Light Infantry reported a forty per cent. increase in volunteers and extra staff had to be called in to handle the flood of recruits. The women of that city rushed to volunteer for war jobs. 'Many were actuated by a desire to avenge the Dieppe casualties' according to the *Spectator*. 'They said they couldn't join the army but if they could do their part by making munitions to send with their compliments to the enemy they would be satisfied.'

The widow of Norman Orpen, killed at Puys, said before setting off to her job in a munitions factory, 'I have little time for grief. I must get back to work. Every part I can make, every bullet and gun, will help to end sooner the slaughter of young Canadians.'

Almost a month had passed before the full extent of the disaster was revealed. There had been rumblings about the Canadian government's reticence in giving complete details of casualties and at a Kiwanis Club lunch in Ottawa on 11 September the speaker complained, 'For three weeks we have been waiting to be told how many of Canada's gallant soldiers were lost.' Four days later the official figures were released and Canada learned that it had lost 3,350 of its men. For the first time since the bloody fighting of the First World War, newspapers printed column after column, and in some cases page after page, of casualties. 'The figures must have shocked and dismayed every Canadian,' commented the *Globe and Mail*. Toronto, whose mayor Fred Conboy had sent a message of 'hearty congratulations', to the local regiments involved immediately after the raid, was the worst-hit city, accounting for one-sixth of the total losses.

Across the country there were memorial services for loved ones lost or believed killed. In Edmonton a service was held for Marcel Lambert of the Calgary Tanks just before his family heard that their son, who would eventually become Speaker of Canada's House of Commons, was after all a prisoner. The faith of Katherine McCool was rewarded when she refused to believe the official report of her husband Brian's death or the telephone call from someone saying he had seen McCool dead on the beach. She would not attend the memorial service held at Toronto's St Paul's cathedral for Dieppe casualties and had even received her first widow's pension cheque before the news came through that McCool was alive in captivity.

Ross Munro, who became publisher of the *Montreal Gazette*, was sent back to Canada to undertake a nationwide speaking tour which drew thousands at each stopping point. 'It was a tough tour to make,' Munro has recalled. 'I was suffering severely from what later became known as battle shock, and nearly collapsed several times. On the positive side I was able to assure hundreds of families that their missing men were probably captured. I took back hundreds of messages from men of the 2nd Division and was able to bring some comfort to others who had men listed as killed in action. I was the personal connection between the raid and those at home and this was a great satisfaction.'

According to a report in the *Albertan*, Munro told a Calgary audience of 3,000 how men of their tank regiment had 'fought their way clean through Dieppe', to the rear of the port. 'On the tour I wasn't conscience-stricken that I wasn't coming out loud and clear about all the facts,' Munro said. 'In the atmosphere of the times it could never have happened. Everything written and said came under censorship and I always felt that I came as close as I possibly could to telling the full story within those imposed limitations.

'It was a disaster that day. I couldn't write it, call it a disaster, but I knew in my heart that it was.'

Dieppe was also a propaganda defeat for the Allies. Delays and muddles in London and the scarcity of information from the British authorities forced the media to carry announcements from German sources which, though decried at the time, were in fact remarkably accurate. Dieppe was ready made for the German propaganda machine and they revelled in it, devoting to the raid what Combined Operations' official report called 'one of the most ambitious and prolonged campaigns yet devised by the enemy'.

Though the first Allied communiqué announcing the raid was issued from London at 0600 hours on 19 August, the second did not appear until seven hours later, by which time the Germans had already broadcast news of tank landings. The third communiqué came out at 2010 hours but there was more than a 24-hour delay before the final announcement at 2250 hours on 20 August and it was admitted later, 'The period of silence between the third and final communiqués enabled the enemy to some extent to seize the initiative.'

On the morning after the raid all the war correspondents who had been assigned to it, with the exception of Wallace Reyburn who was having treatment for his minor wounds, attended a briefing at which it was agreed to release all their stories, most of them already written, at mid-day. Because of 'censorship delays' it was early evening before they were cleared for publication.

When the *Daily Express* rang up Combined Operations Headquarters to ask if they could run a story on the part played by service women during the raid they were turned down. The chief public relations officer, Sqn-Ldr F. C. Gillman, said he feared seeing an article appear with a headline such as 'Hush Hush Girls Behind the Dieppe Raid'.

There were strong complaints when permission was refused for Free French and Belgian pilots who had flown on the raid to broadcast to their own countries. It was finally agreed that the Free French should be allowed to appear on the BBC's European Service six days after the event, with the pompous comment that, 'the exception was made in view of the fact that the raid was carried out on French soil'.

By then there had been loud grumbling in the *Evening Standard*: 'If this is a foretaste of what we can expect when the real invasion comes, I hope there will be no nonsense next time about the names of the outstanding heroes.... The authorities are clamping down on all names. Let the people know their heroes.'

The refusal to permit follow-up stories on Dieppe was part of a deliberate policy to 'kill' an embarrassing defeat as quickly as possible, but the Germans gleefully conducted an extensive post-mortem. Photographs of prisoners and derelict tanks were circulated around the world, even appearing in British and Canadian publications, a carefully constructed newsreel was distributed to occupied and neutral countries, and a four-page leaflet showing pictures of wrecked tanks and landing craft and the dead, wounded and captured and entitled, for Canadian consumption, 'Dieppe: We and the British Invade France' was dropped by German aircraft at night over the areas of Canadian camps in southern England.

Though there had been no mention to the German public of the raid while it was taking place, once success was confirmed the publicity machines went into full production. That evening Berlin radio gave a factual report of what had happened, claiming 'the enemy has suffered an annihilating defeat', and dismissing Dieppe as 'an amateur undertaking'. The words Dunkirk and Gallipoli figured frequently in the comments and for several days it was stressed that Dieppe was to have been the start of the Second Front, neatly making the point that the raid was 'too large to be a symbol, too small to be a success'.

The New British Broadcasting Station, an English-language propaganda station beamed from Germany, said on the evening of 19 August, 'Well, if it isn't a Second Front it darned well ought to be. Only a successful invasion of the Continent could justify the expenditure of life and material which is taking place.'

Churchill, always a prime target, was vilified as 'an unscrupulous and vainglorious amateur driven to despair by the demands of the Kremlin', and Lord Haw Haw also blamed 'this bloody fiasco' on the British Prime Minister's 'willingness to sacrifice his soldiers to appease the Russians'. In a broadcast from Breslau, Edward Roderick Dietze commented, 'Once again Churchill is responsible for the sacrifice, nay one might well say the murder, of brave men who deserved to be led by someone better than an unscrupulous gambler and manipulator of public opinion.'

One glaring source of propaganda material which the Germans missed was the poor recognition afforded to those who had suffered most, the Canadians. This was originally due to a private and confidential memo to editors issued by Francis Williams, Controller of Press and Censorship, at 1330 hours on 19 August: 'For your information I may say that while Canadian troops comprise the main body of the landing force they constitute approximately one-third of the total personnel of all services participating in the raid.' This, combined with the spectacular success of Lovat's Commandos, sufficed to obscure in early reports the part played by Canadians. The next evening Williams attempted to undo the effect of his first memorandum by requesting editors, 'It will be very much appreciated if in their stories newspapers will bear in mind that by far the biggest proportion of troops engaged were Canadian forces. To emphasise Commandos in headlines and stories would be to give an unfair perspective to the operation.'

It was too late, as the issue of *Picture Post* for 5 September showed. Under the title, 'Dieppe: The Full Story', the magazine carried eleven pages of pictures and text, chiefly devoted to the Commandos and Royal Air Force. The only mention of Canadian participation was two obscure sentences on the tenth page.

There was anger in Canada when American-produced newsreels of Dieppe were shown in the cinemas there, and one letter to the *Globe and Mail* complained, 'I was amazed that any Canadian theatre would have the unadulterated gall to show such a definitely American version of a Canadian exploit in Canada. I think it is the most scandalous example of newsreel reporting I have ever seen.'

Churchill attempted to clear up public misconception when, in a Commons speech on 8 September, he said, 'It is a mistake to speak or write of this as a Commando raid, although some Commando troops distinguished themselves remarkably in it. The military credit for this most gallant affair goes to the Canadian troops who formed five-sixths of the assaulting force, and to the Royal Navy which carried them all there and which carried most of them back.'

Still plugging his theme of Dieppe as 'a reconnaissance in force' Churchill went on to tell the House, 'I personally regard the Dieppe assault, to which I gave my sanction, as an indispensable preliminary to full-scale operations.'

In private, Churchill was nowhere near so fulsome about the results of Dieppe. In a personal note to Gen. Sir Hastings Ismay of the War Cabinet Churchill wrote, 'Although for many reasons everyone was concerned to make this business look as good as possible, the time has now come when I must be informed more precisely about the military plans. Who made them? Who approved them? What was General Montgomery's part in it? At first sight it would appear to a layman very much out of accord with the accepted principles of war to attack a strongly fortified town front without first securing the cliffs on either side, and to use our tanks in a frontal assault instead of landing them a few miles up the coast and entering the town from the back.'

Churchill ordered Ismay to collect all the facts available, 'and I will then consider whether there should be a more formal inquiry'. No such inquiry was ever held.

Churchill was not the only one puzzled by Allied tactics at Dieppe. In a report on the 302nd Division's Dieppe experience, Gen. Conrad Haase considered it 'incomprehensible' that the British High Command should think one Canadian division could overrun a German infantry regiment reinforced with artillery. He thought the plan of attack 'mediocre' and the timetable 'too rigid'. Haase added, 'The fact that the Canadians did not gain any ground on the main beaches was not due to any lack of courage but because of the concentrated defensive fire…. The British rather seriously underestimated the quantity of weapons required for such an attack. The strength of naval and air forces was *entirely insufficient* to suppress the defenders during the landings.'

The comments of German officers paralleled all the earlier misgivings put forward by British planners. Gen. Adolf Kuntzen, commander of the 81st Corps, considered it 'inconceivable' that the landings at Pourville were not supported with tanks. 'An attack with tanks from there against the hill west of Dieppe might have been successful. Contrary to all expectation the British did not employ parachutists and airborne [glider] troops. If they had attacked Puys simultaneously with airborne troops and from the sea the initial position of the defenders would probably have been critical.'

Comments on the fighting qualities of the Canadians varied considerably. The 81st Corps report said, 'The Canadians on the whole fought badly and surrendered afterwards in swarms. On the other hand the combat efficiency of the Commandos was very high. They were well trained and fought with real spirit.' But Fifteenth Army headquarters disagreed: 'The large number of prisoners might leave the impression that the fighting value of the units employed should not be too highly estimated. This is not the case. The enemy, almost entirely Canadian soldiers, fought – so far as he was able to fight at all – well and bravely.'

Hitler's chief interpreter Paul Schmidt was sent to Dieppe to question prisoners and reported to the Führer, 'The troops probably fought as well as ever but their top commanders must be frightful. One prisoner bluntly told me, "The men who ordered this raid and those who organised it are criminals and deserve to be shot for mass murder".'

The Germans were impressed by the 'excellent' maps carried into battle and the effectiveness of the smokescreen laid over the beaches, but were not so impressed by the Churchill tanks after examining them. The Churchills were considered 'nothing remarkable, either from the point of view of construction or from a metallurgical or technical point of view'. The guns were felt to be 'poor and obsolete' and the armour 'though strong, is of bad material and cannot be compared with the equivalent Russian or German armour'. The tracks were considered to be brittle, bulky and of clumsy construction, and the report on the tanks came to the conclusion that, 'in its present form the Churchill is easy to fight'. An explanation for the apparent inability of their guns to destroy the Churchills on 19 August was also offered: 'The anti-tank crews fired from too great a distance and badly in addition.'

The Germans were not nearly so concerned as Winston Churchill had been about the fate of French property. After the raid they set about ruthlessly clearing fields of fire and Gen. Conrad Haase ordered, 'All buildings, trees and hedges in which the enemy could conceal himself for close-range combat must be razed regardless of the so-called "destruction of values". The lives of German soldiers exceed all these considerations.' One of the first buildings to be demolished was the Casino.

Eight days after the raid the Germans remained deeply suspicious that Southam's copy of the operational order which had fallen into their hands had been planted on them and Gen. Adolf Kuntzen of the 81st Corps cautioned, 'It is not certain whether it was to serve only purposes of propaganda or deception.' The opinion persisted among high-ranking officers that, had Dieppe fallen, new orders would have been issued and a full-scale invasion launched. Von Rundstedt had the battle plan translated and circulated, and in a covering letter the C.-in-C. West ordered that particular note should be taken about 'how much the enemy knows about us', as well as what he considered the Allies' peculiarities of landing and fighting.

Von Rundstedt felt there were lessons to be learned from such things as the daylight landing. 'Anything is possible, even things which appear most improbable. The English may try to land at any time of the day, even at low tide' and he warned, 'Just as the defending force has gathered valuable experience from the action at Dieppe so has the assaulting force. Just as we are going to evaluate these experiences for the future so is the assaulting force going to do the same, perhaps even more so because it has gained this experience dearly. We must therefore count on the enemy being smarter next time, with still more means at his disposal.'

Von Rundstedt ended with the forecast, 'He will not do it like this a second time!'

Early in the raid Dieppe and its environs had been showered with leaflets to alert the French '*Ceci c'est un coup de main et non pas l'invasion*' (This is a raid and not the invasion) and the leaflets urged the population to 'refrain from all action which might compromise safety ... do not expose yourselves to German reprisals. France and her Allies will need you on the day of liberation'.

In a battle where the fighting, and the damage, was confined almost exclusively to the town's seafront there was little need for the French to become involved and, with few exceptions, they heeded the advice of the leaflet. So pleased was Hitler with what he termed the Dieppe population's 'perfect discipline and calm' that he directed they should be rewarded. Ten million francs was placed at their disposal to help repair damage and suffering caused in the raid. When he was informed of this by Col. Bartelt, CO of the 571st Regiment, M. Levasseur, the mayor of Dieppe, went a stage further and requested the release of French prisoners-of-war whose homes were in the Dieppe area. In generous mood and alive to the propaganda merit of such a move, the Germans agreed, explaining to the world that 'the behaviour of the French people has been more than correct ... they aided the German troops in their combat, rendering services of all kinds, put out fires, tended the wounded and provided the combatants with food and drink'.

It was all carried through with quite remarkable speed. On 12 September a train carrying 1,500 released French prisoners pulled into Dieppe, where the Germans had banned any form of official welcome. Because of the destruction of 813 Battery and reports of French support for the Commandos, no prisoners from the Varengeville area were freed. Nor were any Berneval men released. Claude Lambert, who now operates a seafront hotel in Dieppe, explained why.

'I was 13 years old at the time and had come home from school in Paris to be with my parents at Petit Berneval. My father lost a leg in the First World War and the Germans had a great respect for him because of this. The day after the landing we saw six or seven dead soldiers. We supposed the Germans were going to bury them but on the 21st they were still there and my father went to the German commandant and told him it was a rule of war that they should be buried. The officer told my father he would have nothing to do with them and that he could please himself.

'So we went into the village and asked the people to give horse carts to take the bodies to the cemetery. We asked for one or two and were offered twelve. We were also asking, my brother and myself, for people to give a sheet to wrap the bodies in and we wondered whether we would get any. It was the war, nobody had anything. We were given 25 sheets, everybody wanted to give their sheets. Two carts were enough and all the bodies were covered with flowers. All the village walked behind. The Germans were very angry over that.'

Generally, however, there was honourable treatment for the fallen. On the evening of 19 August the Dieppe town engineer was consulted about the best way of disposing of the bodies. He felt a communal grave was the answer and a huge trench was prepared in Janval cemetery, where the Allied dead were interred with due ceremony.

Soon afterwards, however, the German Army Graves Commission decided they deserved a more decent burial. During the 1940 campaign, when Dieppe had been a British hospital base, a piece of ground had been acquired as a military cemetery near Vertus Wood above the Scie valley on the edge of town. The German High Command ordered that as many as possible of the dead should be moved to Vertus, coffins were provided and 500 German soldiers were detailed to exhume the bodies, which were carried to their new resting place with full military honours. There they lie to this day, only a few yards from the busy junction where the roads to Paris and Rouen divide, with a fine view from the very heights which the Camerons strove in vain to reach in 1942. Dieppe's dead are buried back to back, in the German fashion, and the double rows of headstones are divided by strips of lawn and surrounded by rose bushes, a beech hedge and Canadian maples. Many of the headstones, all engraved with the Maple Leaf of Canada, carry only the stark message 'A Canadian Soldier'. The visitors' book shows that, in the words of the stone of remembrance in the cemetery, 'Their name liveth for evermore'. The children of St Bernadette's School in Kenton, Middlesex, for instance, left this message after their visit: 'Young people thank you for your sacrifice'.

Bitterness, anger and recrimination linger to this day about Dieppe, particularly over the question of whether the Germans had foreknowledge. In letters sent home by Canadian servicemen censors found 'a tremendous volume' of opinion that the enemy had been waiting, and a report prepared by the Canadian government at the end of 1942 came to the conclusion that, 'The Germans seem to have had ample warning of the raid and to have made thorough preparations for dealing with it.' A soldier in the Royal Hamilton Light Infantry wrote, 'Old Jerry knew we were coming. One of our prisoners told us they had been confined to barracks for three days waiting for us.' Another letter home said, 'I guess you folks have heard all about the Dieppe Raid. It was a pretty nice piece of work but someone talked too much and our dirty friend across the Channel knew just about when and where to expect our boys, and naturally there were far more casualties than had it all been a surprise to them.'

Yet the Luftwaffe was clearly unprepared for Dieppe, the Canadians got ashore at Green Beach with no trouble and No. 4 Commando destroyed a gun battery which was indisputably surprised by their arrival in its midst. As Cecil Merritt maintains, 'How *could* the Germans have known if we got in on our beach against defences which were unmanned?' Lord Lovat's opinion probably comes closest to the truth: 'I don't think there was a breach of security as such. It was just that the raid was signposted all the way. We were expected to arrive at a certain date, and we did. Where it mattered, on the beaches, the enemy were waiting.'

Lovat considers the tactics employed at Dieppe 'a first-class blunder', adding, 'The whole approach from Combined Operations was certainly not negligent in any way, but they just hadn't grasped the tremendously powerful German set-up. And the Canadians just weren't trained for the operation, whichever way it was done. Even we in 4 Commando didn't take enough intelligent appraisal of what we were up against. We knew a lot more about it than the Canadians, but that's not a plus mark frankly. After Dieppe you realised how terribly important it was to study your opponent. You have got to do things pretty thoroughly in war, not a half-hearted affair like Dieppe turned out to be, with inexperienced troops attacking in daylight.'

Lovat is also critical of those responsible for planning the raid. 'I think Paget was a bad general both unimaginative, hidebound and hostile to suggestions. His track record in World War Two was not impressive. I speak as a junior officer but one who had to fire the gun: Mountbatten was the cheerful extrovert who had been lucky at sea. Commandos accepted risks but this was a bad overall plan not likely to succeed, ill-conceived and rigid in its execution. Neither man added up to be good enough to take on the Hun – frontally – and in daylight.'

Who *was* ultimately responsible for Dieppe? The responsibility was diffused and Col. Charles Stacey, the Canadian Army's historian at that time, points out, 'The Dieppe plan was the work of a large and somewhat indefinitely composed committee, whose composition, moreover, changed steadily as the planning proceeded. A simpler organisation and a greater concentration of responsibility would have been more likely to result in a sound plan. There were a great many cooks, and this probably had much to do with spoiling the broth.'

Interviewed on Canadian television twenty years afterwards, Montgomery maintained, 'There was no one commander responsible. If you were to say to me, "Who was responsible for this?" I would say I don't know. If it is considered that some Canadian must be to blame it must be General McNaughton, it must be.'

At the same time, Montgomery felt it was the fault of the British High Command that the Canadians were involved so disastrously. 'They should never have allowed inexperienced troops to take it on, and when the buck was passed to me I should have been more emphatic. I did protest verbally; I think I should have protested vehemently and in writing that it shouldn't have been done with those troops. But I didn't, so I suppose I must bear certain responsibilities.'

Montgomery's biographer, Ronald Lewin, says of his involvement, 'There are Canadians who, pardonably, lay the catastrophe at his door. Much of the odium has stuck to his name. Montgomery has not helped matters by the terse and inaccurate accounts he provides in his memoirs. An impartial examination of the facts suggests that he bears a certain responsibility for what occurred, but that if accusations of delinquency are to be made there are a good many others who should first face the firing line.'

The newspaper magnate Lord Beaverbrook believed the raid had been staged deliberately to discredit the Second Front, which he had been advocating energetically in his *Express* newspapers. Further, he felt that his crusade had led to the pointless sacrifice of many of his fellow-Canadians. Beaverbrook was in no doubt where the responsibility lay and launched an ill-tempered attack on Mountbatten when the two men met at a private gathering, accusing the Combined Operations leader of faulty planning and the needless waste of lives. The bad relationship endured for more than 20 years until they were reconciled by Harold Macmillan in 1963 and as late as 1958 Beaverbrook, whose conviction over the years had hardened that Dieppe had been a massacre of his beloved Canadians, wrote to his son Max Aitken, 'Don't trust Mountbatten in any public capacity … in Canada he said he took full responsibility for Dieppe.'

There was no doubt at all about where the buck stopped. As Military Force Commander Maj.-Gen. Hamilton Roberts was made the scapegoat. Although he was awarded the Distinguished Service Order for 'ability, courage and determination to a high degree', at Dieppe, Roberts's reputation was shattered. He was replaced as head of the 2nd Division in April 1943 and finished out the war in command of a recruiting and reinforcement centre. At the war's end Roberts retired and lived in Jersey until his death in 1962.

Roberts admitted after the war that he felt 'a little bitter', about what had happened to him. 'I don't like the word scapegoat very much but I think that's pretty true, that a lot of people think I was to blame because I was in command. But I was only a small man, a small cog in the big machine. My active career was certainly finished and I was really heartbroken that I couldn't command that grand Division and first-class men in its later battles in north-west Europe.'

Montgomery has gone on record to say, 'I don't think Roberts is responsible or should bear any blame. He did his best.' And Lord Lovat says, 'Roberts obviously wasn't the right fellow but I don't know of anybody who could have done it right that way'. Col. Charles Stacey said, 'Given all the conditions at that time I suspect that if the Emperor Napoleon had been in command off the Dieppe beaches that day he couldn't have done very much more. Napoleon would probably have done something that Roberts didn't do, cut his losses and abandoned his troops on shore rather sooner. Roberts was unwilling to do that and perhaps he persisted with the operation a little longer than was altogether wise. That is the sort of judgement one can make years later, but it is not an easy judgement to make at the moment when the guns are firing.'

Roberts was hounded through the later years of his life for a comment he is alleged to have made at a pre-raid briefing that Dieppe would be 'a piece of cake'. Denny Whitaker of the Royal Hamilton Light Infantry says he well remembers Roberts saying it, though Ross Munro recalled in his book, 'There was no question that the officers were impressed by the briefing. I heard one of them say, "This will be a piece of cake".' Roberts himself strenuously denied ever saying it, explaining that it simply wasn't a Canadian expression. Whatever the truth of the matter, some Canadian officers who had been captured at Dieppe sent their general a piece of cake. 'Actually I thought it was a piece of old brown bread, showing me what rations they had while they were in captivity,' said Roberts.

For some years afterwards Roberts regularly received a piece of cake through the post on the anniversary of Dieppe.

Brig. Southam's copy of the Military Plan for Operation 'Jubilee', picked up on the beach before he was able to destroy it, was the direct cause of much hardship to those captured. It was said to be common practice for the British Special Service Brigade to tie up any prisoners taken on their raid against the European coasts and this practice was extended to Dieppe with the instruction 'Wherever possible, prisoners' hands will be tied to prevent destruction of their documents.'

As a result of what they considered a barbaric instruction, the Germans began shackling British and Canadian prisoners on 8 October, first with ropes and later with handcuffs, causing additional misery to men who were already suffering enough. 'We were in shackles for one year, 44 days and 45 minutes,' said Col. Labatt. 'At first we were bound with rope, then graduated to handcuffs and later to shackles – a steel band round each wrist and about 18 inches of chain between. The Germans shackled us at eight in the morning and unshackled us at nine at night. Mind you, we soon found ways of getting out of them but if you were found without your shackles on there were reprisals.'

On the day the shackling began the British War Cabinet announced that it would undertake reprisals against an equivalent number of German prisoners, and the Canadian government reluctantly agreed to this measure. On 10 October German prisoners were handcuffed in Britain and Canada and at one camp in Bowmansville, Ontario, extra guards had to be brought in to subdue a riot and shots were fired. There was strong objection in Canada and in an editorial on 14 October the *Toronto Globe and Mail* deplored the shackling of German prisoners, saying it was 'aping the depravity of the Nazi beasts and discarding civilisation's conventions. We cannot sink to the level of the Huns. It is Canada's duty to say we will have no part of it.'

The Allies quickly discontinued the practice and no German prisoners of war were tied up after 12 December. No reciprocal action by the enemy followed, though the practice became lax in the extreme in the camps. 'In the final days the Germans still came at eight but just put our shackles on a table,' said Labatt. 'Each man picked his up and hung them on a hook. Just before nine at night he put them back on the table for the Germans to pick up.'

At Eichstätt in Bavaria, where the majority of Canadian officers captured at Dieppe were held, handcuffs came to be worn only twice a day at check parades, and as long as prisoners observed the regulations at these times the German guards did not trouble to enforce the rules. Finally, after representations by the International Red Cross, the Germans discontinued the shackling on 22 November 1943.

It was at Eichstätt that Cecil Merritt heard he had won the Victoria Cross and Brian McCool arranged an impromptu celebration. McCool had carried into captivity a small sample of a new mauve settee covering which his wife had sent him and since its colour closely resembled that of the VC ribbon, this material was made up into a makeshift ribbon and an investiture was held in the camp. Canada's other Dieppe VC, John Foote, did not learn about his award until the war was over. On his return to Canada, Foote was ordered to report to Ottawa where he was closely questioned at great length about his activities on the beach. 'I genuinely thought I was about to be disciplined for something I had done wrong, then they told me what it was all about.'

Foote, who has given the medal to the Royal Hamilton Light Infantry regimental museum, says 'When we fought that action I could have pinned that medal on fifty people beside me. I never was so happy as when I gave the medal to the regiment. It doesn't belong to me. All those comrades are my Victoria Cross.'

Not all the men captured at Dieppe remained prisoners long enough to be interned in prison camps. Realising that their best chance of escape would come while they were still in France, many attempted to get away and though most were recaptured several achieved what were known as 'home runs' by getting back to England. French Canadians enjoyed a language advantage and three privates of the Fusiliers Mont-Royal, Conrad Lafleur, Robert Vanier and Guy Joly, escaped from a hospital train outside Dieppe and reached Gibraltar via unoccupied France.

Lucien Dumais, also of the Fusiliers, broke out of the cattle truck in which he was being transported to prison camp and made his way south to the unoccupied zone, where he stayed until October before moving to Marseilles where he was put in touch with an escape organisation by the American consul and, with 65 other escaped prisoners of war, was eventually collected from a beach near the Spanish border by a Polish trawler belonging to the Royal Navy and taken by sea to Gibraltar. On his return to Britain Dumais was recruited as an agent and went back to France to help escaped Allied servicemen get home.

Redvers Prior, the naval officer wounded four times on Green Beach, escaped the day after the raid from a hospital train and followed a similar route, via Vichy France and Spain, to Gibraltar, bringing back with him details of German troop dispositions in France. George Browne, captured with Catto in the woods above Blue Beach, escaped on 27 August but was rearrested while making his way into the French unoccupied zone and interned. He escaped again, was recaptured once more and, following the occupation of the remainder of France by the Germans in November 1942, he fell into the hands of the Italians. While being moved to Grenoble by bus he got away again and after a perilous winter journey through the Pyrenees, entered Andorra in company with two Spanish smugglers, moving from there to Gibraltar.

Perhaps the most daring escape was brought off by John Runcie of the Cameron Highlanders. In camp at Verneuil Runcie feigned an attack of appendicitis and was backed up by captured Canadian medical officers who were assisting the overworked and harassed German doctor. The German sent him to Paris for examination, and he was given a private room adjoining a large ward filled with wounded from the Russian front. An X-ray quickly revealed no problems, and when Runcie was told he would be kept in a further couple of days for observation he managed to persuade a French hospital attendant to help him get away. On the night of 5 September Runcie, dressed only in pyjamas, climbed through a window, was met outside with a change of clothing and taken to an apartment in Montmartre, where he was fed and sheltered for ten days.

On 17 September, with a small amount of food and money, Runcie set off in beret and overalls to walk to Spain, a journey which took him more than two months. Occasionally he received lifts on French lorries and his openness in admitting that he was an Allied officer was never betrayed. On two occasions he was also offered rides by German army drivers, and told them he was a Basque mechanic on his way home. Runcie reached the safety of the British consulate in San Sebastian on 22 November.

Not everyone was so successful. Leonard Keto of the Royal Regiment escaped three times from his camp in Germany, 'but they got me each time, the sons of bitches'. Dick Clark of the Calgary Tanks said he escaped 'several times' before finally managing to cross to the Allied lines at the Falaise Gap during the German offensive early in 1945. Clark explained his persistent desire to escape with the comment, 'I don't like being confined', an unusual philosophy from a member of a Churchill tank crew.

Dieppe was a forceful reminder to the Allies, particularly the eager Americans, that there could be no short-cut to victory in Europe. Churchill maintained bravely, even after the war, that the results of the raid 'fully justified' the heavy cost: 'Dieppe shed revealing light on many shortcomings in our outlook.... We learnt again the value of powerful support by heavy naval guns in an opposed landing and our bombardment technique, both marine and aerial, was thereafter improved. Above all it was shown that ... team work was the secret of success.'

But did the price paid have to be *so* heavy to discover obvious truths? That German strongpoints were well defended; that a frontal assault in daylight required preliminary bombardment of overwhelming power; that it is an expensive and difficult proposition to capture a town when the enemy commands the heights dominating it. Many of the higher-ups involved with Dieppe shared Churchill's opinion, at least publicly, that the lesson was well learned by the time of the Normandy landings in 1944. The Canadian general, Harry Crerar, argued 24 hours after D-Day that the raid's great sobering influence on Allied strategy had been 'a Canadian contribution of the greatest significance to final victory'.

Mountbatten always claimed that the battle of Normandy was won on the beaches of Dieppe but Montgomery, while agreeing that the D-Day planners learned much from Dieppe, pointed out, 'We could have obtained the information and experience without losing so many magnificent Canadian soldiers.'

The price of learning having been so extreme, the lessons were carefully absorbed – the need for truly *combined* operations with all services working in harmony, the necessity for flexibility in planning, the value of heavy armour, special training, careful timing and tight security. The absolutely essential prerequisite of fire-power to reduce defences was the principal lesson, however. Hughes-Hallett, the Naval Force Commander, said in his official report, 'I am satisfied that a capital ship could have operated in the Dieppe area during the first two or three hours without risk', adding significantly, 'It could probably have turned the tide of battle ashore in our favour.' And Roberts, the Military Force Commander, was a changed man afterwards. When the joint commanders were drafting a report for submission to Mountbatten, Roberts recommended 'We should include a paragraph recommending the bombing to destruction of such towns as Dieppe ... the town and harbour could then be mopped up from the rear.' A far cry, this, from his earlier fears about bombing rendering the streets impassable.

The realisation that the sheer weight of the sort of bombardment required to reduce Dieppe would also inevitably render the port useless turned the Allies away from their previously-held views that the seizure of a port was a vital requirement for the Second Front. In the opinion of one of Germany's top generals, Hans Speidel, the raid led Hitler into a major blunder. 'Dieppe persuaded Hitler that the Second Front should be fought on the Atlantic Wall and he gave orders to this effect. The army was told to hold every inch of ground and that the defence must adhere to the coast as the main line of battle. There was no freedom to operate or to envisage the interior of France as a battlefield.'

The Führer ordered the completion of the Atlantic Wall by May 1943, throwing thousands of forced labourers into the work, and directed that priority should be given to the Channel ports. At the same time the Allies were coming to the decision to take their own prefabricated mobile harbours with them and launch the invasion against lightly-defended open beaches. 'The Mulberry harbours were largely developed from our experience at Dieppe,' said Mountbatten.

As a result of that, Mountbatten told a gathering of Dieppe veterans in Toronto in 1973, 'Dieppe unexpectedly but most fortunately became one of the great deception operations of the war.' Perhaps Hitler should have borne in mind that comment of von Rundstedt's: 'He will not do it like this a second time.'

After the Allied break-out from Normandy in the summer of 1944 Montgomery, ever attentive to historical detail, said in his orders of the day for 20 August, 'I am sure the Canadian 2nd Division will attend to Dieppe satisfactorily'. The 2nd Division had every intention of doing exactly that.

This time everything had been prepared to give Dieppe the full treatment as Canadian forces pressed forward along the road from Rouen. A powerful naval force (which included *two* battleships!) stood by to bombard from the seaward side and Bomber Command flexed its muscles to flatten the town if necessary. Even the code name for the attack on Dieppe carried a more determined ring, Operation 'Fusillade'. All the units of the 4th and 6th Brigades which had suffered so heavily two years previously were in the column as the 2nd Division hurried towards its rendezvous with history – the Royal Regiment, Camerons, South Saskatchewans, Essex Scottish and Hamiltons. Each of the infantry battalions involved numbered some survivors of Dieppe among its ranks.

But the German guns remained silent as the Canadians moved into the town on 1 September 1944. The defenders had fled. Dieppe fell without a shot being fired. 'Instead of bullets and blood Dieppe gave the Canadians flowers and wine,' reported Ross Munro who went back with the Canadians. 'A delirious population poured into the streets to shout that the town was free.'

Munro wrote that the official march-past by the 2nd Division through Dieppe on 3 September was 'probably the most impressive and meaningful Canadian parade of the war'. The salute was taken by Lt-Gen. Harry Crerar, now commander of the Canadian First Army, in defiance of an order from Field Marshal Montgomery to join him instead for a conference. Immediately after the ceremony Crerar flew to the headquarters of Montgomery, his superior as head of the 21st Army Group.

Crerar was testily criticised by Montgomery for his tardiness but said afterwards he had told his commander, 'I had a definite responsibility to my government and my country which, at times, might run counter to his wishes.

'There was a powerful reason why I should have been at Dieppe. In fact, there were hundreds of reasons – the Canadian dead buried there.'

BIBLIOGRAPHY

Blore, Lt-Cdr Trevor, *Commissioned Bargees: the Story of the Landing Craft* (London, 1946).
Blumentritt, Guenther, *Von Rundstedt, the Soldier and the Man* (London, 1952).
Brown, Anthony Cave, *Bodyguard of Lies* (London, 1976).
Bryant, Sir Arthur, *The Turn of the Tide, 1939–1943* (London, 1957).
Buchanan, Lt-Col. G. B., *March of the Prairie Men* (Privately printed, 1957).
Buckley, Christopher, *Norway, the Commandos, Dieppe* (London, 1951).
Bull, Peter, *To Sea in a Sieve* (London, 1956).
Carver, Field Marshal Sir Michael (ed.), *The War Lords* (London, 1976).
Churchill, Winston S., *The Second World War*, 6 vols (London, 1948–54).
Dumais, Lucien R., *The Man Who Went Back* (London, 1975).
Durnford-Slater, Brig. John, *Commando* (London, 1953).
Fergusson, Bernard, *The Watery Maze: the Story of Combined Operations* (London, 1961).
Gilchrist, Donald, *Castle Commando* (Edinburgh, 1960).
Goodspeed, D. J., *Battle Royal: a History of the Royal Regiment* (Toronto, 1962).
Greenhous, Brereton, *Semper Paratus: the History of the Royal Hamilton Light Infantry* (Privately printed, 1977).
Hart, Basil Liddell, *The Other Side of the Hill* (London, 1948).
Higgins, Trumbull, *Winston Churchill and the Second Front* (New York, 1957).
Irving, David, *Hitler's War* (London, 1977).
James, Adm. Sir William, *The Portsmouth Letters* (London, 1946).
Jones, R. V., *Most Secret War* (London, 1978).

Jordan, Gerald (ed.), *Naval Warfare in the Twentieth Century* (London, 1977).
Leasor, James, *Green Beach* (London, 1975).
Lepotier, Rear-Adm., *Raiders from the Sea* (London, 1954).
Lewin, Ronald, *Montgomery as Military Commander* (London, 1971).
Lovat, Lord, *March Past* (London, 1978).
Maguire, Eric, *Dieppe, August 1942* (London, 1963).
Majdalany, Fred, *The Fall of Fortress Europe* (London, 1969).
Maund, Rear-Adm. L. E. H., *Assault from the Sea* (London, 1949).
Mellor, John, *Forgotten Heroes: the Canadians at Dieppe* (Toronto, 1975).
Merk, Rev. Charles, *A History of Dieppe* (Paris, 1909).
Mills-Roberts, Derek, *Clash by Night* (London, 1956).
Montgomery, Field-Marshal the Viscount of Alamein, *Memoirs* (London, 1958).
—— *Normandy to the Baltic* (London, 1947).
Mordal, Jacques, *Dieppe: the Dawn of Decision* (London, 1962).
Munro, Ross, *Gauntlet to Overlord* (Toronto, 1945).
Murphy, Ray, *Last Viceroy: the Life and Times of Earl Mountbatten* (London, 1970).
Pakenham, Simona, *Sixty Miles from England: the English at Dieppe, 1814–1914* (London, 1967).
Peis, Gunter, *The Mirror of Deception* (London, 1977).
Rees, Goronwy, *A Bundle of Sensations* (London, 1960).
Reyburn, Wallace, *Glorious Chapter: the Canadians at Dieppe* (Toronto, 1943).
Reynolds, Quentin, *The Curtain Rises* (London, 1944).
—— *By Quentin Reynolds* (London, 1964).
Richards, Denis, and Saunders, Hilary St George, *Royal Air Force, 1939–45* (London, 1953).
Robertson, Terence, *Dieppe: the Shame and the Glory* (London, 1963).
Roskill, Capt. S. W., *The War at Sea, 1939–45* (London, 1956).
Ruge, Vice-Adm. Friedrich, *Sea Warfare 1939–45* (London, 1957).
Saunders, Hilary St George, *The Green Beret* (London, 1949).
Scott, Peter, *The Eye of the Wind* (London, 1961).
—— *Battle of the Narrow Seas* (London, 1945).

Sherwood, Robert, *The White House Papers of Harry Hopkins* (London, 1949).
Shirer, William, *Rise and Fall of the Third Reich* (London, 1960).
Sims, Edward H., *The Fighter Pilots* (London, 1967).
Speidel, Lt-Gen. Hans, *We Defended Normandy* (London, 1951).
Stacey, Col. Charles P., *Six Years of War: Official History of the Canadian Army in the Second World War* (Ottawa, 1955).
Stevenson, William, *A Man Called Intrepid* (London, 1976).
Swettenham, John, *McNaughton*, vol. 2, 1939–43 (Toronto, 1969).
Taylor, A. J. P., *Beaverbrook* (London, 1972).
Thompson, R. W., *Dieppe at Dawn* (London, 1956).
—— *The Price of Victory* (London, 1960).
Trevor-Roper, H. R., *Hitler's War Directives, 1939–45* (London, 1964).
Truscott, Lt-Gen. L. K., *Command Missions* (New York, 1954).
Wamper, Hans, *Dieppe: Test of the Coastal Ramparts* (Berlin, 1943).
Whitehead, William, *Dieppe 1942: Echoes of Disaster* (Toronto, 1979).
Young, Peter, *Storm from the Sea* (London, 1958).
—— *Commando* (London, 1969).
Zuckerman, Prof. Lord, *From Apes to Warlords* (London, 1978).
The Canadians at War (Toronto, 1969).
The *RCAF Overseas: the First Four Years* (Toronto, 1944).

NEWSPAPERS AND PERIODICALS

A. *Britain*
Brighton and Hove Gazette
Brighton and Hove Herald
British Army Review
Daily Herald
Daily Mail
Daily Mirror
Daily Sketch
Daily Telegraph
Evening News, London
Evening Standard, London
London Gazette
News Chronicle
Picture Post
Radio Times
Sunday Express
Sussex Express and County Herald
The Times, London

B. *Canada*
The Albertan
Armed Forces Digest, Toronto
Calgary Herald
Dieppe Veterans' Journal
Edmonton Journal
Hamilton Spectator
Montreal Gazette
Montreal Standard
Montreal Star
Ottawa Journal
Toronto Globe and Mail
Toronto Star
Toronto Telegram

C. *United States*
Colliers, New York
New York Daily News
New York Times

SOURCE NOTES

DND	Department of National Defence, Ottawa
PAC	Public Archives of Canada
PRO	Public Record Office, London

Foreword
The German convoy, Combat report of Lt Wurmbach, File 981 GN (D1 and D2), DND.

Chapter One: The Plan
'Defeat is one thing ...', Trumbull Higgins, *Winston Churchill and the Second Front*, p. 128; 'England on the toboggan', Sir Arthur Bryant, *The Turn of the Tide*, p. 312; 'We should immediately ...', Bernard Fergusson, The Watery Maze, pp. 46–7; 'The horizon was black ...', Bryant, p. 266; 'An incurable wish ...', ibid., p. 337; 'It had no strategic prospects', ibid., p. 341; 'Quite the most wonderful man', ibid., p. 252; 'Winston never had ...', ibid., p. 415; Mountbatten's appointment, Fergusson, pp. 51–2, 86–9, 124–5; 'Rather a waste of time', Terence Robertson, *Dieppe: the Shame and the Glory*, p. 34; 'Dickie was hankering', Bryant, p. 370; 'This meeting with Winston', ibid., p. 372; Hughes-Hallett's decision, Report No. 159, Historical Section, Cdn. Military HQ, DND; Dieppe's English connection, Simona Pakenham, *Sixty Miles from England*, pp. 23–4; 'His bathing costume rolled down ...', ibid., p. 209; The raid plans, Combined Operations Report, Document DEFE2/551, PRO; A forty-eight-hour raid, Report No. 159, CMHQ, DND: 'On 25 April ...', Mountbatten address to Dieppe veterans, Toronto, 29 Sept 1973; 'Not one in which I was involved', ibid.; Montgomery's denial, 'Close Up', CBC TV, 9 Sept 1962; 'Do you want it?', Robertson, p. 55; 'A bold

decision', CBC TV; McNaughton backs Rutter, Special Report of Historical Officer, CMHQ, 11 Feb 1943, DND; 'In a few months' time ...', Jacques Mordal, *Dieppe: the Dawn of Decision*, p. 99.

Chapter Two: Rutter

'No plan ...', Trumbull Higgins, p. 126; 'We had no equipment', Lucien Dumais, *The Man Who Went Back*, p. 6; 'The ultimate weapon', Robertson, p. 6; 'It would surely be a mistake', ibid., p. 8; 'My men of steel', D. J. Goodspeed, *Battle Royal*, p. 378; The regimental mascot, *Dieppe Veterans' Journal*, Toronto, 1977; The camouflaged trees, *March of the Prairie Men*, p. 8; Poor discipline, Essex Scottish Offence Report, Appx. 9, Essex Scottish War Diary, DND; 'Monty go home', Robertson, p. 41; The chewing gum, *March of the Prairie Men*, p. 10; 'I have organised canteens', Charles Stacey, *Six Years of War*, p. 421; Army crime statistics, Record Group 24, CMHQ File Block 20, PAC; 'Touch her bare flesh', *Brighton and Hove Gazette*, 22 August 1942; Rape report, ibid., 17 January 1942; 'One night I had just gone to bed', John Durnford-Slater, *Commando*, p. 101; Wallace inquest, *Sussex Express*, 2 Jan 1942; 'These disturbances at night', *Brighton and Hove Gazette*, 3 Jan 1942; 'Why Canadians seem boisterous', ibid., 7 Feb 1942; 'No Canada, you've had enough', ibid., 2 May 1942; 'If you really want to take Berlin', Jackdaw C8; 'A big hefty guy', *Evening Standard* 20 Aug 1942; 'We earnestly regret', Robertson, p. 15; 'They were very nice boys', BBC Radio Brighton programme on Dieppe; 'Happy-go-lucky chaps', ibid.; 'You could sense the lethargy', Ross Munro, *Gauntlet to Overlord*, p. 297; 'We enjoyed going out ...', Ray Geoffrion interview; 'Fanstastic conception', Report No. 100, 'Jubilee': The Preliminaries, DEFE2/337, PRO; Outline plan for 'Rutter', Combined Operations Report, pp. 3–6, PRO; 'You must be mad, Dickie', Mountbatten speech, 29 Sept 1973; Churchill approves bombing, Combined Operations Report, p. 3, PRO; McNaughton's cable, Special Report of Historical Officer, CMHQ, 11 Feb 1943, DND; Isle of Wight training, Robertson, pp. 75–9, Munro, pp. 299, 301, Combined Operations Report, pp. 6–7; 'The condition of the men ...', Report No. 100, DEFE2/337, PRO; 'A revelation', Munro, p. 299; 'You wouldn't know the regiment ...', DEFE2/550, PRO; 'We were welded ...', John Foote interview; 5 June meeting, Combined Operations Report, p. 6, PRO; 'Useless sideshows', Robertson, p. 93; 'This is one passage ...', Fergusson, p. 170; 'Convenient lapse of memory', Ronald Lewin, *Montgomery as Military Commander*, p. 41; 'Bare hands and fists', Goronwy Rees, *A Bundle of Sensations*, p. 146; 'Really taken aback', Mountbatten speech, 29 Sept 1973; Exercise Yukon, Combined Operations Report, p. 7; 'These are anxious days', Munro, p. 301; 'We sailed back to Cowes', Rees, p. 156; 'We have waited more than two years', Report No. 100, DEFE2/337, PRO; 'Everyone left the room', Munro, p. 303; 'Launching against a defended port', 'Close Up', CBC TV; 'I am satisfied ...', Report No. 100, DEFE2/337, PRO; The Downing Street meeting, Mountbatten speech, 29 Sept 1973, Report No. 159, Historical Section, CMHQ, DND; Mrs Hans-Hamilton, DEFE2/552, PRO; 'The day is coming', Canadian House of Commons Debates, Official Report, 1 July 1942, p. 4134; 'It took a month or so', Prof. Lord Zuckerman, *Apes to Warlords*, p. 153; Peter Bull's LCT, Peter Bull, *To Sea in a Sieve*, pp. 42, 60; 'Barometer is our idol', Munro, p. 305; 'I was still in kip', Charles Surphlis interview; 'It was a hateful decision', Adm. Sir William James, *The Portsmouth Letters*, p. 178; 'God, what a blow', Munro, p. 306; 'Off for all time', File 220C1.009 (D3), DND; Montgomery 'delighted', 'Close Up', CBC TV.

Chapter Three: Jubilee

'Dieppe gave the Allies ...', Jackdaw C8; Newspaper stories of Rutter, Report No. 100, DEFE2/337, PRO; 'Most important that a large-scale ...', Winston Churchill, *The Second World War*, Vol. 4, p. 509; 'Rather bold proposal', Mountbatten, BBC TV, 19 Aug 1972; 'I put the idea', Mountbatten speech, 29 Sept 1973; 'It was all done verbally by me', Mountbatten, BBC TV; 'Get cracking as soon as possible', Robertson, p. 134; 'I knew we were in for it', ibid., p. 158; 'You didn't go to Dieppe, eh?', Jack Poolton interview; 'The Canadians made no secret', Lord Lovat interview; 'Doors were open', Robertson, p. 130; 'Hanging on by our eyelids', Bryant, p. 356; 'We hold strongly the view', ibid., p. 406; 'Carrying a large lump of ice ...', Higgins, p. 160; 'If the British would only ...', ibid., p. 162; 'Had I been asked ...',

Robertson, p. 135; 'I turned my attention', Mordal, p. 120; 'I suspected that …', Rees, p. 157; 'Valuable but painfully dull', Durnford-Slater, p. 14; 'His ideas were old-fashioned', Peter Young, *Storm from the Sea*, p. 21; Recruiting methods, Durnford-Slater, p. 90; 'Rabble in arms', Lord Lovat, *March Past*, p. 229; 'Honeycombed with rooms', ibid., p. 238; Picture postcard anecdote, Lord Lovat interview; 'A nice fellow but …', ibid.; 'Roberts took practically no part', Mordal, p. 125; 'What the hell do you know …?', Lord Lovat interview; The US Rangers, L. K. Truscott, *Command Missions*, pp. 18, 39–40; The Achnacarry graves, Donald Gilchrist, *Castle Commando*, p. 23; 'Most invigorating', Durnford-Slater, p. 96; 'Usually a battle is fought …', Lovat, p. 241; 'Five mile sprint marches', Bill Portman interview; 'They were not supermen', Gilchrist, p. 17; 'One or two blokes', George Cook interview; Armfuls of British bayonets', Gilchrist, p. 108; The operational plan, Combined Operations Report, PRO; 'Given an even break', File 220C1.009 (D3), DND; 'Everyone was so confident', Munro pp. 313–5; Re-equipping the force, Robertson, pp. 151–2; The Free French Commandos, DEFE2/339, PRO; Breaches of security, Combined Operations Report, p. 172, PRO; The Sylvan Flakes ad., DEFE2/328, PRO; 'Take a last look …', RG24, Vol. 10873, File 232C2(D.59), PAC; 'I knew that our previous …', Bull, p. 63; Contradictory weather reports, James, p. 185; 'Uninformed had been clamouring', Bryant, p. 487.

Chapter Four: Departure

'Invasion mustn't …', DEFE2/328, PRO; Hitler's directive, File SGR 1/90, DND; The 302nd Division, Report No. 36, Historical Section, CMHQ, DND; 'Woefully inadequate', Mountbatten speech, 29 Sept 1973; The German recruits, DEFE2/324, DEFE2/338, PRO; 'Shoemaker and a Communist', Maurice Mallet interview; Captured weapons, Joachim Lindner interview; Shortage of guns, File 594.009 (D1), DND; 'With the weak forces …', 81st Army Corps Report, File 981.023 (D10), DND; The batteries, Mordal, pp. 107–9, Stacey, p. 354; The Casino, DEFE2/330, PRO; Unwin's protest, Robertson, p. 174; German jealousies, Lindner interview, and File 981 GN (D10), DND; Von Rundstedt's order, File 594.013 (D9), DND; The death oath,

Stacey, p. 357; Gen. Haase's orders, DEFE2/330, PRO and File 594.013 (D9), DND; 'Life was a paradise', Lindner interview; 'We used to barter', Friedrich Waltenheimer interview; 'Our relationship …', Richard Schnösenberg interview; 'It was very quiet', Lindner interview; 'All of a sudden', Allan Glenn interview; 'New set of battledress', Austin Stanton interview; Camerons' departure from camp, DEFE2/335, PRO; 'The people emptied their houses', Durnford-Slater, p. 102; 'On arriving at Newhaven', File 232C2 (D59), PAC; 'Some girls were standing', ibid.; Fusiliers Mont-Royal departure, FMR War Diary, DND; 'One can only guess …', Lovat interview; 'I didn't take notice …', John Foote interview; The Chasseurs, Mordal, p. 208; 'When I got the job …', Wallace Reyburn interview; 'A peashooter armada', Robertson, p. 202; Ammunition confusion, File 232C2 (D53), PAC; Empty ammunition boxes, Combined Operations Report, p. 11; Grenade accidents, DEFE2/337, PRO; 'With high spirits', Essex Scottish War Diary, Appx. VI, DND; 'Few of the Royals', Munro, p. 309; 'There was no cheering', Ron Beal interview; 'Stolid dead pans', Jerry Wood Report, DND; 'The sea was smooth', Munro, p. 320; The hunting songs, Truscott, p. 63; 'Relief and exhilaration', John Hughes-Hallett, BBC TV; 'Give him the works', DEFE2/548, PRO; 'All units stationed near Puys …', Schnösenberg interview; The Luftwaffe party, Hans Wamper, *Dieppe, the Test of the Coastal Ramparts*; 813 Battery's daily orders, DEFE2/328, PRO; Passing through the minefield, Combined Operations Report; 'The Lord is my light', Foote interview; Letters home, Harold Price interview; 'I don't think anybody …', Poolton interview; 'A first-class dinner', Wood Report, DND; Labatt's meal, Robert Labatt narrative of experiences at Dieppe, DEFE2/338 Appx. D (ii), PRO; 'The plan is good', Robertson, p. 201; 'There was no doubt', Labatt narrative, PRO; 'I had been posted …', Bill Stevens interview; Priming the grenades, Poolton, Stevens, Reg. Hall interviews; 'I struggled into my battle kit', Labatt narrative, PRO; 'Everywhere men were applying', Gilchrist, p. 1.

Chapter Five: Yellow Beach

'From a political point of view ...', File SGR190, DND, Ottawa; 'A rifle bullet would ...', Wally Dungate interview; 'Fast but vulnerable', Durnford-Slater, p. 103; Group Five details DEFE2/334, 2/336, PRO; Wyburd's report, DEFE2/334, PRO; 'Although we were left behind', John Smale interview; German shipping figures, Friedrich Ruge, *Sea Warfare 1939–45*; Faulty radar, DEFE2/324, PRO, Mordal, pp. 160–1; 'A horrible, quivering semi-daylight', DEFE2/335, PRO; 'My God, now look out', Durnford-Slater, p. 103; 'It soon became very apparent', DEFE2/334, PRO; 'Like a thousand snakes', Durnford-Slater, pp. 103–4; Larry Maier's report, DEFE2/329, PRO; The first man wounded, Denis O'Connor interview; Collins and the compass, DEFE2/335, PRO; Smale's swim, Smale interview; German reports on the engagement, File 981 GN (D1), DND; *Slazak* and *Brocklesby*, Combined Operations Report, p. 13; 'Filled us with foreboding', DEFE2/324, PRO; 'A customary attack', Report of C.-in-C. West, DND; 'This naval launch', Albert Moore interview; 'Most outstanding feature' DEFE2/326, PRO; 'The hottest tracer fire', DEFE2/335, PRO; 'Most unpleasant moment', Young (1), p. 61; 'All right, you lot', Stephen Saggers interview; 'The barbs were very close ...', Young (1), p. 64; 'Some of the soldiers ...', ibid., p. 64; 'Young was flamboyant', Saggers interview; 'When we were going in', Dungate interview; The German defences, File 594.003 (D2), DND; 'The first bloke to get killed', Dungate interview; 'Stinking with landmines', Ron Grove interview; *Franz* attacked, DEFE2/336, PRO; Other German ships escape, File 981GN (D1), DND; 'Young soldiers will follow', Young (1), p. 58; The attack on the battery, Combined Operations Report, p. 14, Hilary St George Saunders, *The Green Beret*, pp. 16–17; 'We gave him a telescope', DEFE2/335, PRO; 'They had now got their blood up', Young (1), p. 65; 'There seemed to me ...', ibid., p. 66; 'A bloody great bang', BBC TV; 'I never saw a more heartening sight', Saunders, p. 18; 'Followed at a respectful distance', ibid., p. 18; 'When we began to withdraw', Saggers interview; 'It was like those dreams', Young (1), p. 69; 'Automatically I waved', Smale interview; 'Distinctly warm ...', Young (1), p. 69; Smale's swim, Smale interview; Blücher Force, File 594.003 (D2), DND; 'Nothing like the scale model ...', Geoffrey Osmond interview; 'It was a shambles', Dungate interview; Beach party's withdrawal, DEFE2/334, PRO, Combined Operations Report, p. 14; 'I collected seven bullets ...', Osmond interview; 'Only people in the world', Moore interview; 'We had to lie in the grass', Grove interview; Connolly's swim, ibid.; 'There was a bunch of us', ibid.; American Joe, Moore interview; 'I made everybody pack up', Osmond interview; 'There were masses of Germans', Dungate interview; Berneval 'cleaned up', File 594.003 (D2), DND; 'I found him ...', Durnford-Slater, p. 105; 'I can but reproach myself, DEFE2/334, PRO.

Chapter 6: Orange Beach

'My task ...', Lord Lovat, *March Past*, p. 268; 813 Battery description, DEFE2/330 PRO, Combined Operations Report, p. 15; 'He struck me as a grand guy', DEFE2/326, PRO; 'He did not appear ...', Derek Mills-Roberts, *Clash by Night*, p. 17; 'The usual depressed crowd', ibid., p. 20; Tin helmets discarded, Lovat interview, Mills-Roberts, p. 21; 'Like sticks of shaving soap', Cook interview; 'I kept low when we landed', Portman interview; 'Flower of the British Army', *Daily Herald*, 21 Aug 1942; 'We were warned', Cook interview; 'I was dead accurate with it', Lovat interview; 'A warm wind was blowing', Peter Scott, *Battle of the Narrow Seas* p. 96; 'It flashed three times', ibid.; 'Thanks largely to the fact', DEFE2/336, PRO; 'Blimey, they're waiting for us', Cook interview; 'A cricket pitch apart', Lovat interview; 'A nasty beach', ibid.; Gilchrist's trousers, Gilchrist, p. 3; Finney cuts the wire, DEFE2/327, PRO. 'Its beams swept across', Mills-Roberts, p. 22; 'As we nosed in ...', *Daily Herald*, 21 Aug 1942; 'I realised it was likely', Report SS/131/G22, Operation Cauldron, DEFE2/337, PRO; 'Had the Germans prepared ...', *Daily Herald*, 21 Aug 1942; 'I could not help thinking ...', DEFE2/339, PRO; 'I felt sorry for the poor old chap', Mills-Roberts, p. 24; The local prostitute, DEFE2/330, PRO; 'The marksman settled himself ...', Mills-Roberts, p. 26; 'The screams and cries', DEFE2/337, PRO; 'Father and mother of explosions', *Daily Herald*, 21 Aug 1942; 'I found a splendid spot', DEFE2/336, PRO; 'A few had been hit ...', James Pasquale interview; 'One of the remarkable things ...', Lovat interview; 'She was shouting *bonjour*', Cook interview; 'There is no finer target', Lovat interview; 'We watched amazed', Gilchrist, p. 5; 'I was against a tree', Cook interview; Portman and the grenades, Portman interview; 'It was a stupendous charge', DEFE2/337, PRO; 'We were asphyxiated', Gordon Webb interview; 'There were two Germans ...', Portman interview; Porteous wins the VC, *London Gazette*, 2 Oct 1942; 'The morale of the enemy ...', DEFE2/330, PRO; 'I couldn't take him prisoner', *Daily Herald*, 21 Aug 1942; 'I did much better ...', Webb interview; 'Half-witted gesture', Lovat interview; 'I got a pan of water', Portman interview; 'For their songs and snipers ...', Lovat, p. 223; 'Shot 'em up the arse', Lovat interview; The new-laid eggs, Saunders, p. 112; Morning coat and striped trousers, Saunders, p. 109; 'He was bubbling with happiness', *Daily Herald*, 21 Aug 1942; 'They needed a little encouragement', *Radio Times*, 17 Aug 1972; 'OK by you?', DEFE2/337, PRO; German casualties, Report of C.-in-C. West, DND; Cook's capture, Cook interview; Horne's Jewish papers, George Horne interview; 'We circled the ship', Lovat interview; 'All through the afternoon', *Daily Herald*, 21 Aug 1942; 'They may have been tired ...', *Daily Sketch* 20 Aug 1942; 'There was my picture', Webb interview; Lovat in London, Lovat pp. 264–6; 'Men with blackened faces', File 594.013 (D7), DND; 'A classic example', Notes from Theatres of War, War Office, Feb 1943; 'I was quite flattered', Lovat interview.

Chapter Seven: Blue Beach

'It was only ...', Poolton interview; Puys description, Pakenham, pp. 78, 92, Goodspeed, p. 394; 'It would have been difficult', Goodspeed, p. 395; Contingency plans, DEFE2/336, PRO; The Royals' task, Combined Operations Report, p. 17; Catto and the wire, Brian McCool interview; Landing craft delayed, DEFE2/337, PRO; Germans alerted, Schnösenberg interview; Bill McLennan's story, *Toronto Star*, 19 Aug 1972; 'I leapt in the water', Leonard Keto interview; 'If the Navy boys ...', McCool interview; 'The remainder had to be urged', DEFE2/336, PRO; 'There were definite instances', Report No. 159, Historical Section, CMHQ, DND; 'We kept our heads down', Munro, p. 332; 'Talk about a display of fireworks ...',

Poolton interview; 'The grimmest of my life', *Ottawa Journal*, 20 Aug 1942; 'They plunged into ...', Munro, p. 326; 'They didn't even have to take aim', Poolton interview; 'I don't know whether', ibid.; 'Splash, we were in deep water', Al McDonald interview; 'I don't think a man ...', Beal interview; 'Slipping and sliding ...', Surphlis interview; 'I took one look', Price interview; 'Being a Bren gunner ...', Stevens interview; 'It's hopeless ...', DEFE2/337, PRO; 'Another seven hours of hell', File 232C2 (D53), PAC; 'Cut down in front of our eyes', Munro, p. 328; 'Forcibly made to disembark', Robertson, p. 253; 'I heard the sailors yelling', File 232C2 (D53), PAC; 'Each floor had six windows', ibid.; 'The hand of God ...', Munro, p. 328; Edward Force lands, DEFE2/337, PRO; 'No sense of foreboding', Reg Hall interview; 'I was right beside ...', DEFE2/337, PRO; 'We couldn't move', Hall interview; 'A young fair-haired guy', Poolton interview; 'They didn't get more than ...', DEFE2/337, PRO; 'No lack of brave acts', Poolton interview; 'That Mr Woodhouse ...', DEFE2/339, PRO; Wedd's bravery, DEFE2/337, PRO; 'Bill McCluskey got shot ...', Stevens interview; 'The lanyard from his revolver ...', McDonald interview; 'There he was ...', Stevens interview; 'Stewart kept hollerin ...', Price interview; 'I got right to the top', Poolton interview; '... Or for us to go back', DEFE2/328, PRO; Catto's party, DEFE2/337, PRO; 'He was last seen', DEFE2/339, PRO; Ellis ashore, DEFE2/327, PRO; 'Halfway down the beach ...', File 232C2 (D53), PAC; 'The skipper yelled at them', DEFE2/339, PRO; 'Every man for himself', 232C2 (D53), PAC; Ellis's escape, DEFE2/327, PRO; McLennan's escape, *Toronto Star*, 19 Aug 1972; 'I remember a feller', McDonald interview; 'We were swimming around for hours', DEFE2/339, PRO; 'They took all my clothes', ibid.; Jack Catto's escape, File 232C2 (D85), PAC; 'We were only about ...', File 232C2 (D53) PAC; 'If anybody moved ...', DEFE2/337, PRO; The Eureka rescue, DEFE2/335, DEFE2/337, PRO; 'The boat only slowed down ...', File 232C2 (D53), PAC; 'Although there was the odd German ...', Surphlis interview; 'There was a sergeant', Schnösenberg interview; 'If we had only had ...', Poolton interview; 'I shall always remember ...', Jackdaw C8; 'It was low-level bombed ...', DEFE2/328, PRO; Catto's capture, Schnösenberg interview; The casualty figures, Goodspeed, p. 400; 'I congratulate you ...', Mordal, p. 187.

Chapter Eight: Green Beach

'We were very glad ...', Merritt interview; Green Beach plan, DEFE2/337, p. 32, PRO; SSR tasks, Buchanan, *March of the Prairie Men*, p. 15, DEFE2/337, p. 32, PRO; Jack Nissenthal, James Leasor, *Green Beach*, p. 15; 'The first streaks of dawn', Wallace Reyburn, *Glorious Chapter*, p. 55; 'As our small boats ...', Buchanan Report, SSR War Diary, DND; 'Like a herd of elephants', Robertson, p. 276; 'There was some humour ...', Reyburn interview; 'We seemed to be lying ...', Reyburn, p. 59; 'Many a wisecrack', Buchanan Report, SSR War Diary, DND; 'They were scruffy stuff', Reyburn interview; Samulewitsch's capture, DEFE2/338, PRO; 'I was lying down', Reyburn, pp. 69–70; 'What seemed to be pebbles', *Sunday Express*, 23 Aug 1942; RSM Strumm, File 232C2 (D85), PAC; I'm sorry to see you hit ...', Cecil Merritt interview; 'Several Frenchmen came out ...', SSR War Diary, DND; 'Considerable time was lost ...', DEFE2/328, PRO; Berthelot and Haggard, SSR War Diary, DND; 'Rather snivelling ...', ibid.; Sawden's bravery, ibid.; 'They were mortaring us ...', Reyburn interview; 'Matchless gallantry', *London Gazette*, 2 Oct 1942; 'Twirling his tin hat', SSR War Diary, DND; 'There is no danger here' DEFE2/337, p. 38, PRO; 'I gave 'em a lead', Merritt interview; 'I asked him afterwards', Reyburn interview; 'We must get ahead lads', DEFE2/337, p. 38, PRO; 'I've just bombed out ...', *Ottawa Journal*, 22 Aug 1942; 'Full of inspiring courage', SSR War Diary, DND; 'Half as many mortars', File 232C2 (D78), PAC; 'Sten guns are no damned good', SSR War Diary, DND; 'The German soldier seemed ...', ibid.; 'The Germans hated ...', File 232C2 (D78), PAC; Fenner's bravery, DEFE2/337, p. 39, PRO; 'It sure felt good ...', DEFE2/328, PRO; 'In the best of spirits', ibid.; 'Gostling was very cool ...', DEFE2/335, PRO; Capt. Young's group, DEFE2/337, p. 45, PRO; 'I was kind of worried ...', ibid.; Young's death, File 232C2 (D83), PAC; 'Snipers and machine-guns ...', DEFE2/328; 'We were met with very heavy ...', DEFE2/337, p. 36, PRO; 'We were at no time able ...', Hawkins and Nissenthal report contained in Secret Report of 2nd Canadian Field Security Section, DND; 'When it became apparent ...',

DEFE2/337, p. 41, PRO; 'Jerry had plenty of reinforcements ...', SSR War Diary, DND; The propaganda leaflets, Reyburn, pp. 66–7; 'They wanted to fight with us', File 232C2 (D78), PAC; 'There was this kid', Reyburn interview; 'Suddenly soldiers appeared ...', Maurice Mallet interview; Major Law's group, DEFE2/335, PRO; 'Presumably they were halted ...', DEFE2/338, PRO; The hospital platoon, File 594.003 (D2) DND; 'Vanquish' ordered, DEFE2/337, p. 49, PRO.

Chapter Nine: Red and White Beaches

'They say war ...', Foote interview; The main beach tasks, Combined Operations Report, p. 21; Air Force support, Annex 7, Combined Operations Report, Appx. D (ii); 'Ideal for our purposes', Labatt Report, p. 2, PRO; 'A regular fireworks display', ibid. p. 4; 'Single targets were registered', Report of C.-in-C. West, p. 4, DND; 'Destroyers and many other vessels', Report of Dieppe Port Commandant, File 981 GN (D13), DND; 'As I looked out ...', Schnösenberg interview; 'It was not nearly so heavy', Truscott, p. 67; There was a roar overhead,' Labatt, p. 5; 'We had been told ...', Brereton Greenhous, *Semper Paratus*, p. 196; 'Some fields were burning', Schnösenberg interview; 'As the landing craft ...', Report of Port Commandment, File 981 GN (D13), DND; 'I only remember the sound ...', Greenhous, p. 197; 'The troops rushed out ...', MacRae Report, Appx. VI to Essex Scottish War Diary, DND; Tom McDermott, John Mellor, *Forgotten Heroes*, p. 65; 'The first blast ...', File 232C2 (D57), PAC; 'It is amazing ...', MacRae Report, Essex Scottish War Diary, DND; 'Every time you showed your head ...', File 232C2 (D57), PAC; The Casino defences, DEFE2/327, PRO; 'Suddenly the towers ...', Labatt, p. 5; 'I put a dressing ...', RHLI War Diary, DND; 'We could go no further', ibid.; 'It was really terrible', ibid.; 'I must have made a burrow ...', *Hamilton Spectator*, 5 Sept 1942; 'As I crawled up ...', BBC TV; 'They could land ...', RHLI War Diary, DND; 'It touched neither of us', Labatt, p. 6; 'Standing right up ...', RHLI War Diary, DND; Wichtacz's bravery, File 232C2 (D85), PAC; 'Seconds later I saw ...', Labatt, p. 6; 'He started at once', ibid.; 'Sten guns are no good', RHLI War Diary, DND; 'When we attempted ...', ibid.; 'My number one man ...', Al

Richards interview; 'I demanded as a final phase …', Report of Port Commandant, File 981GN (D13), DND; The tank landings, Combined Operations Report, p. 23; 'I had a clear view …', Black Watch of Canada War Diary, DND; 'The tank, now released …', ibid.; 'I opened fire …', Cliff McKenna interview; *Bel esprit de combat*, DEFE2/328, PRO; 'So riddled by shrapnel', File 232C2 (D59), PAC; 'I can't do anything more …', DEFE2/326, PRO; 'Wait on my orders to go', File 215C1 (D244), PAC; 'Fire was so intense', Black Watch War Diary, DND; 'Whole beach was a pillbox', ibid.; 'The Navy fellows just disappeared …', Foote interview; 'About 200 yards out …', Eldred report, Calgary Regt War Diary, Appx. C, DND; 'A shell took off my hand', *Toronto Globe and Mail*, 13 oct 1942; 'I glanced across the deck', Wood report, DND; 'I dashed to the wheelhouse', Ross report, DND; 'We yelled and beat on the sides', Wood report, DND; Lt. Cheyney's report, DEFE2/339, PRO; 'I gave orders to turn …', 'Close Up,' CBC TV, 1962; 'All the infantry except thirty …', Robertson, p. 322; 'Badly wounded and half-drowned', File 232C2 (D59), PAC; 'The front door is down …', Bill Lynch, unpub. MSS; 'The first wave was supposed …', Vic Sparrow interview; Sinasac's luck, *Ottawa Journal*, 22 Aug 1942; 'I was one of about six or seven …', File 232C2 (D59), PAC; 'Stuff was falling inside', Wood report, pp. 4–6, DND; Engineer casualty figures, Engineers' report, File 594.013 (D14), DND; 'Afterwards you ask yourself …', File 232C2 (D59), PAC; 'I climbed a ladder …', Southam report, DEFE2/338, PRO; 'After picking myself up,' Edwin Bennett report, File 594.011 (D1), DND; 'The least of my troubles', ibid.; Southam's landing, Southam report, DEFE2/338, PRO; Stanton's landing, Austin Stanton interview; 'The first tank was stopped …', File 232C2 (D59), PAC; 'The most conspicuous case …', ibid.; 'When I looked again …', ibid.; 'For Christ's sake, don't', Robertson, p. 322; 'We were really catching it', DEFE2/335; Bobby Parks-Smith, DEFE2/326, PRO; Capt. Alexander's bravery, File 232C2 (D85), PAC; Lett wounded, CBC TV; Andrews's tank drowned, DEFE2/328, PRO; Badlan and Garneau, DEFE2/335, PRO; 'These losses have been a blow …', DEFE2/335, PRO; 'One thing that irks me', Dick Clark interview; 'We realised it was hopeless', Glenn interview; 'It was a pretty grim trip', Bennett report, 594.011 (D1), DND; 'Only a red spot left', RHLI War Diary, DND; 'We made a dash for the Germans', File 594.011 (D1), DND; 'It took a terrible toll …', RHLI War Diary, DND; 'Better get out of here', DEFE2/327, PRO; 'I spotted the three enemy …', RHLI War Diary, DND; 'I looked around upstairs …', ibid.; 'We also found one sniper', ibid.; George Hickson, DEFE2/327, PRO; Comments on prisoners, RHLI War Diary, DND; Von Rundstedt's situation appreciation, Report of C.-in-C. West, DND; The 10th Panzers, Appx. H to report of C.-in-C. West, DND; Destroying secret documents, 981G Int. (D1), DND; Von Rundstedt's criticism, File 594.013 (D9), DND; 'The enemy did not take advantage …', Report of Naval Commander Channel Coast, 981 GN (D11), DND; 'Operation has greater extent …', Report of C.-in-C. West, DND; U-boat request refused, ibid.; Luftwaffe unprepared, Appx. F to Combined Operations Report; Hill's group in Dieppe, RHLI War Diary, DND, DEFE2/327, 328, 329, PRO; The milk cart, Georges Guibon Diary, DND; 'French motor vehicles', DEFE2/338; Hickson's group in Dieppe, DEFE2/327, PRO; Stapleton's group, DEFE2/324, PRO; 'One of the most unfortunate errors', DEFE2/328, PRO.

Chapter Ten: Disaster

'People felt …', Richards interview; 'Good luck boys', Dumais, p. 18; 'It was a grand sight', ibid., p. 19; Fifty bullet holes, 594.019 (D4), DND; 'One continuous roar', Dumais, p. 19; 'I had no rifle', Marc Pilote interview; 'I was in charge of five boats …', Guy Vandelac interview; 'I began to think …', Dumais, p. 21; 'They did not touch down …', Ross report, p. 4, DND; 'It burned me up …', Wood report, p. 5, DND; 'I sank like a stone', Ray Geoffrion interview; 'Unable to accomplish anything', DEFE2/328; 'I ran under the cliff', Geoffrion interview; 'On my right hand side', 'Close Up', CBC TV; 'Like they were set in jelly', Vandelac interview; 'Don't open fire', 594.011 (D5), DND; 'We realised it was hopeless', Vandelac interview; 'I had taken three steps', *Canadians at War*, pp. 196–7; 'What we went through …'', *Ottawa Journal*, 22 Aug 1942; 'I wasn't frightened', Pilote interview; The Marine Commando landing, DEFE2/328, PRO; 'This meant a mere walk ...', Mordal, p. 211; 'It was not long before I realised ...', DEFE2/328, PRO; 'Immediately the fire became intense ...', DEFE2/339; 'The scene on the beach ...', BBC TV; 'We fired 946 rounds ...', ibid.; 'The minute you showed ...', Vandelac interview; 'I thought at first ...', Greenhous, p. 205; McCool's landing, McCool interview and 232C2 (D53), PAC; 'It was a grim feeling ...', Labatt report, p. 8; 'By God, sir', ibid., pp. 9–10; 'Mortar and shell splinters', DEFE2/328, PRO; 'Coming along on all fours', Dumais, p. 27; 'He informed me they were nearly blind ...', Southam report, p. 3; 'I was looking through ...', Stanton interview; Alf Collingdon's Red Cross, Greenhous, p. 208; 'It was very uncomfortable ...', Foote interview; 'We ran out of stretchers,' Wood report, p. 6; 'I just lay on the beach', *Ottawa Journal*, 22 Aug 1942; 'We didn't even know ...', ibid.; 'Crying his heart out', Dumais, p. 31; 'Mr Prince said no ...', DEFE2/328, PRO; Alan Humphreys report, *News Chronicle*, 21 Aug 1942; 'General, I am afraid ...', Truscott, p. 70; 'By nine o'clock ...', Naval Commander's report, DEFE2/336, PRO; 'He was loath to abandon hope', Report No. 159, CMHQ, Historical Section, DND; 'Bring them home', *Colliers*, 19 Sept 1942; 'Roberts then informed me ...', Naval Commander's report, DEFE2/336, PRO; 'I have seen the greatest ...', *Daily Sketch*, 20 Aug 1942; 'Almost continuously ...', *Daily Herald*, 20 Aug 1942; Squadron details, Annex 7 to Combined Operations Report; Wheels lowered, Munro, p. 324; 'Rapidly laid and efficient', DEFE2/330, PRO; 'A waste of resources', DEFE2/333, PRO; The Mustangs, War Office File 106/4196, PRO and 181.002 (D412), DND; 'Neither Spitfire nor Dornier', *Colliers*, 19 Sept 1942; 'I was standing beneath ...', 232C2 (D53), PAC; Johnny Johnson, Edward Sims, *The Fighter Pilots*, pp. 30–1; 'We must drive this lesson home', 215C1 (D244), DND; Charlie Stover, *Ottawa Journal*, 20 Aug 1942; Jack Godfrey's story, Personnel Records, DND; 'The air attacks were serious ...', Report No. 159, Historical Section, CMHQ, DND; The Dornier squadrons, DEFE2/324, PRO; 'Steaming slowly along', Scott (2) pp. 97–8; Drew Middleton's report, DEFE2/329; PRO; Exaggerated claims, DEFE2/334, PRO; The Dieppe Buffet, *Daily Mail*, 22 Aug 1942; 'The Americans did not waste ...', *Daily Herald*, 20 Aug 1942; Don Morrison's story, *Ottawa Journal*, 24 Aug

1942 and *The RCAF Overseas*, pp. 57–9; 'The wreckage floated …', Rees, p. 167; German pilots rescued, DEFE2/336, PRO; 'He was a likeable youth …', Scott (2), p. 107; 'He walked up to me …', Schnösenberg interview; 'Allied Fliers Bag 280', *Toronto Globe and Mail*, 21 Aug 1942; 'Extremely satisfactory …', DEFE2/328, PRO; German air losses, Sims, pp. 187, 217; RAF losses, DEFE2/337, PRO and 594.065 (D4), DND; 'Trailing its coat', Bryant, p. 488; 'With a feeling of …', Naval Commander's report, DEFE2/336, PRO; 'Their fire was extremely accurate …', ibid.; 'Each time it became harder …', Robertson, p. 264; Dobson, Norris and Lee bravery, DEFE2/326, PRO; 'There were seldom fewer …', DEFE2/336, PRO; 'We have plenty of ammo', Scott (2), p. 101; Lt F. M. Foggitt, DEFE2/339, PRO; Cdr H. V. McClintock, DEFE2/336, 2/328, PRO; Germans' Second Front suspicion, Report of C.-in-C. West, and 594.013 (D7), DND.

Chapter Eleven: Withdrawal

'We were sent …', 'Close Up', CBC TV, 1962; Early withdrawal, Combined Operations Report, p. 54; 'I was running around', Merritt interview; 'As we set off …', Reyburn, p. 111; 'Classic scene for a movie', Reyburn interview; 'As they neared the beach …', Hayter report, 232C2 (D53), PAC; 'I knew it was going to be hell', DEFE2/328, PRO; 'Many of the lads …', RHLI War Diary, DND; The landing craft arrive, DEFE2/336, PRO; 'As it touched the beach', Hayter report, 232C2 (D53), PAC; Reyburn's escape, Reyburn, pp. 112–121 and Reyburn interview; 'Some completely bewildered …', DEFE2/965, PRO; 'The vessel was badly overloaded', Ed Dunkerley interview; Cpl Salmond's story, BBC TV; Finlay's story, *Armed Forces Digest*, Spring 1978; 'He crossed the beach', DEFE2/335, PRO; Waltenheimer's story, Friedrich Waltenheimer interview; 'It would have been suicidal …', DEFE2/335, PRO; 'No words of mine …', RHLI War Diary, DND; 'In spite of the extremely difficult …', DEFE2/337, PRO; Casualty figures, ibid., and Stacey, p. 389; 'The only thing they had forgotten', Stanton interview; 'Large deviations …', Combined Operations Report; 'Enemy along headlands', DEFE2/328, PRO; 'They were flying …', Labatt report, p. 10; 'Worse than moving pictures', Wood report, p. 7; Boarders beaten off, DEFE2/328, PRO; 'Trying to make ...', Dumais, p. 41; 'Great guys ...', Lynch, unpub. MSS; James Maier's escape, DEFE2/327, PRO; Menard rescued, *Canadians at War*, p. 197; MacRae's escape, DEFE2/328, PRO; Jardine's escape, *Toronto Globe and Mail*, 12 Sept 1942; 'Machine-guns on the cliffs ...', Wood report, p. 7; 'The Germans were determined ...', BBC TV; 'I tied my footwear ...', ibid.; 'Well, it was pretty cold ...', 232C2 (D59), PAC; 'He begged me not to leave him', DEFE2/335, PRO; Labatt's story, Labatt report, pp. 10–12; 'A few minutes later', Southam report, p. 4; 'We had to throw out ...', RHLI War Diary; George Hickson anecdote, DEFE2/327, PRO; Al Richards's story, Richards interview; Beach messages, DEFE2/328; 'We were six or eight deep', Lynch, unpub. MSS; 'The injuries were appalling', Labatt report, p. 12; 'I was fortunate', Bennett report, 594.011 (D1), DND; 'I added that disobedience ...', Southam report, p. 5; 'Nobody moved', Wood report, p. 7; 'One of the rescuers ...', ibid.; George Skerrett, 232C2 (D85), PAC; 'The calmness of this heroic officer ...', Greenhous, p. 209; 'The enemy is withdrawing', Report of C.-in-C. West; 'He was shot ...', Labatt report, p. 12; Fusilliers Mont-Royal surrender, DEFE2/337 and 328, PRO; 'We put them on the mess deck,' BBC TV; 'They looked as if ...', Rees, p. 170; 'I wasn't scared ...', Reyburn interview and *Sunday Express*, 23 Aug 1942; HMS *Berkeley* sunk, DEFE2/336 and Scott (2), pp. 102–3; Col. Hillsinger, Truscott, pp. 70–1; Lt. England saved, Buchanan, p. 18; 'Enemy closing in', DEFE2/328, PRO; The tank bombs, Stanton, Glenn and Clark interviews; 'Keeping a landing craft', DEFE2/336, PRO; 'A mass surrender', 232C2 (D59), PAC; Roberts's pigeon message, DEFE2/328, PRO; Casualties on main beach, Stacey, p. 389.

Chapter Twelve: Surrender

'Like the German nightmare ...', Schnösenberg interview; 'I told them that ...', Beal interview; Shooting the wounded, Poolton interview; 'A German soldier came in ...', McDonald interview; 'I don't think anybody ...', Beal interview; 'I saw no instance ...', DEFE2/328, PRO; 'Made up from murderers', 594.013 (D7), DND;

'The other two ...', John Lerigo interview; 'I must admit ...', James Pasquale interview; 'A German officer offered ...', Dungate interview; 'It was a scorching day', Moore interview; 'The process of realising ...', Merritt interview; 'As we had no ammunition', DEFE2/965, PRO; 'Lefty' White's objection, Buchanan, p. 18; 'Women approached us', 232C2 (D66), PAC; 'The most unpleasant decision', Labatt report, pp. 12–13; 'Shame and humiliation', Wood report, p. 9; 'I heard somebody shout ...', Pilote interview; 'There was a crunch ...', McCool interview; 'Sorry lads ...', Southam report, p. 5; 'I raced to the brigadier ...', Robertson, pp. 379–80; Dumais surrenders, Dumais, p. 45 and DEFE2/335, PRO; 'I stood up ...', Greenhous, p. 212; 'Two six-foot skinny youths ...', Wood report, p. 9; 'So long, gentlemen ...', ibid., p. 10; 'One little fellow ...', Stanton interview; 'Before going in the water ...', Foote interview; 'I was tired, I was hungry ...', BBC TV; 'We were all very thirsty ...', Lynch, unpub. MSS; Stanton and the beer, Stanton interview; 'Caused some casualties', DEFE2/337, PRO; 'We had just given up ...', Keto interview; 'I had my boots ...', McDonald interview; 'Those who could march ...', Hall interview; 'Whatever its effect ...', Southam report, p. 6; 'I've led you this far ...', Wood report, p. 12; 'A picture of horror', Haussmann report in Wamper, *Dieppe: A Test of the Coastal Ramparts*; John Gilchrist story, DEFE2/324, PRO; 'When they finally ...', Stevens interview; 'All the way down the street ...', Lynch, unpub. MSS; 'As they marched past ...', Georges Guibon, *Diary*, p. 17, DND; 'As we passed through ...', Greenhous, p. 213; 'English pigs', Geoffrion interview; 'Singing the Marseillaise', Poolton interview; The V-sign curtains, Price interview; The wedding procession, Geoffrion interview; 'In the church ...', Foote interview; McCool's bullets, McCool interview; 'I was asked in perfect English ...', Osmond interview; 'They put us in a Volkswagen', Foote interview; 'Mostly they pumped you ...', Poolton interview; 'They tried to bully me ...', McCool interview; 'The officers all showed ...', Appx. G to Report of C.-in-C. West; The cigarette story, Geoffrion interview; 'Struck by the contrast', Jorgensen report, Wamper; 'The concussion was frightful', *Colliers*, 19 Sept 1942; 'As we approached the boat ...', Scott (2), p. 104; The casualties are landed, 229C1.7

(D4), PAC, DEFE2/332 and 339, PRO; Casualty figures, Stacey, pp. 387–8; 'Before midnight ...', Godspeed, p. 402; 'The sun is bright but ...', Essex Scottish War Diary, DND; 'Instead of a hundred ...', BBC TV; 'When I came out ...', *Radio Times*, 17 Aug 1942.

Chapter Thirteen: Aftermath

'The Duke of Wellington ...', Mountbatten address to Dieppe Veterans, Toronto, 1973; 'We have captured ...', Guibon, *Diary*, p. 12, DND; Equipment captured, 981.023 (D10), DND; 'It is a scene of death', Jørgensen report in Wamper, DND; 'Battered to destruction', Report of C.-in-C. West, p. 16; German wounded rewarded, 594.013 (D9), DND; German losses, Report of C.-in-C. West, p. 24, 981.023 (D10), DND and DEFE2/328, PRO; Telegram to Churchill, DEFE2/330, PRO; Churchill's reply, Prem. File 3/256, PRO; *Daily Mail* stories, *Daily Mail*, 20, 21 Aug 1942; 'Did we bring back ...?', *Daily Sketch*, 21 Aug 1942; 'Heartening news', *The Times*, 20 Aug. 1942; 'Even hard-boiled ...', *News Chronicle*, 20 Aug 1942; American headlines, *Daily Herald*, 22 Aug 1942; The New York cat, Jackdaw C8; Canadian Press reaction, *Daily Telegraph*, 22 Aug 1942; 'The name that thrilled ...', *Toronto Globe and Mail*, 24 Aug 1942; 'Many were actuated ...', *Hamilton Spectator*, 4 Sept 1942; 'Little time for grief, *Ottawa Journal*, 22 Aug 1942; 'For three weeks ...', *Toronto Globe and Mail*, 12 Sept 1942; 'Shocked and dismayed', ibid., 15 Sept 1942; Mrs McCool's faith, McCool interview; 'It was a tough tour ...', Munro letter to author, 15 March 1979; 'Fought their way clean through ...', *Calgary Albertan*, 9 Sept 1942; 'It was a disaster', CBC TV; 'One of the most ambitious ...', Appx. C to Annex 14, Combined Operations Report; 'The period of silence ...', ibid.; Story delays, DEFE2/329, PRO; 'If this is a foretaste ...', *Evening Standard*, 20 Aug 1942; 'Too large to be a symbol', DEFE2/328, PRO; 'Well, if it isn't ...', ibid.; 'Churchill is responsible', DEFE2/329, PRO; Memos to editors, DEFE2/328, PRO; 'I was amazed ...', *Toronto Globe and Mail*, 9 Sept 1942; 'It is a mistake ...', *The Times* 9 Sept 1942; Churchill's note to Ismay, Prem. File 3/256, PRO; German comments on raid planning, DEFE2/338 and 330, PRO, 594.003 (D2), 594.013 (D9), 981.023 (D10) and Report of C.-in-C. West, DND; Canadians' fighting qualities, Stacey, p. 392; 'The troops probably fought ...', David Irving, *Hitler's War*, p. 409; Report on tanks, 594.013 (D9), DND; French property razed, 594.003 (D2) DND; The operational order, Report of C.-in-C. West; Von Rundstedt's comments, ibid.; French prisoners released, ibid., p. 240, DEFE2/329, PRO; The Berneval burial, Claude Lambert interview; The dead re-buried, Mordal, pp. 246–7, Leasor, p. 212; Canadian letters home, DEFE2/334, PRO; 'How could the Germans have known?', Merritt interview; Lovat's comments, Lovat interview; 'The Dieppe plan ...', Stacey, p. 399; Montgomery's comments, 'Close Up', CBC TV, 9 Sept 1962; 'There are Canadians ...', Lewin, p. 39; Beaverbook and Mountbatten, A. J. P. Taylor, *Beaverbrook*, pp. 538, 638. 'I don't like the word ...', CBC TV; 'I don't think Roberts ...', ibid.; 'Not the right fellow', Lovat interview; 'Given all the conditions', CBC TV; 'Piece of cake', ibid. and Munro, p. 304; Shackling of prisoners, Stacey, pp. 396–7; 'Aping the depravity ...', *Toronto Globe and Mail*, 14 Oct 1942; Dumais escapes, DEFE2/328, PRO and Dumais, pp. 54–5; Runcie's escape, 232C2 (D66), PAC; 'They got me each time', Keto interview; Clark's escape, Clark interview; 'Dieppe shed revealing light ...', Churchill, Vol. 4, pp. 457–8; 'A Canadian contribution ...', R. W. Thompson, *Price of Victory*, p. 48; 'We could have obtained ...', Mordal, p. 87; 'I am satisfied ...', Naval Commander's Report, DEFE2/336, PRO; Roberts changes his mind, 215.C1 (D244), DND; 'The defeat persuaded Hitler ...', Lt-Gen. Hans Speidel, *We Defended Normandy*, p. 49; 'Dieppe unexpectedly ...', Mountbatten speech, 29 Sept 1942; Dieppe captured, *Canadians at War*, p. 521–2, Mordal, p. 273; Crerar takes the salute, *Canadians at War*, p. 536.

ACKNOWLEDGEMENTS

My grateful thanks to the following for their assistance during the researching of this book: the indefatigable Henry Brown of the Commando Association; Dr W. A. B. Douglas, Director of the Directorate of History, National Defence Headquarters, Ottawa; Winston MacIntosh, National Defence Headquarters, Ottawa; Ray Geoffrion, Harold Price, Bill Stevens and, particularly, E. J. 'Dal' Dalrymple of the Dieppe Veterans Association; Lou Lisko, U.S. Rangers historian; the staffs of the Public Archives of Canada, Ottawa, the Toronto Public Library and the Public Record Office, London; and Heather Abraham (French) and Rosemarie Fischer (German) for their work in translating documents and tapes.

Also my thanks and appreciation to the following participants in the Dieppe Raid who submitted to interviews, questions and other forms of harassment: Ron Beal, Dick Clark, George Cook, Wally Dungate, Ed Dunkerley, Ross Finlay, John Foote, Ray Geoffrion, Allan Glenn, Ron Grove, Reg Hall, George Horne, Leonard Keto, Claude Lambert, John Lerigo, Joachim Lindner, Lord Lovat, Bill Lynch, Brian McCool, Joe McDermott, Al McDonald, Cliff McKenna, Maurice Mallet, Cecil Merritt, Albert Moore, Ross Munro, Denis O'Connor, Geoffrey Osmond, James Pasquale, Marc Pilote, Jack Poolton, Bill Portman, Harold Price, Wallace Reyburn, Al Richards, Stephen Saggers, Richard Schnösenberg, John Smale, Vic Sparrow, Austin Stanton, Bill Stevens, Bill Stockdale, Charles Surphlis, Marcel Swank, Romauld Tyminski, Guy Vandelac, Friedrich Waltenheimer, Gordon Webb, Peter Young.

Printed in Great Britain
by Amazon